Music and Theatre in France

in the 17th and 18th Centuries

AN AMS REPRINT SERIES

A
GENERAL HISTORY
OF THE
STAGE

AMS PRESS, INC.
NEW YORK, N.Y.

A

GENERAL HISTORY

OF THE

S T A G E,

From its ORIGIN.

In which the

Several THEATRES of EUROPE,

Those Particularly of

ITALY, SPAIN, FRANCE, ENGLAND,
HOLLAND, FLANDERS, and GERMANY,
with Regard to their Excellencies and Defects,
are Critically Compared with each other;

THE

VARIOUS MANAGEMENT of them Described;

AND THE

CHARACTERS, MANNERS, and PERSONS of the
PRINCIPAL PERFORMERS considered.

Together with

T W O   E S S A Y S;

On the ART of SPEAKING in PUBLIC,

AND A

COMPARISON between the ANTIENT and MODERN
D R A M A.

Translated from the Eminent LEWIS RICCOBONI.

The SECOND EDITION.

To which is Prefixed,

An INTRODUCTORY DISCOURSE concerning the
Present State of the ENGLISH STAGE and PLAYERS.

L O N D O N:

Printed for W. OWEN at *Temple Bar*, and LOCKYER DAVIS
near *Salisbury Court* in *Fleet Street*. 1754.

608186 *dc*

Library of Congress Cataloging in Publication Data

Riccoboni, Luigi, 1676-1753.
  A general history of the stage, from its origin . . .
together with two essays, On the art of speaking in
public, and a Comparison between the ancient and modern
drama.

  (Music and theatre in France in the 17th and 18th
centuries)
  Reprint of the 1754 ed. printed for W. Owen, London.
  Translation of Réflexions historiques et critiques sur
les différens théâtres de l'Europe.
  1. Theater—History. I. Title. II. Series.
PN2100.R6 1978   792'.09   76-43937
ISBN 0-404-60187-1

FEB 0 1981

3772397

First AMS edition published in 1978.

Reprinted from the edition of 1754, London, from an
original in the collections of the Cornell University Library.
[Trim size and text area have been slightly altered in this
edition. Trim size of original: 13 x 20.2 cm; text area:
7.9 x 15.8 cm.]

MANUFACTURED
IN THE UNITED STATES OF AMERICA

T O

David Garrick, Efq;

SIR,

AN *Author, who, with the fole Intent of farther improving the prefent State of* the Britifh *Theatre, by pointing out the Excellencies and the Defects of thofe of other Nations, tranflated* RICCOBONI; *in the fame Spirit, and from the fame Motive, addreffes this Second Edition of that Tranflation to you, who have moft Power to employ it to the defigned Purpofe.*

I fhould add a great deal to this Addrefs of mere Civility, if I had not intended that, in an Introduction written before this Work. To that, Sir, I refer you for the Senfe I entertain of the great Services fuch a Performance may be of in fo laudable a Defign:

A 2 *All*

DEDICATION.

*All that I need say here is, that as the Tran-
slator has no mercenary Views in this Dedication, it will come with the better Grace from
his Hand; that he is sure your Discernment
will see the Propriety of all that can be urged
from such Examples; and that he doubts not
but that Applause and that Encouragement you
have deserved so fully, and received so liberally
from the Publick, will engage you in the Design; and give you a new Spirit, in the Attempt
of adding every thing to their reasonable Entertainment.*

*Accept the Thanks of one who has as often
been charmed with your Performances as he has
seen them; and believe him to be not the less
sincere in that Declaration, because he sub-
scribes to this Address no other Name than
that of*

The AUTHOR.

AN

A N
INTRODUCTORY DISCOURSE
To the SECOND EDITION,
BY THE
TRANSLATOR.

N confidering the Progrefs of Theatrical Entertainments in the feveral Parts of the World, as delivered by this careful and judicious Writer, it is natural to turn our Eyes particularly upon the prefent State of them in our own Kingdom ; and to apply to that, what he obferves concerning the feveral States, the particular Perfections or Defects of the others.

This is the Ufe of Reading : this the Intent of Study. One who knew more of the true Ufe of Hiftory than any who wrote it, has faid that its principal Value is the fetting before us, in the Lives of other Men, Inftances of what will be worthy, what infamous ; what advantageous, and what deftructive, in our own. It is not lefs the Cafe, in this Story of the Theatres, than in thofe more important Writings which he names : And however trivial the Confideration of Men's Amufements and Entertainments may

A 3 feem,

feem, in Comparifon to their authorized Butcheries of one another ; yet the Obfervation holds. He will read of the *Italian*, *French*, and *Spanifh* Theatres to little Purpofe, who employs not the feveral Remarks made upon their Excellencies and Defects to the Improvement ; or, if that be not in his Way, at leaft to the better underftanding of our own.

It has been lefs the Cuftom of the *Englifh* to invent, than to improve. We acknowledge it in general when we fpeak of Things of more Confequence : and although a *Locke*, a *Newton*, or a *Clarke*, afford eminent Exceptions, yet in general it is true : and it appears not lefs the Circumftance in thefe of leffer Moment. The Author of thefe Accounts tells us the *Englifh* did not begin Theatrical Reprefentations fo foon as many other of the civilized Nations ; but he tells us alfo, that they have found the Way to excell them all. He gives the Palm to the Players of our Nation, againft the *Italian* and the *French*, whatever Merit he may have allowed to thofe. This was his Opinion, when the *Englifh* Theatre, however diftinguifhed by a few good Actors, was far from the Eminence at which it is arrived now ; and there is no doubt but that, under a Manager fo judicious and fo indefatigable as he who is moft confpicuous at prefent, it will continue to rife in Excellence.

Poffibly,

Poffibly, fome who doat upon the paft, and fuppofe the Players of this Time to want Merit, becaufe themfelves want the Spirit that fhould tafte it, may fay there have been Players more eminent than thofe who grace the prefent Theatre; but 'tis from the Reafon only that has been juft given. They will thunder in our Ears the *Booths* and *Bettertons*, of whom, not remembring them, they will expect to take their Account: but in that we have a Right to be excufed. The very Defcriptions of them by Mr. *Cibber*, who was one among them, and who is free e- nough in his Applaufes of them, confefs they had their Faults: I would not fay that Author is always free in making this Con- feffion; but 'tis eafy to fee them in the ge- neral Character he draws. It would be well to reft the Comparifon on what we fee of the prefent, and what he fays of the paft Actors, not regarding how he fays it: we fhall then find thefe the Superiors.

Give a Man of Mr. *Cibber*'s Talents a Player of Mr. *Garrick*'s Merit to praife, and fee how he will lead you through all the Epithets of Dignity and Power, Variety, and Elegance, of Harmony and Feeling; and when he comes to point out the pe- culiar Characteriftic of this Actor, that Fire, that native Spirit that glows in all his Parts, that double Portion of the Promethean Heat, that animates the little Lump of Clay;

A 4   you

you will know how much a good Caufe im-
proves under the Tongue of a judicious
Council ; how much of that fuperlative
Excellence thefe are faid to have poffeffed,
you owe to his Eloquence who tells you of
it. Mr. *Cibber* is old, and he is partial : he
remembers the Things that pleafed him
when he was young, with an old Man's
Fondnefs ; and he has the old Man's Imperfection, Want of Relifh for whatfoever is
new. But ftill making thefe Allowances for
his Manner, and taking thefe Peoples Characters, as you can fee in his Writings without adopting every florid Epithet of his Defcriptions, you will own the prefent Players
better.

This is a Point of fome Importance, becaufe the contrary is continually faid ; and
thofe who fee Things fuperficially are carried away by it. 'Tis to the Credit of our
Nation that we fhould improve in all polite
Entertainments ; and certainly this has a
Place among them. It is an undoubted
Truth, that we do improve in them ; and
let that Truth be acknowledged. The Encouragement that is given to thefe Entertainments is vaftly greater than it ever was;
and the Tafte of the prefent Time, with refpect to them, is good : This ought to be a
Proof. Mr. *Cibber*, to whom it is moft proper to refer, becaufe he knows moft of the
former Theatre, will tell us that an Audience

ence to the Amount of Thirty-five Pounds was esteemed a good one, when all those famed Actors and Actresses play'd together. At present Mr. *Garrick* seldom plays to less than a Hundred and Sixty; and the Merit of Mrs. *Gregory* (Novelty apart) has never brought into the larger House so little. We have seen the Prices of the Places raised a Fourth, upon the Appearance of some new Entertainment of particular Expence; and we have seen those advanced Prices continued (without any one's murmuring) to all Plays; and now made universal. We have seen the full Price of Admission demanded for half a Play, when there was a new Entertainment of this Kind, without Disturbance; and we see at this Time the same strict Rule observed in favour of the Harlequin *Fortunatus*, after the first Run has been long over; and when tacked to Plays in which Mr. *Garrick* has not acted.

The Readiness with which all People submit to this, is a Proof how perfect an Encouragement they are willing to give to the present Theatre. There is no Question but it will be easy to abolish that Custom of receiving half the Price for two thirds of the Evening entirely: and he must deserve ill of the Publick, who, under such Encouragement, would not endeavour every thing in his Power to add to the Entertainment. It does not seem that Mr. *Garrick* will ever

be

be deficient in this Particular; and perhaps
we have nothing to wiſh ſo much as that
the Management may continue in his Hands,
to ſee the Stage riſing continually in Credit.

It would be very unfair to deliver this
Praiſe partially; and by ſaying ſo much of
the principal Manager of one of the Theatres, to caſt a tacit Reflection upon the o-
ther. Mr. *Rich* has never been deficient in
Care and Application: No Manager, not
only not the preſent of the other Houſe, but
none ever ſhew'd more Readineſs to engage
whatever might be pleaſing to his Audiences: But Mr. *Garrick* is a younger Man;
he has more of the buſtling Spirit of the
World, and he is himſelf an Actor. We
are accuſtomed to ſee the principal Parts of
Plays done as well at his Houſe as at the
other; but at the other we are accuſtomed
to ſee all done well. There is a Pleaſure in
this which an Audience never fails to reliſh
highly: And the Preſence of a Manager
who treads the Stage himſelf is a great Advantage.

This is a very due Praiſe to Mr. *Garrick*,
and he feels what is more valuable than
Praiſe from it. But it may be carried farther;
nay, it ought: it is neceſſary; and even at
his Houſe ſome very fine Scenes are ſpoil'd
for want of it. It were fooliſh to join the
Mob in hollowing at the thin Seats in a *Venetian* Senate; for that is right: a Council of
Six

Six determines all Things of Importance there; but then the Six might look like Counfellors. One is offended at the dirty Faces and the dirty Shoes of thefe *moft potent Grave and Reverends*; and in the fame Manner one cannot help being difgufted with the Confpirators who join with *Pierre*. We conceive of them as great Men engaged in a great Enterprize; the principal Perfons in one of the moft powerful States in the World, joined to its Deftruction: How is this Idea fatisfied, when we fee the Band of Big-coated Candle-fnuffers? Embroidery and Dirt; unfit Embroidery, and Dirt that fits too naturally, ftriving at an impoffible Union: and when we hear the better Sort of them fpeak, thofe who are judged fit to be intrufted with a Line and half, how are we difgufted! Thefe, Men to form Confpiracies, to overturn States, and fet the World in Uproar! Senfe and Reafon contradict it! The Force of the Scene is wholly deftroy'd by the unnatural Afpect. We cannot expect *Pierre* fhall be fuccefsful; we fee thefe People muft betray him. When he is in the midft of them he feems a Hero encircled by a Race of Pickpockets; and we blufh to fee him embrace Men who are fitter to wipe his Shoes.

There are many Inftances of the like Kind in other Tragedies; and they are the great Difgrace of the prefent Theatre. The Manager

nager will fay 'tis difficult for him to remove
them ; for Men who have a Mein and Afpect have generally Parts joined with it, and
will not be placed as Cyphers : and thofe
who are able to perform a Character of Confequence will not accept thefe Parts of a
Line or two. It may be difficult to get the
better of this ; but it cannot be impoffible.
It will offend thefe Gentlemen of better Figure, and higher Rank, to be ufed occafionally in low and trifling Characters ; but they
fhould remember it is only occafionally : and
he fhould remember that they are his Servants. The Army fubmits in fome degree
to thefe Regulations ; and the beft Players,
probably, would not be for demanding a
Rank above the fuperior Officers : if fo, the
Secondaries cannot be placed higher than
Subalterns. The Remedy will follow. The
Superior among the Forces has Power to
make thefe ferve in any Capacity. The Ser-
jeant raifed from a private Man muft defcend into a private Man again, if the Neceffity of the Service require it ; and why
fhould not the fame be practifed in thefe
Forces of the Stage? This is wanting : This
is the great, nay, one might almoft fay, it is
the only Thing wanting to raife the prefent
Theatre to the higheft Pitch of Excellence :
And why fhould it not be done ? The Publick give fufficient Encouragement ; the Manager has Abilities and Spirit ; and if this be

the

the only Reform neceſſary, why ſhould he delay to make it ? As to the Gentlemen themſelves, to eaſe their tender Minds, and reconcile the Practice to their Notions of Honour, they ſhould conſider (continuing the Alluſion with which the Profeſſion has been honoured) That when Works of Importance are preſſing, Generals themſelves will take up the Pickaxe and the Spade ; but in the ordinary Courſe of Things, and when that preſſing Neceſſity is over, they leave thoſe Tools in the Hands of thoſe who are deſtined to the Uſe of them, and return to their own great and important Characters.

The true Taſte of the preſent Audiences will extremely favour any Attempt of a Manager upon this Foundation : The Actors whom he would offend by it are not of the capital ones on whom he depends ; and therefore they depend on him : They depend alſo upon the Favour of the Publick. They may be aſſured that the Publick would receive them with moſt Favour when they took moſt Pains to pleaſe them ; and would never ſupport them againſt a Manager who had endeavoured to make them the moſt uſeful, whatever, in their own romantick Opinions, their Honour might have ſuffered by ſuch forced Condeſcenſion.

It is from this Taſte of the Audiences that we are to expect the great Improvements in the Theatre : the Manager, when that

Taſte

Tafte happens to be bad, muft conform to it; much more is it neceffary, as well as commendable, when it is good as now. Even the Galleries at this Time contain no *Dutch* Spectators, who would roar with Satisfaction to fee a Bear act the Part of an Executioner, or a Criminal hang'd upon the Stage : Even our Harlequin Entertainments do not defcend to any thing quite fo contemptible as this. But it were well if they could be abolifhed, becaufe they come much nearer to it than any thing elfe of our Reprefentations. Mr. *Garrick* feemed once to be of Opinion that this was practicable; nay, his City Friends talk of a Kind of Promife, that if ever he were raifed to the Patent, no fuch Buffoonery fhould difgrace his Theatre : Little Minds alone will fuppofe it poffible he fhould be influenced by Views of Intereft only to continue thefe Follies. It would be as eafy for him to receive the full Price for half a Play during the Seafon, with one of his own Farces after it, as with a Pantomime; and it would be as reafonable to demand it : this would at once encourage him to employ his Talents as a Writer, as well as Actor, to our Entertainment, and tend more than any thing to difplace thofe Scenes which never fail to difguft the better Part of an Audience, and are a Scandal to a Theatre which has in its Service fuch a Set of Players.

This laft Particular is the more ftriking

at *Drury-Lane* Houfe, becaufe the Perfon who acts the Harlequin has very great Talents for more rational Performances. He has fhewn alfo, that he is capable of Improvement : and, far from thinking that even the Applaufe of the Injudicious could make wrong right, he has, particularly of late, left off many exceptionable Things in his Manner, and come nearer to Nature. The Confequence is what it ought : he receives that Applaufe from the Pit which ufed to come from the Top of the Houfe; and he receives it, as he deferves, in a double Portion.

What might not be expected from a Player who ftudies to mend even in thofe Things, in which he receives Applaufe ! and what Pity he fhould be interrupted in thofe Improvements by the Practice of what might be better done by an Alehoufe Tumbler. Thofe who faw Mr. *Woodward* in Sir *Fopling Flutter*, and, notwithftanding fome little Faultinefs, diftinguifhed fuch great Merit in the Performance, muft have been difgufted beyond fufferance to fee him hop about in his chequered Coat, a Quarter of an Hour after, in *Fortunatus*; and play the Part of a Monkey after he had rally'd with fo much true Spirit one of the moft delicate Foibles of his own Species.

The fpeaking Harlequin of the *Italian*, and the *Graciofo* of the *Spanifh* Theatre, mean as they may be, are yet much more
tolerable

tolerable than this Abuse of the Character: Persons of Humour always play them, and there is Novelty in the Place of greater Merit. This would not do with the juft and dif-cerning Tafte of an *Englifh* Audience; but furely the dumb Folly ought to be lefs coun-tenanced than the Impertinence.

If this Tafte of the *Italian* be as much below our Approbation, as the Abfurdity or Barbarifm of a *Dutch* Comedy, there is fome-thing yet to be learned from the Performers of that Nation. Inferior as they are to ours in the Expreffions of the greater Paffions, they excel us as much in the lighter and more trivial Circumftances: and if they want the Force of that ftudied Deportment, by which our tragick Actors fometimes per-form Wonders, they have a Freedom and bold Eafe in the comic, which we fhould do well to imitate, and a Variety, of which we feem at prefent to have no Conception. This is the Ufe to be made of Obfervations on the Cuftoms and Manners of other Theatres: this is the Purpofe with which we ought to fee the foreign Performers; and this the real Advantage we may draw from reading Ac-counts of the *Italian* and *French* Theatres, when written with the Spirit and the Can-dour of this Author, when they are as free to point out their Defects as Beauties.

We have heard of one of the eminent Performers in fome of the firft ferious Operas

that

that were introduced in *England*, who was acknowledged to exceed all the others upon the *Englijh* Theatres at that Time, in the Juftice, Elegance, and Grandeur of his Deportment. He gave Senfe to the moft paltry Words, and even Majefty to Nonfenfe. In this the *Italian* Stage might have then been a Pattern to the *Britijh*; and we have a prefent Example of the fame Thing, not lefs eminent or lefs acknowledged, though in another Way,

The Burletta's acted at this Time, fhew us one Performer, a Girl, who excells all the Actreffes or Actors we have feen in comic Deportment. Often its Extravagance carries it to Farce, but ftill even there it is pleafing. We call it in fome Particulars unjuft, that is, unnatural; and a fober Judge of thefe Things where he has feen the Girl making Grimaces at the Pit, and putting fome bafhful *Briton* out of Countenance, has afked whether there were any thing in the Words of the Song to fupport this Extravagance of Gefture ? The fame Anfwer may be given to both thefe tacit Cenfures. It is *Italian* though not *Englijh* Nature : and the Cuftom of the Country fupports this Violence of Tone and Manner, even when the Words are trivial.

To relifh thefe Performers properly, we fhould conceive that they are rallying *Italian*, and not *Englijh* Follies and Extravagancies;

gancies ; and that nothing can be too extravagant for such a Design. As to the Action
of this young Person, it must therefore be
acknowledged just as well as free ; altho'
at first Sight it may strike us as improper.
And knowing where, according to our Taste
it is exceffive, those who imitate it, may there
drop the Original.

We have admired the *Italian* Dancers for
that perfect Command of their Persons, by
which they throw themselves into Attitudes
of every graceful Kind ; this Girl has brought
that Command of Limbs and Features into
Comedy in their Way : And certainly if
some of our tolerable Actresses would ex-
change their *English* Stiffness for some of
this foreign Ease, they would do themselves
new Honour. In Farces, all that we have
seen in this Person might be introduced in
our own Language, and by our own Performers ; for, Thanks to those who write
them, we have Characters as extravagant
represented there as any these can mimick ;
and the utmost of this Excess would become them.

The other Thing it would be well that
our Actors would imitate from the *Italians*,
is their Variety : This would do them much
more Honour than their constant Sameness,
and certainly would give their Audiences
greatly more Pleasure. With us the same
Scene is always play'd in the same Manner,

not

not only by the fame Actor, but by every Actor who performs it : We know, therefore, before it comes, all that we are to admire. Perhaps there never was a greater or a jufter Piece of Action upon the Theatre of any Country, than that confummate Player Mr. *Barry* threw into his Character of the Earl of *Effex*, when his Wife fell into a Swoon, and he was going to Execution ; but 'twas every Night the fame. In this Manner alfo that beautiful, though perhaps not proper, Attitude of *Romeo* at the Tomb, is always the fame, not only in Mr. *Barry* and in Mr. *Garrick*, every Time each plays, but 'tis the fame in both : On the contrary, let an *Italian* pleafe ever fo greatly once in his Scene, he never courts a fecond Applaufe by the fame Attitude. It feems that thofe of our Performers are practifed at the Glafs, thofe of the *Italians* rife from Nature : thefe People having that true Enthufiafm to conceive themfelves really the Perfons they reprefent. In Comedy this Fault is more frequent and more confpicuous in our People than in Tragedy; with the *Italians* it is more avoided.

When the Burletta's were performed fome Years fince at the *Hay Market*, People were vaftly pleafed with a Quarrel between an old Scholar and a Fop, and which was continued with a Multiplicity of bold and expreffive Geftures at leaft ten Minutes : The Audience did a Thing very uncommon ; they

called

called for the whole Scene again. They were
obeyed : The Father and the Fop entered,
renew'd their Quarrel, and continued it as
long as they had done before, and enforced
it with as many as violent and as expreffive
Attitudes and Geftures; but thefe all different.
They trufted to Nature to give them a proper Deportment for the Scene, and fhe did
not fail them : They had Recourfe to the
fame Inftructrefs again, and they fucceeded
as well, though in a perfect Variety ; for the
Fund is inexhauftible.

It would be well that our Performers in
both Ways, inftead of fervilely practifing
ten Hours before a Glafs, what is to be
palmed upon their Audience as the fudden
Effect of a Paffion ; or inftead of coldly copying one another, would follow Nature as
thefe People do ; and give us fomething
new every Time we faw them ; although
we were prefent at the fame Play for eight
Repetitions.

The Want of this feems one of the great
Caufes why new Plays are fo much difcountenanced, or at beft fo coldly received ;
not that I would venture to fay they have all
deferved better Treatment. However, we
may in this Point fet their Merit quite out
of the Queftion ; and yet fee why it is very
natural they fhould be difcountenanced. We
are weary of feeing the fame Thing in the
fame Manner, though we could very well
receive

receive it with the Advantage of but a little Variety. If we are content to recollect the Sentiments, and from our imperfect Remembrance of the Words in which they are cloathed acknowledge a Sort of Novelty, that greatest of all Charms, in the Repetition of them ; we are difgufted at having the fame Geftures, Looks, and Attitudes repeated to us nine Times over. To remember thefe, and expect them over and over again, is infupportable ; and it argues a ftrange Dearth of Invention in thofe who practife them ; at leaft it would argue this, if Cuftom did not too much authorife it : and it will when that Cuftom fhall be condemned by all Perfons as unnatural and vicious.

In the Tragedy of *Boadicea*, which but for this cloying Repetition would certainly have pleafed more than nine Nights, we had an Inftance of the Fault in the greateft Player in the World : It is no particular Cenfure to charge him with it, becaufe 'tis cuftomary ; and nothing elfe was expected from him ; but he will own the Impropriety when he fubmits the Queftion not to Cuftom, but to his own difcerning and impartial Reafon.

Mr. *Garrick*, in the Character of *Dumnorix*, in this Play, drew his Sword on the firft Night in the midft of a Prayer ; and full of the Uprightnefs of his Caufe, brandifhed it in the Face of Heaven : It was

2   difputed

difputed whether this were proper; but there could be no Difpute whether a Repetition of it could be proper : that was impoffible. The Suddenneſs of a virtuous Emotion might excufe him once in doing it; but nothing could juſtify the cold Repetition ; nor could any thing be more unpleaſing to an Audience than to know beforehand what was to happen as the Start of a Paſſion, and to be able to fay at what Word the Hero was to draw forth his Weapon. This, taking away the Appearance of Nature and Reality, debaſes in the greateſt Degree a Player who is full of her true Feelings, and places Mr. *Garrick* upon almoſt a Level with the Automatons, who attend upon him in that Scene, to whom he is to give a Look as their Cue for drawing their Swords, as the Word in the Prayer is his.

Theſe Things are not named as private Cenſures : for not being particular to the Perſon, they can bring no Difgrace upon him. It was proper to bring an Inſtance of the Fault that had been named ; for one Example fpeaks plainer than a thouſand Explanations ; and nothing could do fo much Juſtice to the general Nature of the Cenſure, as producing that Inſtance from him who would, if any could be fo, have been above the Reach of the Fault. It is incumbent on fuch Players as this to remedy the common Follies of the Stage ; and their

Example

Example will give Authority and Weight to the Practice. The World will easily discern that he who dedicates his Labours to this Gentleman can have no Pleasure in distinguishing his Foibles; and he will call that Person most his Friend who points them out: It might be decent to do this privately, if they were his particularly; but when they are the Foibles of the Time, and all fall into them, there needs not the Reserve.

The Women of the present Stage are much less liable to this Censure than the Men; they may therefore with Justice, and greatly to their Honour, claim a Reserve for themselves in the Sentence: Not that they are wholly free from the Fault, but that they are not so guilty of it; and this is the more to their Honour, because if they had fallen into it, and pleaded the Example of the Men, it would have been an Authority. Whoever observes Mrs. *Cibber*, in her repeated playing of *Indiana*, will find continually something new in her Manner, her Gesture, and Deportment. All her Attitudes in her Distress speak the same Emotions of Despair; but the whole Frame is as capable of Variety in Expression, as the Voice. This is not the only Proof we have of that Actress's really possessing that Enthusiasm of the Theatre; on which all great Acting depends, and of her perfectly losing herself in the Character: of her being not Mrs.

Cibber,

Cibber, but very *Indiana*; very Lady *Mac-beth*; and very very *Conſtance*.

Her Variety is no where ſeen ſo much as in this laſt named Character : It has been indeed ſo great, that many have queſtioned whether ſhe now play'd it ſo well as ſome Years ſince; but they anſwer themſelves by the very Conduct of the Queſtion. While one inſiſts ſhe is not equal to her former ſelf, and another that ſhe is greater than ever : Enquire more ſtrictly, and you find they ſaw her on different Nights : The Queſtion is not, whether Mrs. *Cibber* acted *Conſtance* better ſome Years ago or now, but whether ſhe acted it better on *Tueſday* or on *Thurſday*, and the whole Reſult is, that Mrs. *Cibber* has great Variety. The Spirit and Geſture of one Night pleaſe ſome; thoſe of another Night others; according to their different Judgments. Mrs. *Cibber* is equal and alike worthy their Applauſe in all.

It were Injuſtice to paſs by Mrs. *Pritchard*, without her Share of this Praiſe; and thoſe muſt have ſeen *Merope* but once, who want a lively Inſtance of it. But this Variety is more ſurpriſing in that new Actreſs named before, who, tho' always the ſame haughty, jealous, fond *Hermione*, never was twice indebted to the ſame Set of Attitudes and Geſtures to expreſs that Excellence.

REFLECTIONS

REFLECTIONS

UPON

DECLAMATION, or, *The Art of Speaking in Public*, &c.

 PERSON who does not profess an Art, is excusable if he is ignorant of its Principles; but if he professes it, he is answerable to the Public if he is not completely Master of it both in Theory and Practice. The different Callings of Mankind in Civil Society are the Effects of the wise Dispositions of an all-ruling Providence, and it is blameable in us to neglect the most minute Consideration that may contribute either to our Instruction in the Theory, or Perfection in the Practice.

Experience however teaches us, that many look upon their own *Profession* as the *Tyrant* of their *Genius*, and exclaim against their Fate for subjecting them to Labours which are their Aversion, and leading them into

Pursuits

Purfuits in Life, in which, for want of the neceffary Talents, they have no Profpect of fucceeding. Hence it proceeds, that many neglect their own Profeffion, and are ignorant in the Rules of an Art, which has employed their whole Life to practife.

It would be eafy to demonftrate the Folly of this; and the Hiftory of the great Men, who have excelled in the Sciences and fine Arts, are fertile in Examples of a contrary Conduct. Even Daily Experience may convince us, that a Man, whom Nature has indulged neither in the neceffary Talents nor in the Inclination for an Art which he profeffes, can, by Application, fupply thefe Defects fo perfectly, as to arrive at the fame Excellence with thofe who fhare largely in every Gift of Nature and Judgment, that is requifite to attain *Perfection.*

Among the Arts, there is one which is either quite given up, or neglected, the Moment that a Perfon, after a faint Effay in it, finds that he is deftitute of the Qualifications that can make him fhine. This proceeds from a common Prepoffeffion that *Excellence* is not to be acquired, that *Defects* are not to be fupplied, nor the *Difficulties* that lye in the way furmounted, without the Affiftance of *Natural Genius.* The Art I mean is that of *Declamation,* an Art in which *Demofthenes* is a ftanding Inftance to reproach

proach the *Indolent*, and a glorious Example to promote the *Industrious*.

The Art I treat of unites the Expreffion of Action to the Propriety of Pronunciation, in order to give the Sentiment its full Impreffion upon the Mind or Heart.

A tuneable Voice, a great and a graceful Deportment, are not fufficient to make a Speaker fucceed in every Province of Oratory. We every Day fee Speakers who with all thefe Advantages are grown grey in a falfe manner of Action, and this becaufe they did not reflect that Nature does not beftow the Polifh upon the Diamond fhe forms, and that it is Labour and Art which gives it Water and Lufture.

Could we trace the Progrefs of the greateft Orators of our Times, I am perfuaded we fhould find that their firft Effays were but faint and unpromifing, nay, that their Manners were ungraceful and awkward, and that it required a long Courfe of Study and Application to correct the original Abfurdities of their Action. The great Mafters of Antiquity are thought by many to be but weak Authorities upon this Head; the *learned Few* indeed efteem them, but by moft Speakers they are difregarded; as if every Deviation from their *Principles* was not at the fame time a Deviation from *Truth* and *Nature*. Men of Genius, when they read

their

their Works, perceive that their Precepts are no other than a Repetition of what their own Underftanding had before fuggefted; fometimes the fame *Ideas* recur, which after a ferious Examination we find were expreffed by the Ancients; and this leads fome Moderns into a Miftake that *Antiquity* is only an ufelefs Piece of *Reading*; but I maintain that this is the very Quality which recommends it.

It is true, that when we reafon upon an Art which derives its Principles wholly from Nature, a Man, tho' of a very indifferent Underftanding, may acquire it of himfelf, but never can acquire it fo as to *excell*; for tho' in Oratory the Uninftructed finds in his Mind every Faculty which is requifite to have a clear Conception of the fundamental Truths of that great Art, yet, would he be completely Mafter of them, he muft be directed by Acquirements unattainable by an untutored Capacity. On the other hand, a Man of Genius ought to cultivate an Acquaintance with thofe ancient Mafters, both as they regulate the Range of his Imagination, and fupply Ideas to his Judgment.

Eloquence and *Action* were found neceffary, and practifed from the moft remote Antiquity; they have civilized the Manners of the moft barbarous, they have recommended themfelves to the Efteem of the moft polite, Nations.

Nations. The Art of *Declamation* is called
Exterior Eloquence; and indeed the moft
forcible and the moft irrefragable Arguments,
when committed to Paper, can never affect
us with the fame Force as when animated by
the Energy of Expreffion and the Beauty of
Action. When thefe meet, we may pronounce the Perfon who poffeffes them a complete Speaker.

The Initiates in the Art of *Declamation*
ought never to expofe themfelves to the
Neceffity of appearing in Public: For even
their firft Appearance demands the Abilities
of a Mafter. I do not know if there is any
thing in Life more irkfome than to hear a
Speech pronounced in a fhocking manner:
One can excufe himfelf from fitting a long
time before a wretched Picture, or before a
Statue where the Proportions are unjuft and
ill-difpofed; but when a Man enters into an
Affembly to hear a Speech or a Difcourfe,
Good Manners oblige him to fit it out to the
End, and it unfortunately happens that one
has too many Opportunities of exercifing his
Patience, both by the frequent Occafions
that offer, and the numerous Profeffors of the
Art. The Pulpit, the Bar, Academies, Colleges, Clubs, Coffee-Houfes, the Parliament
and the Play-houfe have all their Votaries,
who eagerly purfue this Art.

It is a Miftake if we imagine, among the
diffe-

different Professions I have named, that there are any who are under no Necessity of cultivating this Art. Even Authors who only appear in Print are interested; for there is no Author, who, if he has any Friends, does not, before he submits his Work to the Censure of the Public, appoint a Set of Company to whom he causes his Work to be read, that from the Effects which it has upon them, he may form a Judgment of its Success with the Public. As to Poetical Compositions we need not hesitate a Moment; for your Poetical Gentleman, tho' perhaps he has no Intention to appear in Print, loves to have his Verses repeated all over the Town: Thus Writers both in Verse and Prose are under a kind of Necessity of understanding the Art of Speaking; for a bad manner of Pronunciation sometimes throws the Audience into a *Disgust* and *Languor*, which is but a very indifferent Omen of Success with the Public; tho' perhaps all the Matter is, that the Merits of the Work are not perceived thro' the Unskilfulness of the Repeater.

I am sensible that among the Ancients, whom we must own to be our Masters in the Art of *Declamation*, there were a great many bad Orators; therefore it is not at all surprizing that the same thing should happen now. I own it is not, and in some measure it is easily accountable for; but this Obser-

vation

vation can be no Excuse to those to whom Nature has denied Talents for succeeding in *Declamation*, yet persevere in a bad *Manner*, without endeavouring to correct it.

Besides, I comprehend under the Art of *Declamation*, every Intercourse of Conversation which is communicable by distinct, intelligible Language, no Discourse is so familiar, no Chat so indifferent and undesigning, as not to have its own Peculiarities of Expression pointed out by Nature herself; and it is a Mistake to imagine that an *Academic*, for Instance, is not obliged to be acquainted with the Rules of *Declamation*, provided every thing that he reads in the Assemblies where he is conversant, is delivered in an intelligible, and almost familiar, manner. I maintain the contrary, and affirm that there is no familiar Discourse but what has Modulations of Voices that are proper or improper for its Subject. Every Man is obliged to a minute Search into the proper manner of expressing even the smallest Trifle that falls in his way; if he wants that, the Matter he has to communicate cannot have its due Effect.

I shall not here point out that immense Variety of Accents of which the Voice is susceptible, and which ought to be employed on different Occasions in order to do Justice to the vast Crowd of Sentiments that arise in

the

the Mind. I am perfuaded that it is impoffible to write fo upon this Subject as to leave
nothing unfaid that may illuftrate it; and
to obviate every Difficulty that may occur.
If *Quintilian*, treating of the Action of an
Orator, fays, that he ought not always to be
tied down to Precepts, but fometimes to confult his own Genius, I believe I am juftified
in making the fame Reflection upon the
Turns of the Voice; I even think that
Rules are unneceffary, becaufe, generally
fpeaking, thefe Turns are not to be regulated
by Precepts, and are indeed infinite, if every
one, following his own Genius, be it *fevere*
or *eafy*, *foft* or *violent*, varies them fuitably.

Nature in forming Mankind feldom throws
even the moft minute Parts of two different
Men into the fame Mould; we find it very
rare that two Faces have a ftrong Refemblance of one another, but it never happens
that they cannot be diftinguifhed: We do
not even find that the Eyes, the Hands, the
Mouth, the Ears, or the Nofe of two different Men are exactly the fame in Colour,
Form, and Symmetry. This wondrous Conduct of the Father of Nature, who has
ftampt fuch a Difference not only upon the
whole, but upon the Members of a different
Body, naturally leads us to another Reflection. Amidft that furprizing Variety we
may obferve, that the Voices of Men never
exactly

exactly refemble one another, which can only
proceed from the Difference betwixt the
interior Organs of the Human Body in feveral Perfons. How then can one imagine
himfelf capable to mark out the different
Turns and Cadencies peculiar to fo many
Millions of Men, each of whom has a different Voice adapted to his own particular
Genius, and immediately under its Direction?
It would require a great deal of Pains to
point out in general thofe different Sounds,
the *melancholy*, the *chearful*, the *furious*, &c.
and I even believe it is ufelefs to put the Examples fuitable to each in Writing; thefe
muft neceffarily be conveyed by animated
Expreffion, and their Propriety can only be
perceived in the fine Action of an able
Mafter.

Could we penetrate and lay open our Soul
to the Bottom, it would be no hard Matter
to perceive the Source of every Modulation
of the Voice; fhe comprehends them all,
becaufe they are neceffary to her communicating to us thofe wonderful Excellencies entrufted to her by the Author of Nature. But
as the Matter into which fhe is pent obftructs
her Operations, fhe muft *fhake her Plumes*,
and detach herfelf as much as poffible from
the Subftance which confines her. In order
to fucceed in this in fome meafure, we muft
firft deliver the Soul from the Incumbrance
of

of the Senſes; an Operation which, tho' violent, is by no means impracticable.

The Enthuſiaſm of Poets, and the deep
Reſearches of Sages, in whatever Age they
lived, were no other than the Effects of that
profound Recollection of their intellectual
Faculties which penetrated to the Bottom of
the moſt retired Sentiments and Paſſions of
the Soul. Here they ſurveyed Anger, Pity,
Revenge, and the reſt of the Affections, un-
diſguiſed by Cuſtom, and unfettered by Intereſt. Thus every Expreſſion, every Linea-
ment of the Pictures, which they gave of the
Human Soul, was *warm*, *animated* and *juſt*,
becauſe all drawn from the Life. Thus the
Readers found nothing in their Works that
could either be *improved*, *mended*, or *corrected*.

It was aſtoniſhing ſometimes to ſurpriſe
theſe great Men in the *Criſis* of their *Enthuſiaſm*, when they appear'd quite *abſent*, without the Uſe either of Eyes or Ears. They
were looked upon as Fools till they were
awakened and rouſed from their profound
Meditations; and then they at once left their
beautiful *Viſions* and enchanting *Ideas*, into
which they had been worked by their long
Application. A Loſs that was generally
irreparable; for too often it happened that
theſe Sages and Poets could never more recall
thoſe exquiſite Pleaſures of Imagination, nor
recollect the inſtructive Reflections in which
their

their Souls were wrapt before they awakened.

The Ancients termed *Poetry* a *Divine* Language, an Epithet that has been adapted by Posterity; the first Divines among the Heathens were all Poets, they treated of their Gods in their Poems, and their Oracles were all delivered in Verse. But whence comes it that we, who have a *System of Faith*, different from that of the Heathens, should likewise call fine Poetry a *Divine Language?* For my own Part I am convinced, that the chief Reason, which both the Ancients and we had to give it this Appellation, was because Poetry is regarded as a Language above Humanity; since in effect, when the noblest *Enthusiasm* of the Poet speaks the Language of the Soul, we hear something that is amazing, and which can admit of no other Character but that of *Divine*.

But how can we repeat or represent such Compositions, otherwise than by cloathing them in the *Language of the Soul* likewise? Hence it appears to me by an unavoidable Consequence that their Orators, Sages, and Poets entered into the same *Enthusiasm* when they repeated, which they felt when they composed, their Works. If the Soul which inspired their Thoughts equally operated in pronouncing them, their Pronunciation must have been always just and infinitely variated

variated, from the moſt ſublime Heroics down to the moſt familiar Proſe. But one may eaſily conclude, that the Enthuſiaſm they fell into in *declaiming* was far leſs *intenſe* than that which aſſiſted in *compoſing*. Nature dictates this, and we ſee it every Day, at leaſt in appearance, put in Practice.

Every Orator after he ſalutes his Audience remains for ſome Moments motionleſs and ſilent; very often he ſhuts his Eyes; and it is generally believed that he does this in order to give the Spectators time to compoſe themſelves, that they may be more attentive to what he has to deliver: I even think that it is with this View that the greateſt Number of Orators obſerve ſuch a Practice; but both the Speakers and Hearers are under a Miſtake. Thoſe Moments which the Orator obſerves to himſelf ought to be employed in *recollecting* his *Ideas*; and a Minute is ſufficient for him to forget all Nature, and to fill his Mind entirely with his Subject. If he afterwards opens his Eyes when he begins his Diſcourſe, he ſeems to ſend them over all, but fixes them on no particular Object; and if by Accident his Looks ſhall reſt on one Point, he diſtinguiſhes it by no extraordinary Emotion; and this perhaps happens in the very Criſis of his Recollection. It is then that entering upon his Diſcourſe, be his Subject what it will, he feels that *Enthuſiaſm* which

is

is neceſſary to make him declaim in the *Sounds of the Soul.*

It is not a random Obſervation when we commonly ſay, *Such a Speaker does not animate his Expreſſion*; or *that there are ſome Paſſages in ſuch a Work that ought to be more animated.* It is becauſe the *Enthuſiaſm* I have mentioned is wanting both in the Compoſition and Delivery, and neither the *Speaker* nor *Author* have endeavoured to *animate themſelves*, that is, to write and to ſpeak according to the pure genuine Sentiments of the Soul, detached as it were from all Matter.

Words alone are not the only Means by which the Art of *Declamation* expreſſes the Sentiments of the Soul: Nature has implanted in the Eyes ſuitable Expreſſions which convey the Sentiments of the Soul to the Mind; and we may venture to ſay, that in Speaking and Action the Eyes poſſeſs the faireſt Place. *Cicero* and *Quintilian* have not forgot their Effects; and at preſent how many Orators do we ſee whoſe Excellencies would be more complete, did they not ſhut their Eyes during half the time they are ſpeaking? I ſhall not adviſe an Orator to go too much into this Method, whatever Reaſons may be given for the Practice; whether that an Orator, being conſcious of a treacherous Memory, is afraid that he may be
diſcon-

difconcerted ; or that he imagines, fhutting
his Eyes for an Inftant, and then opening
them all of a fudden, they ferve as the Light-
ning that precedes the Bolt, which the
Eloquence of the Orator is ready to dif-
charge, and which indeed is a Mafterpiece of
Action. In fhort, whether it is the Effect of
Precaution or *Art*, it is a Practice that is
both ways dangerous; for by a Speaker frequently fhutting his Eyes, his Expreffion in
a great meafure lofes its Force.

The Eyes therefore ought indifpenfibly to
attend the *Enthufiafm* of Action, becaufe it
is certain that by them the moft inconfiderable Sentiments of the Soul may be expreffed. We may even go fo far as to fay,
that without the *filent Language* of the
Eyes *Words* would fink under *Expreffion* ;
that almoft *Divine Expreffion* communicated
by, and imparted to, the Soul ; and we ought
not one Moment to doubt that both in the
great and the minute Parts of Oratory, the
Eyes infinitely contribute to the Succefs of
the Speaker. If we obferve narrowly, we
fhall find that our Eyes, without the Help of
Words, can difcover Fear, Fury, Shame,
Refolution, Archnefs, Tendernefs, Indifference, Envy, Joy, Grief, and that inexpref-
fible Number of Paffions that crowd the
Soul of Man.

If a Speaker is deeply fkilled in his Art
he

he will not be fatisfied with barely making the Expreffion of his Eyes attend that of his Tongue, but take care that the former fhall have a Moment's Start of the latter. For Inftance, in a Period, which ought to fet out with a burft of Anger, if the Speaker, in a little Paufe which he artfully makes before he fpeaks, fhall by a fingle Look exprefs his Anger, he can fo effectually prepoffefs the Spectator with what he is to fay, that he will all of a fudden mould him into that Temper which moft eafily admits of the Impreffions that he defigns to convey in the reft of his Difcourfe. The fame Obfervation holds of all the other Paffions.

Amongft all the expreffive Operations of the Eye, there is one of great Confequence. A Speaker ought to take care not to work himfelf up to Tears: Yet if they fhall naturally flow, he fhould not ufe the leaft Efforts to ftop them. The Grimaces of a Speaker, who forces himfelf to cry, are either *difguftful* or *ridiculous*; but when his Tears flow fponta-neoufly, it rarely happens that the Emotions which attend them are *difagreeable*. The Speakers who endeavour to weep never can thoroughly feel what they fay; for when it is the Soul that fpeaks, Tears require no intermediate Affiftance to make them flow. If they are affected, the Cheat is eafily difco-vered, and the Effect they have is either none at all, or very bad; but if they are natural, they touch the Heart, and steal the good Wishes of the Spectators.

One can scarcely be persuaded that the rest of the Face enjoys the same noble Qualities of the Eyes, for expressing the Sentiments of the Soul; yet it contributes so much to Expression, that the Words and the Eyes can never of themselves succeed without its Help. We often find in a Speaker a Set of inflexible Features which the Spectators express by a Phrase which we daily hear, *An unmeaning Face.* The Language of the Face consists in the Muscles of which it is composed, with the Blood that animates them; and when these two are put in Action, they both by their Colour and Movement very sensibly paint the Sentiments of the Soul. The great *Shakespear* contains many Instances of this kind: In that Scene where *Othello* murders his Wife, after he gives her a Hint of his Intention, he makes her say:

—— *And yet I fear you, for you're* fatal then
When your Eyes roll so. Why I should fear
    I know not,
Since Guilt I know not: Yet I feel, I fear.
   Oth. *Think on thy Sins.*
   Des. *They're Loves I bear to you.*
   Oth. *Ay! and for that thou dy'st.*

                      Des.

Def. *That Death's unnatural, that kills*
    for loving.
Alas! why gnaw you fo your nether Lip?
Some bloody Paffion fhakes your very Frame:
Thefe are Portents: But yet I hope, I hope,
They do not point on me.

In *Henry* VIII. when that Prince leaves
Wolfey, the latter fays,

— *He parted frowning from me, as if Ruin*
Leapt from his Eyes.

But the fineft Inftance of that kind I know,
is in King *John*, when *Hubert* acquaints
that Prince with the Death of *Arthur*. The
Earl of *Pembroke*, who had never feen *Hubert*
before, obferving King *John* and him in clofe
Conference, fpeaking of *Hubert*, fays to the
Earl of *Salifbury*,

The Image of a wicked heinous Fault
Lives in his Eye; that clofe Afpect of his
Does fhew the Mood of a much troubled
    Breaft.
And I do fearfully believe 'tis done,
What we fo fear'd he had a Charge to do.

C   Sal.

Sal. *The Colour of the King doth come and*
  go,
Between his Purpofe and his Confcience,
Like Heralds 'twixt two dreadful Battles fent:
His Paffion is fo ripe, it needs muft break *.

It would be endlefs to multiply Inftances
of this kind from this Divine Writer: The
only Reflection we fhall make is, That thefe
Paffages fhew to what *Excellence*, *Action*
may be carried, if it copies immediately after
Nature. We may obferve at the fame time
that when *Shakefpear* wrote, it is probable
that the Actors, who played the Parts of King
John, *Henry*, *Hubert*, and *Othello*, muft have
entered fo far into Nature, as to be able to
exprefs by their Features, and that too at the
proper Inftant, thofe Paffions which the
Poet has fo beautifully defcribed in his Lines.
Otherwife the Action muft have been miferably faulty, and the Excellence of the Poet
would have chiefly ferved to point out the
grofs Defects of the Actor, by putting the
          Audience

---

* The Author in the Original gives a Quotation from
Racine, but it falls fo infinitely fhort of what we find in almoft
every good *Englifh* Dramatic Poet, that I believe the Reader
will, when he looks into the Original, eafily pardon my
fupplying it from *Shakefpear*. I have likewife ventured to
throw what he infers, from the Inftance he brings, into another Light which may accommodate it more to our Stage,
and avoid a Repetition of fome Part of what goes before.

Audience in mind of what the latter ought
to do. I am of opinion that the greateft
Actor, when he is to play a Part in a Scene
where this dumb Action happens, has Reafon to be ftrongly alarmed with the Appre-
henfions of his not fucceeding. It is not
enough that he feels all that a Man in the
Circumftance of the Character he reprefents
may be fuppofed to feel, but he muft likewife
feel for others. This requires the deepeft
Recollection and the moft exquifite Senfe of
the Paffions of Mankind; a Senfe that can
arife only from a humane Difpofition, for
one of the chief Characters of *Ill-nature* is to
be *infenfible* of another's Anguifh. Therefore what *Quintilian* fays of an Orator may
be juftly applied to an Actor, that he ought
to be a Man not only of great Good-Senfe,
but of great Good-Nature. His Bufinefs is
to move, and it is by the Language of. the
Heart alone that he can hope to fucceed.

We muft however take Care to diftinguifh
the Difference betwixt an Alteration of the
Features, in order to exprefs the Sentiments
of the Soul, and the Grimaces that attend a
Play of the Mufcles. The firft makes a
Speaker valuable; the other makes a *Scaramouch diverting.* If a Man enters ftrongly
into a proper Enthufiafm, and fpeaks in the
Accents of the Soul, his Features will naturally form themfelves into an Agreement with

his

his Subject by the Alteration both of his Colour and Muscles. This Correspondence of the Eyes and the rest of the Features is absolutely necessary in Expression, in the same manner as in Music, the Charms of a fine Voice are heightened by the Instruments that play in Concert; for if the Eyes and Features do not correspond with the Action, it is the same as if the Violin and Bass, which play along with a fine Voice, should leave off playing; and thus both the Pleasure of the Music must be diminished, and its Effects weakened.

If the Movements of the Body and the Arms do not possess so conspicuous a Place in the Art of *Declaiming* as the Operations of the Eyes and Features, they are, however, neither useless nor despicable. A perfect Speaker, who has not the Advantages of a fine Attitude and graceful Air, loses a great deal of his Merit; the Arms as well as the Face have their Eloquence; and if the Spirit of this Art, when strong and lively, adds no Grace to Nature by the Management of the Arms, it must be owned that she at the same time communicates less Force to her. For I readily agree that to move the Arms with Dignity and Grace is the Gift of Nature alone. It is a Right of Nature to form the human Body in what manner she pleases. We see two Persons equally well made, yet the

the Motions and Deportment of the one may
be extremely awkward in every thing he
does, and thofe of the other very genteel and
agreeable. If an Orator happens not to be
endowed by Nature with the Talent of
properly managing his Arms, he is defective
in a very material Point. The Affiftances
he may borrow from an affiduous Practice
before his Looking-Glafs, and great Application, may give him an affected, but never
the true, Motion of the Hand and Arm;
and tho' it is faid that *Demofthenes* took the
Advice of a Mirror in regulating his Movements, I am of a quite different Opinion.
Who knows if the Pains he took were not
in order to bring to Perfection the Talents
which he already poffeffed, rather than to
purfue thofe which he did not poffefs; and
that he did not chufe this Method to increafe
the Beauty rather than to correct the Faults
of his Action?

An Orator who is confcious that his Action
is imperfect in this refpect ought, inftead
of practifing the *Action* of the *Arms,* to
reftrain himfelf from moving them at all;
all his Cares ought to be directed to bring
the other Parts of his Action to as high a
Degree of Perfection as poffible. If he once
can attain to fpeak with the *Enthufiafm* of
the Language of the Soul, he will, without
his own perceiving it, move his Arm, for the

Soul

Soul will then direct it, and therefore his Gesture never can be unjust.

As to those to whom Nature has been so favourably partial as to endow them with this Embellishment, tho' they are under no Necessity of studying their Gesture, yet they ought to take care not to be too lavish of their Talents. It happens to them as it does sometimes to certain Speakers, who having deep Lungs and a strong Pipe, are always plying them with so much Violence, that they lose the Merit of giving to their Expressions that Variety of Accents, so necessary for painting and understanding their Thoughts; in the same manner a Speaker, who is too lavish of his Gestures, finds so much Work for the Eyes of his Auditors that they are quite fatigued, and their Thoughts wandering and confused.

The Turns of Expression, and the Motions of the Body and the Arms, exactly correspond and go hand in hand with one another; so great is the Harmony with which they act, that if the one is faulty it immediately affects the other; for let the one of these Qualities be ever so perfect, it never can prevent the Disadvantage that arises from a Defect in the other. And indeed, how can the Eyes of a Spectator, for Instance, be agreeably entertained by the great or graceful Management of the Body or the Arms,

or

or prepare themselves to communicate to the Mind the Pleasure which she ought naturally to feel, if at the same Instant his Ears shall be struck with the Sound which gives his Mind a Sensation quite different from what she expected to receive from the Eyes?

In every Part of the Structure of the human Body, from the greatest to the least, it is easy to discover the Finger of a Divine Operator in forming that Masterpiece of the Creation. We see it so ordered by Nature, that all these Parts of our Body concur in the Art of Speaking. It is not so with other Arts, not even in those that are mechanical. *Painting* *, for Instance, employs only one Part

---

* The Author in this Observation is too partial to his own favourite Art. Had he consulted the History of *Painting* in his own Country, he would have found Painters, whose Senses were as much abstracted by the Enthusiasm of their Art, as any Poet, Philosopher, or Actor that ever was. And indeed, according to the Principles which he himself has laid down, it requires as deep a Recollection of Imagination, and as thorough an Acquaintance with the Images imprest upon the Heart, to throw them out in *Painting* as it does in *Poetry* or *Acting*. Let any Man of Taste or Genius but consider the Divine Enthusiasm that appears in the Figure of St. *Paul* preaching, in the *Cartoons* at *Hampton-Court;* let him consider the Attention, the Recollection, and the Reverence of the Spectators: Let him look upon any other Piece in that Gallery, he will find in every one of them Expressions which demonstrates that *Raphael* has possessed, besides the *Talents* of the finest Painter that ever was, those that distinguish the best *Poets*, *Orators*, and *Actors*.

Vassari, in his Lives of the Painters, informs us, that when *Michael Angelo* worked as a Statuary, he appeared to be quite

an

Part of our Senses; and when one paints he can sing, talk, hear, &c. The same may be said of the other Arts. In the Art of Action, even Reflection is forbidden; and if that Operation of the Soul, which is so absolutely Master of our Will, shall come athwart our Mind, and surprize us while we are speaking, she is forced back; because the Intensenefs of what we are about drives her out of our Head and disclaims her Company. Nor indeed are we Masters of our Reflection even in other human Operations, during which, Thoughts crowd upon one another against our Will. Here we may conclude that this Art, which as it were enchants our whole Senses, is almoft *Divine*; that our Soul is the *Agent*, and our Members and Organ the *Ministers* she employs. I will therefore repeat it, that we can declaim only in the Accents of the Soul, and that without these there can be no Action.

I

---

an Enthufiaft, and not poffeft of the fame Degree of Reafon as other Men, and it has been a very general, and a very juft Obfervation of the moft eminent Painters, that when they wanted to give a ftrong Expreffion to any Paffion, their own Features involuntarily altered according to the Refemblance they wanted to create.

Our Author's Obfervations, though he confines them to Action, are applicable, not only to Painting and Statuary, but to Mufic, Architecture, and to every Art which has *Beauty* and *Truth* for its Foundation. This Application indeed can only be partial, but had our Author acknowledged it, it would have been fo far from difparaging, that it muft have done Honour to his Profeffion.

I have elſewhere obſerved that the Theatrical Objects ought to be rendered very
ſtrong and ſtriking, even tho' the Rules
of Nature ſhould be a little tranſgreſſed,
that the Expreſſion and Action may not be
loſt to ſuch Spectators as ſit at a Diſtance
from the Stage. I ſay the ſame thing both
with regard to the Pulpit and the Bar;
but both the Speaker and the Player ought
to do this with great Caution, and only to a
certain Degree, left he diſguſt the Spectators
who are more near, by introducing too great
a Deviation from *Nature*, and too ſtrong an
Inconſiſtence with *Truth*.

I ſhall not take notice of the indiſpenſable
Neceſſity of a proper Pronunciation, becauſe
all the World is convinced of it; only I muſt
obſerve, that the Man who cannot correct the
Viciouſneſs of *habitual Dialect*, or *defective
Nature*, ought never to act in Public, becauſe
he runs the riſque of exciting Laughter
when he ought to draw Tears.

In ſhort, to render the Propoſition I have
advanced about Declaiming in the *Language
of the Soul*, on which the good or bad Succeſs of a Speaker depends, more intelligible,
I ſhall once for all take notice that this kind
of Declamation is no other than *one's feeling
the thing he pronounces.* I do not by this
mean that which is commonly called *Good
Senſe* in ſpeaking, and an intelligible manner

in

in delivering, becaufe to *feel* is another thing;
and in order to demonftrate it, I muft make
a Digreffion.

It is certain that an Orator, when upon an
important Point, ought to endeavour to work
his Audience into a Perfwafion that he be-
lieves what he advances. This is the *whole*
of his Art. A Man commonly before he
alters his Opinion is in fome doubt; he
endeavours to inquire of himfelf whether
the Change of his Sentiments is founded
on Reafon, or upon the enchanting Delufion
of the Speaker. The Speaker is therefore
obliged in his own Vindication to prevent
fuch a Sufpicion from gaining Ground in the
Mind of his Audience, or the Judges. For
this end he muft fpeak fo naturally as to
force, as it were, the Spectators to believe
every thing he is then faying, and that he
fpeaks from the Heart. For if the Audience, inftead of hearing, were to read what
he delivers, they would infallibly prefume
that, in compofing it, a thoufand Arts and
Subtleties had been employed to make it
fucceed. On the contrary, that which feems
to be as it were poured forth Extempore,
carries with it an Air of *Truth* and *Sincerity*,
which prepoffeffes the Audience in favour of
every thing that is faid. If therefore a Speech
is thus far juft to Nature, the Illufion is then
complete; and if it fhall be afterwards
printed,

printed, the Juftnefs with which the Orator delivered it will be ftill admired, a Circumftance that is highly advantagious to his Character. If a Player in his Part fhall act fo as to perfuade us that the Characters we fee are not *fictitious* but *real*; if a Counfel fpeaking for a Client fhall fucceed fo far as to convince the Judge and the Audience that it is the injured Perfon himfelf who petitions for Redrefs, or the Offender who pleads for Mercy; I repeat it again, the Illufion becomes then complete, then all that is *faid* is *felt*, and every thing paffes in the *Language of the Soul.*

It is eafy to underftand that all I have faid of Speaking in general is applicable equally to *prophane* and *facred* Orators; however I cannot difpenfe with touching more particularly on what regards the latter.

As to the manner in which a Preacher ought to deliver himfelf, his Subject is too ferious not to make us fenfible that it ought to be expreffed in Accents *fimple*, indeed, but full of *Dignity* and always *juft*. Among thofe who mount the Pulpit, a great many form themfelves upon *Theatrical Action* without following that natural Method commonly practifed at the Bar. Therefore I think it will be neceffary for us to examine this *Theatrical Action*, its Strength, and the Nature of its *Accents*, before we can decide whether

whether it is proper for the Pulpit. Except in Theatrical Declamation, (where every Period commonly begins or ends with an Elevation of the Voice) it muſt be granted that Words, when protracted and drawled out with a *Sameneſs of Accent*, as well as the Straining of the Voice, whether too vehement or ill-judged, are the perfect Averſion of Nature. A manner of ſpeaking different from what is practiſed, either in Muſic or in Speeches, is required in Tragedy. A Lawyer therefore will never think proper to plead in the ſtudied affected manner of Theatrical Declamation. Orators have in all Ages laid it down as a Maxim, that when they ſpeak, it is as Man to Man, and that therefore they ought to communicate their Thoughts in no other Accents than thoſe which are natural to Mankind.

I am perſuaded that it has been a great Error of the *French* Divines in imagining true *Theatrical Declamation* to be ſuch as is practiſed in *France*. The great Buſineſs of the Stage is, as I have already ſaid, to enchant the Spectators into a Perſuaſion that the Tragedy they are beholding is no *Fiction*, and that they who ſpeak and act are not *Players*, but *real Heroes*. But Theatrical Declamation in *France* has quite a contrary Effect; the firſt Words that are heard evidently perſuade the Audience that all is a *Fiction*, and the
Players

Players fpeak in Accents fo extraordinary, and fo removed from Truth, that it is impof-fible for one to be impofed upon. Is this Theatrical Declamation then a proper Pat-tern for the Pulpit? No, furely. A *prophane Orator* is under no fuch ftrict Obligation to declaim according to Truth, and in the *Ac-cents of the Soul*, as a *facred Orator* is; and it is certain that a Preacher who fhall deliver a Sermon in the manner of a *Theatrical De-clamation* can never make himfelf be *felt.* It may be here objected, that if an *Actor* can touch the Paffions in a *Tragedy*, a Preacher may do the fame in a *Sermon*, if he is a per-fect Mafter of *Theatrical Declamation.* I anfwer in the Negative, and my Reafons are as follow:

Moft Part of *Spectators* in *France* are inca-pable of difcerning that which may be called the *Juftnefs of Action.* They are early ac-cuftomed to *Theatrical Declamation*: Young People do not trouble their Heads much about Reafoning, and they grow old before they make any folid Reflections upon this Point. If an Audience thus difpofed is touched in feeing a Tragedy, it is becaufe they are under an *habitual Illufion*, in which *Truth* has no Share. All the World knows that *Cæfar*, *Alexander*, *Hannibal*, &c. were Men like us; and every Body is perfuaded that they felt their ftrongeft Paffions, and per-formed

formed their moſt Heroic Actions in the ſame
manner as the great Men of our own Age; yet
the very Spectators who are convinced of this,
being prejudiced in their Youth in favour of
the bombaſt manner of *Theatrical Declamation*, form their Ideas of theſe Heroes according to theAppearance they make, as perſonated
by *Players:* That is, as Men quite above the
common Level of Mankind, with a manner
of walking, ſpeaking, and looking, different
from the reſt of the World. But according
to thoſe fictitious Ideas which the Spectators
have adopted, and which deeply affect them,
they form ſo ſtrong an Illuſion, that they ſuf-
fer themſelves to be tranſported beyond Truth
in every thing they ſee and hear. If Players
therefore touch others with the Part they
repreſent in Tragedy, it is only becauſe by
Habit the Audience reconcile themſelves to
the unnatural Method of Declamation, and
thus the Effect that it ought to produce, by
degrees, wears off. For could they ſee Nature and Truth in their genuine Appearances, they would ſoon ſhake off the Preju-
dices of Cuſtom. I ſhall only give two Inſtances of what I have advanced here, which
ought to be tranſmitted to Poſterity, and
eternally engraved upon the Minds of Players. Whoever remembers to have ſeen *Bet-
terton*, or *Booth*, in *England*, muſt readily own
that the whole Houſe was touched by their
ſimple

simple natural manner of Action; and Good Sense dictates to us that we never seek for Pleasure in *Fiction* when we can find it in *Truth*, especially in a Profession such as that of a Player, which borrows its chief Excellencies from Nature herself.

In *France*, when a Stranger goes to a Playhouse for the first time, he is extremely disgusted with their *Theatrical Declamation*. It is true that the *universal Applause* which their Actors meet with, sometimes debauches them into the prevailing Taste of the Country; but I have found at *Paris* a great many *Frenchmen* who never go to see a Tragedy from an Aversion to this kind of Declamation, but it is an Aversion which prevails only with Men of great Genius and Taste, who abhor, they say, to see *Nature* and *Truth* so mangled upon the Stage. How is it possible then that such Declamation should be a proper Pattern for a Preacher, who, if by a mistaken manner of Pronunciation he disguises the great Truths he delivers, may indeed convince the Reason, but never can touch the Passions, of his Audience? A *Grain of Falshood*, if I may express myself so, will sowr a whole *Lump of Truth*, and the human Understanding can never bear to see them associated.

It is likewise incontestibly true that the general manner of Declaiming in a Preacher,

tho'

tho' it ought always to be true and natural, yet ought ftill to admit of three different Diftinctions in its Character. One accommodated to *Sermons*, one to *Panegyrics*, and one to *Funeral Orations*. *Zeal*, *Admiration*, and *Grief*, ought to regulate the manner in which thefe three Subjects are treated, fo that the Speaker may always fuftain, and in his Difcourfe give the Predominance to that Manner which is moft fuitable to his Subject.

It is eafily perceived that each of thefe three Manners, *Zeal*, *Admiration*, and *Grief*, does not exift independant of the other, and that an Orator may have occafion to practife them all in handling the fame Subject. For Inftance, in a Sermon where *Zeal* ought to predominate, the Accents of *Admiration* and *Grief*, as well as other Paffions, are admitted according as the Thoughts, that fall in, require. In the fame manner in *Panegyric*, where the predominant manner ought to be that of *Admiration*, at the glorious Actions of the Perfon who is celebrated; all other Manners, fuch as *Zeal and Grief*, may be employed as Occafion offers, and may even be indifpenfible. I fay the fame thing with regard to *Funeral Sermons*; and tho' it would feem that they are of the fame Nature with *Panegyric*, and that *Admiration* of the great Actions of the Perfons who are celebrated to the Audience fhould have a large Share in the

the manner of delivering them, yet here Grief ought to be the predominant Manner. For it is certain that tho' the glorious Actions of Saints and Heroes claim the same Degree of *Admiration*, yet it is with this Difference, that we remember the first with † *Admiration* mixt with *Joy*, because they are looked upon as happy in Heaven; and the great Actions of the others must be celebrated with *Admiration* mixed with *Grief*, arising from the Remembrance of the Loss we have just sustained by their Death. These are the Reasons why *Grief* ought to predominate in a *Funeral Oration*, not only over *Admiration*, but over all the other Manners that fall within the Compass of an Orator's Practice. Thus, as to the different Manner of employing these three different Passions, the Art of an Orator consists in disposing the immense Variety of the Accents which he uses so as that they may never in the least obscure that which ought to predominate in his Subject. I shall say no more on this Subject in Writing, because the most instructive Precepts on that Point, and even those that may be really useful, ought to be communicated by the

D   Voice,

---

† The Reader thro' all this Passage will no doubt make Allowance for our Author's being a *Roman-Catholic*, and living in *France*.

Voice, as I have obferved before, and not by Paper.

As I have faid in the Beginning of thefe Reflections, that a young Orator ought never to appear in Public, until he has attained a certain Degree of Perfection; I own I cannot help repeating the fame thing here: He ought not to expect that his Audience will fit patiently hearing him for thirty Years, till he has obtained Perfection in his Art; for I grant he may acquire it by long Experience. A young Orator may anfwer me, that it is the *Exercife of an Art that forms the Artift.* I know it well, and according to the Reflections I have made, I know likewife that in practifing it he ought to follow the Method of *Demofthenes.* This great Man, it is well known, fet out by practifing his Art two or three times in Public; he found he did not fucceed, he then fhut himfelf up for fome Years, and then emerg'd into Public the Wonder and Miracle of *Greece.* Let a young Orator do the fame, let him make an Effay of his Art in Public, and if he finds he is deftitute of Talents to fucceed, let him either throw it entirely up, or never appear again until he is a complete Mafter. How abfurd muft a contrary Conduct be! The great Men of all Sciences are at Pains to conceal the Productions of their Youth, becaufe they know them to be imperfect. Painters, Sculp-

tors, and Poets never put their Name to their
firſt Eſſays. Workmen can never paſs for
Maſters if they don't produce ſome finiſhed
Maſterpiece, which proves that they deſerve
that Title. And ſhall a young Orator be ſo
imprudent as to declaim in Public, without
having beforehand exerciſed his Talents and
corrected his Faults in Private?

It is amazing that in all Ages and Nations
of polite Learning, no Schools for *Declamation* have ever yet been eſtabliſhed. The
Maſters of public Schools and Colleges give
Boys ſome ſlight Notions which they never
reduce to Practice in any of the Stages of
Civil Life; but indeed as the principal End
of their Employment is to teach the dead
Languages, they have no Time to beſtow on
other Studies; beſides the Boys whom they
have commonly under their Care are too
young and incapable either to make ſolid
Reflections by themſelves, or to comprehend
the Precepts of their Maſter. Should an
old Orator fill a public Chair and teach the
Art of *Declamation*, he would be as uſeful
to Society as moſt of the fine Eſtabliſhments
that are in great Cities. Young People
would then ſtudy Oratory when moſt of
their other Studies were over; when they
were advanced in Age, and conſequently
more capable to comprehend the Reaſons
that would be offered, but above all, they

D 2   would

would retain the natural and ſtriking Impreſ-
ſions conveyed by animated Speech in the
Practice of *Declaiming* in all the different
Branches of that Art.

THE

THE

ITALIAN THEATRE.

HE Remarks which in another Work I have † already made upon the Rife of the Drama in *Italy*, fufficiently juftify me in fuppofing, that it has admitted of no Interruption fince it ceafed to be exhibited on the *Latin* Theatres. But when it forgat its original Grandeur, it grew fo low as to ftrole from Town to Town, where it was performed in their open Places; and tho' the infipid, indecent Buffoneries, reprefented in this manner, are far from deferving the Name of Comedies, yet we can in them at leaft trace the Seeds of that barbarous Weed which throve fo well, till abolifhed by Religion.

The *Italian Drama* languifhed for a long time in this Condition, till towards the Beginning of the twelfth Century; it then by Degrees recovered its Vigour, and admitted the Embellifhments of Dialogue, but as

D 3 yet

---

† See my Hiftory of the *Italian* Theatre.

yet it was only exhibited in private Houses. About that Time, taking Advantage of Subjects and Characters borrowed from Religion, the Drama began to appear with more Pomp, and the Invention of Printing introduced her to the Acquaintance of the Public: Some Comedies printed about sixty Years after this great Discovery, that is, about the Year 1520, are yet extant; and tho' the Names of the Authors are unknown, yet it is easy to discern from the Uncouthness of the Language that they must have been composed more than a Century before, and their very Titles imply that they were printed long after they were wrote. It is therefore very probable that there were some others worse wrote, consequently older than these, and perhaps now extant in Manuscript; but the printed Comedies which I speak of are so licentious, both in the Conduct and Sentiments, that from them we may easily form a Judgment of the Merit of those which preceded them.

Bibiena in his *Callandra, Machiavelli* in his *Mandragola* and *Clitia,* and *Ariosto* in his *five Comedies,* with the other best Dramatic Writers who flourished in the first forty Years of the sixteenth Century, for the most part, formed themselves upon these ancient Models in their own Language, tho' full of Impiety and Indecency; all they have done being to correct the Form and
Conduct

Conduct of the Fable in order to render it more regular and complete. But notwithstanding the undoubted Proofs which may be drawn from their ancient Comedies that have come to our Hands in Print, (and of a much older Date than the Age of *Callendra*, which was acted for the first time towards the End of the 15th Century,) the *Italians* date the Commencement of this Drama no higher than that Period; and they reckon all the Pieces written in the preceding Ages to be no better than so many *Farces*, tho' they are very long, and divided into *five Acts*. Some Pieces of this kind are called in the Title-Pages *Farces*, and others, *Comedies*. It is likewise remarkable that a great many others in the Title-Pages are named *Farces*, and in the Epilogue, *Comedies*. From this, it is plain, that their ancient Poets, by these two Words, understood the same thing. But the *Italian* Writers, without reflecting upon this Circumstance, very violently deny them the Rank of *Comedies*, and place them only in the Class of *Farces*. For my own Part, by their Leave, I call them all Comedies, but *defective* ones, and the Product of an *Infant* THEATRE.

The Modern *Italian* Writers have chosen to stifle the Merits of their Predecessors to recommend their own Correctness in Dramatic Performances. It appears as if they

had

had it in View to conceal from the Public the Writings for the Stage almoſt for two Ages, that they may glory in thoſe of one Period which does them Honour; their Aim being to perſuade the World that the *Infancy* of their *Theatre* produced only *Maſterpieces*, and not *trifling*, *lame Performances*, as has been the Caſe of all the Theatres in the World, ſince the Time of the *Greeks* and *Latins*. We can eaſily perceive that theſe proceeded gradually, and for a long time as if it were in Leading-ſtrings, before they arrived to Perfection, or even before they had corrected their original Abſurdities. As therefore the ancient *Italian* Comedies, which have come to our Hands, and which are not very numerous, are deſigned in their Frontiſpieces only under the Title of the *Ancients*, but without any Information to the Reader, or the leaſt Light by which we can be enabled to determine their Date, let us enquire if their Repreſentations of Subjects taken from Scripture can furniſh us with any Helps for aſcertaining the Period that gave Riſe to the Modern *Italian* Drama.

Anciently the Paſſion of our Lord was repreſented at *Rome* in the *Colliſee*. The moſt celebrated *Italian* Authors leave us no room to doubt of this, and if we take the Pains to examine them, we ſhall find in their Works plain and indiſputable Proofs of the Point
we

we are now treating; but nothing confirms this Truth more ftrongly than the Tragedies that are extant upon the Paffion of our Lord.

It is no lefs certain that the Cuftom of reprefenting the Paffion of our Lord was entirely abolifhed towards the End of the Pontificate of *Paul* the third, that is to fay, in the Year 1546, or at moft in 1549. This we exprefsly learn from the * Authors here referred to; but it will be very difficult for us to determine at what time the Cuftom of reprefenting the Paffion commenced, or to afcertain its Original. We find indeed that it is of old ftanding; for the Authors I have quoted, unanimoufly concur in favour of its Antiquity: They fix the Period when thefe Tragedies were abolifhed, but leave us entirely in the dark as to the time of their Rife, probably becaufe they themfelves were fo: Therefore all we can advance on this Head muft be founded on mere Conjecture.

Some able Antiquaries of Modern *Rome* are however of Opinion, that the Reprefentations

---

* Andreas Fulvius, Page 146.

La Defcription de Rome, 8vo. Printed Anno 1643, Page 487.

Il Ritratto di Roma Moderna. Printed in 1645. Page 435.

Roma Ricertaca. Printed in 1699. Page 73.

Guido Pancirolli in Roma Sacra e Moderna. Printed in 1725. Page 37.

Crefcembini ne Commentarii de la Volgar Poefia. Page 242.

tations of the Paffion of our Saviour at the
Collifee, could not have been introduced fooner
than in the Year 1449; fo that, according
to this Authority, they muft have lafted for
near a hundred Years, becaufe they ended
under *Paul* the third, towards the Year
1549. This Opinion is founded on the
Teftimony of *Crefcembeni*, in his *Hiſtory of
Poetry in his Mother-Tongue*, where he cites
Cionnacci, and fpeaks in the following manner of *Pious Reprefentations*. I fhall tranflate
his own Words: " The moft ancient that
" have come to our Hands, fays he, is, ac-
" cording to *Cionnacci*, (who fays that he
" had the Manufcript) that of *Abraham* and
" *Ifaac*, by *Francis Beliari*, who died in
" the Year 1484." The fame *Cionnacci*
adds, that at the End of the Manufcript he
read thefe Words; " The above Piece was
" played, for the firft time, at *Florence*, in
" the Church of *Saint Mary Magdalen*, in
" the Year 1449;" and *Crefcembeni* affirms,
that this was the firft from Holy Writ that
ever was compofed or acted in *Italy*. But
if I am not miftaken he is in the wrong,
becaufe the Manufcript affirms no fuch thing;
it only informs us, that the Play of *Abraham
and Ifaac* was reprefented, for the firft time,
in the Year 1449. But it does not fay that
this was the firft Poem of the kind that
ever had been compofed in *Italy*. Had it

been

been fo, the Author would not have failed to have challenged to himfelf the Honour of the Invention, and to have let us know that he was the firft that brought the Sacred Tragedies upon the Stage; therefore Mr. *Crefcembeni* attributed to him an Honour which the Author could not claim, and which if he had, all *Italy* might perhaps have given him the Lye.

Some Pages before, *Crefcembeni*, in fearching for the Original and Rife of Sacred Reprefentations, rejects a Fact which I look upon as decifive in this Point, and therefore fhall tranflate the Paffage literally. " We " cannot, fays he, by any means fix upon " the Time when they began; tho' *Vafori*, " in his Life of *Buffalmacco* the Painter, " gives us an Account of this Feaft which " was made upon the *Arno* in the Year " 1304, where a Machine, reprefenting " *Hell*, was fixed upon the Boats, and " which *Cionnacci* imagines may be that of " *Teofilo*, at the End of which, as he afferts, " Hell was reprefented, *fince it is remarked* " *that towards the End of it, the Devil is* " *returning to Hell with a* Jew, *and an* Angel " *difmiffes the Spectators. Or rather that of* " Lazarus *the rich and* Lazarus *the poor,* " *at the End of which the rich* Lazarus *in* " *Hell in vain begs Relief of the poor one* " *who is in* Abraham's *Bofom.* However, from

" from the Time and Place of Reprefenta-
" tion, (it happening about the Calends of
" *May*, when every thing that was exhibited
" was of the prophane kind,) we fhall not
" place this Entertainment among the Sa-
" cred Feafts, nor affirm that this was the
" firft that ever was reprefented in *Italy*."

I am far from thinking this Conclufion of our Author juft. This Entertainment might have been reprefented on the River *Arno* as a prophane one, but ftill the Subject on which it is built is facred or moral; fo that if it was not of the one kind, it ought always to be underftood to be included under the Rank and Denomination of the other. Therefore inftead of refuting this Opinion, I fhall make Ufe of the Difcovery itfelf as a Direction for tracing, to more remote Antiquity, Works of this Nature, and endeavour to fix the Foundation of a probable Conjecture on this Subject.

If I might venture to give my Opinion on a Point fo obfcure, efpecially after the Authority which I have quoted above, I own I fhould be very much of the Mind that the Reprefentation of the Paffion of our Saviour at the *Collifee* took its Rife much about the Time of the Eftablifhment of the Frater-nity *del Gonfalone*. This I think we may reafonably conclude from the *Statutes* of that *Company*, which were printed at *Rome*

by

by *Bonfadino,* in the Year 1584, Page 74, an Abstract from which I shall here translate.

" The principal Design of our Fraternity
" being to represent the *Passion of* Jesus
" Christ, we ordain, that in case the
" Mysteries of the said Passion are repre-
" sented, our ancient Orders shall be observ-
" ed, together with what shall be prescribed
" by the *General Congregation.*"

Two Reflections naturally arise from this Passage. It appears from thence, that the principal and essential *Constitution of the Fraternity del Gonfalone,* was in order to represent the *Passion of our Lord;* it appears likewise that they had certain Regulations to direct them in the Management of these *Representations,* and in the *Execution* of the *Tragedy.* But is it credible that the Brethren, *del Gonfalone,* had deviated from the principal Regulations of their Order, especially if we consider that the Observation of these Statutes was not only agreeable to their Genius, but even pleased the general Taste of the whole Nation? Every Body is very well acquainted with the *Passion* the *Italians* have for Shows; besides the Public knows with what Earnestness all new Establishments are embraced. But this Fraternity was founded in the Year 1264, as appears by the Preface to the Statutes of the Company, and

and by *Octavio Panciroli*, in his *Teſoro naſ-coſti di Roma*, Page 488. According to theſe Authorities, the Repreſentation of our Lord's Paſſion muſt have begun about the Year 1264, and continued for two hundred and eighty eight Years. This is upon a Suppo-ſition that the Authors I have already quoted are in the right, when they affirm that they were aboliſhed towards the End of the Pon-tificate of *Paul the third*, that is to ſay, about the Year 1549. This is my firſt Conjecture.

The *Italians* boaſt that their Theatre is the Original and Model of all the others in *Europe*. I know they are in the right of it; but this Aſſertion is founded only on an ancient Tradition. And without their ſearch-ing into the Original of the *French*, *Spaniſh*, and *Engliſh* Theatres, they having firmly and implicitely believed that at whatever Time the *Italian* Theatre was opened it muſt have been the firſt. Therefore they were at no Pains to fix the preciſe Æra, and did not care whether it was two Centuries ſooner, or two Centuries later. They have one poſitive Inſtance of a Repreſentation of a *Divine* or *Moral* Nature, exhibited upon the *Arno* in the Year 1304, but this they reject, in order to fix it one hundred and ſixty Years later; by this means they deſtroy another Æra, which is that of the Frater-nity *del Gonfalone*, eſtabliſhed in the Year 1264

1264, and fix the firſt Repreſentation of a Holy Subjeſt ſo late as the Year 1449. Were this Computation incontestably true, the *Italians* could have no Reaſon to boaſt of their being the Fathers of the Drama in *Europe*, but ought to be contented with admitting that they are but the Scholars of other Nations, ſince no Faſt is more certain than that the Myſteries of the Old Teſtament were repreſented at *London* in the Year 1378, and in *France* in the Year 1398, or rather ſooner, as we ſhall prove in a proper Place. It is therefore evident that the *Italians* muſt have learnt the Dramatic Art from the *Engliſh* and *French*, if we admit that their Plays did not begin at the Time when the Fraternity *del Gonfalone* was eſtabliſhed, which was in 1264, or about the Time of the Entertainment preſented on the *Arno* already mentioned, which was about the Year 1300; and if, as *Creſcembeni* and the other modern *Roman* Antiquaries contend, their firſt moral Repreſentation was ſo late as the Year 1449.

What we have quoted from the Statutes of the *Fraternity of the Gonfalone*, ſuggeſts another Refleſtion on this Head. They enaſt, " That in caſe the Myſteries of the Paſſion " ſhould be repreſented, they ſhould con " form to the *Ancient Orders*, and to what " ſhould be preſcribed by the *General Con-* " *gregation*,"

" *gregation.*" Therefore the Reprefentation of our Saviour's Paffion was prohibited only with regard to the Place where it was exhibited, and *Paul* the fecond only abolifhed it at the *Collifee*. It is even rational to prefume that the Fraternity exhibited them fince that Time; but in other Places, for thirty fix Years after the Prohibition by this Pope, it appears by new Statutes that they had a Privilege of playing, *if they thought fit.* For if the Reprefentation of our Lord's Paffion had been abfolutely prohibited by the Pope in the City of *Rome*, the Infertion of this Claufe was quite ufelefs, nor would it have been lawful to have inferted it at all, had it been exprefsly contrary to the Orders of the Holy See.

All Holy Tragedies have been written in Verfe; but we ought not to rely upon the printed Editions to determine whether the moft ancient that we have were acted in the fame Shape in which they are printed. Thefe Editions inform us that they were tranfcribed, in order to render them more legible and more agreeable to the Modern Tafte; and this was done as often as a new Edition was publifhed, or the Play, after fome Interval, was revived. Among others, there remains an Edition of one of thefe Tragedies, where the principal Point I have been endeavouring to prove, is clearly explain-
ed,

ed, and the Tranflation of the Title Page is as follows. " Of the Paffion, Death, and " Refurrection of Jefus Chrift, being a Tra- " gical Reprefentation, by *John Baptift Fila-* " *ur*, the third Edition, corrected from a " great many Miftakes, and enlarged with " the Addition of a great Number of Lines " by *Salvatore Maffonio*, and played in the " City of *Aquila* on Holy Thurfday, in the " Year 1614." The Reprefentations there- fore of the Paffion were not abolifhed in *Italy* fixty five Years after the Prohibition iffued out by *Paul* the third. This too ferves to confirm the Opinion I have advanced, that this Prohibition extended only to the Place of Reprefentation, and not to the Thing reprefented.

Reprefentations from *Holy Writ* continued in *Italy* to 1660, that is, three Years after the Pontificate of *Paul* the third; and that not only in private Places, but much oftner in Churches upon the Celebration of the Feftivals of the Saint who gave Name to the Church ; as we may gather from the Title- Pages of a great Number of Plays; but had they been prohibited and abolifhed by the Pope, the *Italian* Bifhops never would have fuffered them to have been reprefented within their *Bifhopricks*, much lefs in their *Churches*: But the Medley of *Sacred* and *Prophane*, together with the Loofe Comedy, interfperfed

in

in thefe Performauces, difgufted the Spectators, and in a little time they were quite
laid afide.

From all I have faid above, I believe we
may fairly conclude, that if the Paffion of
our Lord was not prefented at the *Collifee*
for the firft time, in theYear of the Eftablifhment of the *Fraternity of the* Gonfalone,
which was founded in 1264, it appeared
there very foon after. Admitting this, I believe, it will naturally enough follow, that
this Fraternity were not the firft Inventors
of thefe kind of Reprefentations, but that
they had before been privately exhibited upon
the Stage, tho' in a very bungling manner,
and that the Fraternity had it in View to act
them with greater Magnificence, and in a
more correct manner at the *Collifee*. What
End would the Inftitution of this Fraternity
have ferved, fuppofing this to be the principal Object they had in View, if they deferred
putting it in Execution for a *hundred four-
fcore and five Years?* It is therefore reafonable to believe that the Execution of this
Project was not deferred very long; and it
would be a Contradiction to all the Rules
of Probability, fhould we affirm that they
did not commence till the Year 1449.

Forty Years intervened betwixt the Eftablifhment of the Fraternity, and the Entertainment exhibited upon the *Arno* at *Florence,*

rence, in the Year 1304. And I take it for an undisputed Fact, that during the intermediate time, the Passion of our Lord, with the other Holy Representations, as well as other prophane Comedies or Farces as they are sometimes termed, begun already to be in Vogue, and that they even had appear'd a long time before the Establishment of the Fraternity; tho' perhaps they were the first who erected a kind of a Theatre in a public Place, such as the *Collisee*, where they were to be represented.

Dante was the first who introduced Poetry among the *Italians*; and without relying upon what *Leonardo Aretino* makes *Dante* himself say, in his Life *, ' that Poetry had commenced a hundred and fifty Years before his Time,' it is sufficient for my Purpose, that it began to prevail in the Days of *Guido Guinicelli*, *Guittone*, *Bonaguinta*, and *Guida da Messina*, who lived before *Dante*, as they flourished in the Year 1200; this confirms my Conjecture, that the Drama was introduced into *Italy* towards the Year 1200, which is before the Establishment of the Fraternity *del Gonfalone*, who probably formed the Plan of their Institution upon the Custom which prevailed in the Country of representing the Passion, on some other Entertainment, the Subject of which was either Moral or Divine.

E 2   The

* Page 97.

The *Italian* Writers never advance any thing as Fact for which they have not *Ocular Demonſtration*; and when they once ground an Opinion upon Facts, if they happen to differ amongſt themſelves, they are perpetually at odds; the Contradiction goes round, and the Difference for ever remains irreconcilable: Conſidering the Uncertainty in which they have left us, I am very ſenſible that if any Body ſhall adopt the Conjectures, which appear to me to be well founded, I ſhall be the means of bringing him into a great deal of Trouble and Diſpute, but far contrary to my Intention. The Invention of Printing happened at a Time when *Italy*, of all the Nations in *Europe*, poſſeſſed the greateſt Share of Learning, and by this means the Works of their Anceſtors ſuffered not a little; for their Men of Learning did not apply themſelves to the Publication of any Work (eſpecially of the poetical kind) that was not in a poliſhed Stile, and a correct Turn. Thus it is by great Chance, that any thing which was otherwiſe has at all came to our Hands. In this Conduct they were not imitated by the other Nations in *Europe*, as we ſhall ſhew in a proper Place; theſe laſt having printed every thing compoſed by their Anceſtors be it good, bad, or indifferent, if written two or three hundred Years before, and by this they have a conſiderable Advantage over the

Italians,

Italians, in tranfmitting to Pofterity many Works which ferve as the Documents and the Guides of Hiftory. Had the *Italians* done the fame thing, we fhould not have at this Time been at a Lofs how to fix the Date of the *Italian Drama.*

Since the Year 1500 no *Italian* Poet has profeffed to write for the Theatre, in order to pick up Money; Dramatic Poetry having fince that Time been an *Art,* but not a *Trade.* The Dukes of *Ferrara, Florence, Urbin,* and *Mantua,* fuffered Plays to be acted only within their own Palaces. The Academy of *Sienna* was the firft that, by its own Example, encouraged other Learned Bodies to compofe and reprefent correct Comedies. Their Example was followed during the xviith Century; and the hired Actors, who till that Time had always acted extempore, never acted any Piece that had not before been printed.

As to what regards the modern *Italian* Theatre, I fhall begin by giving the Reader fome Notion of the Structure of the Stage itfelf, and the Character of the Spectators. The Spectators in almoft all the Cities of *Italy* are *reftlefs* and *noify,* even before the Play begins. In their Applaufes they are violent; and when they would diftinguifh a favourite Poet or Actor, they cry as loud as they can *Viva—Viva.* But if they have a

E 3   Mind

Mind to damn the one, or hifs the other, they bawl out *Va dentro*, and very often they make the poor Actor feel a further Proof of their Indignation by pelting him with Apples, and loading him with a great deal of Abufe. But the Actors who have Reputation and Merit meet with great Efteem and Applaufe; and in the very Cities where the Audiences are moft unruly, they immediately become calm when a favourite Play or Actor appears on the Stage.

But there are fome Cities where the Audience is always quiet and civil, even tho' neither the Play nor the Players are agreeable; the Spectators fhewing no other Refentment than by not returning to the fame Entertainment, after having fat it out two or three times; and inftead of Noife and Bawling, they exprefs their Difpleafure by a Contempt that is a tacite but an equally ftrong Proof of Diflike. This Conduct prevails in the Cities of *Genoa*, *Lucca*, and *Florence*; however the Audiences there know how to difcern and do Juftice to a Poet or Actor of Merit.

In *Italy* they are entirely Strangers to the Cuftom of exhibiting Theatrical Entertainments thro' the whole Year, the Towns where they are at all eftablifhed having their ftated Times for Playing, which do not happen always at one Time of the Year: The Comedians, during the Space of twelve Months,

Months, visit a good Part of *Italy*. The Theatres of *Venice* are open from the Month of *October* to the first Day of *Lent*. In many Cities of the two *Lombardies*, the Spring of the Year is allotted for Comedies; and they are represented in the Day-time without any Lights, because the Play-houses are built in such a manner as to be sufficiently enlightened by the Sun. These Play-houses, or rather Halls, are sometimes a plain Booth erected in large *Areas*, almost like that of *Verona*, where every Year such Booths are built in the *Arena* of the great Amphitheatre.

In the Cities where Comedies are acted by the Day-light, the Representation goes on with great Regularity, which arises not so much from the Characters of the Spectators, as from the Difficulty they would find to escape public Censure.

The Theatres are open in *Rome* only the last eight Days of the *Carnaval*. And ever since *Innocent the Eleventh* prohibited Women from acting on the Stage, young Men supply their Places in Habits of Women.

The *Italian* Theatres are magnificent, they commonly having four Rows of Boxes, besides a lower one, which forms as it were a Partition round the Pit. There is at *Venice* a Theatre with seven Rows of Boxes; this is distinguished by the Title of *Saint Samuel*,

according

according to the general Cuftom of defigning their different Theatres by the Name of their refpective Parifhes where they are built. It is an eftablifhed Cuftom all over *Italy* to fit in the Pit.

In *Venice* one may fee a Comedy for fixteen Sols of *Current* Money, which is paid at the Door, where they receive a Ticket. But then, if one defigns to fit, he muft pay ten Sols more; but if the Pit is not full, they are fuffered to ftand on the Floor, towards the Bottom of the Houfe. As to the Boxes, every Body who is admitted there muft pay for a whole one to himfelf.

The Theatres at *Venice* commonly contain *four and twenty,* and fometimes *thirty* Boxes in a Row; but thefe Boxes can hold no more than fix Perfons, fo that admitting they were all full, they would contain no more than fourteen hundred Perfons in all *. The great Theatre in *Milan* is one of the largeft in *Italy*; but none of them are comparable to that of *Parma,* which, like thofe of Ancient *Rome,* has no Boxes, but Benches arifing in form of an Amphitheatre.

At *Venice* the Spectators go mafqued to the public Diverfions, which is a great Conveniency to the Nobles, efpecially the Senators and

---

* The Author muft mean *the whole Houfe being full.*

and the other Perfons who are in great Offices; becaufe while they are mafqued they have no Occafion to diftinguifh themfelves by the Habit that is peculiar to their Quality or Employment, and even the *Doge* himfelf in this Difguife, may go without his Attendants. But if they have a Mind, they may go with their bare Faces, which gives an Opportunity for the Women of Quality and Diftinction to be feen.

There are commonly in that City eight Theatres open; four for Comedies, and four for Operas. As the Diftinctions of Ranks muft be obferved here, theWomen of Quality place themfelves always in the Front-Boxes; and the *Courtezans*, who for fome time paft have ufed to mafque themfelves, fit in the Row immediately below. The Men and the Women, who are to fit in Chairs in the Pit, take great Care not to put on fine Cloaths, it being the Cuftom to fpit out of the Boxes into the Pit, and to throw into it the Remains of what they have been eating, which renders it extremely difagreeable.

The Boxes are hired either for a Year or a Day. But what they call their Year begins, as we have obferved before, in the Month of *October*, and ends on the laft Day of the Carnaval. The Price of thefe Boxes are not fixed, it being regulated according to the Pieces that are reprefented; the Licencer of
the

the Stage is the Judge how much they shall be enlarged or how much diminished; and that again is commonly regulated by the Merits of the Piece and of the Actors; the Success of a new Piece having sometimes mounted an Upper Gallery to the Price of a Sequin, or ten *French* Livres; a Front Box to ten Sequins, and the others in Proportion. There are very few Cities in *Italy* which have not more than one Theatre; they having generally two or three, and the Prices paid at the Door are commonly regulated according to the Rules that obtain at *Venice*.

Having thus spoken of the Structure of the Stage itself, I proceed now to the Pieces represented on it. Since the Year 1500, the *Italians* may boast with Justice that their Drama has been very complete. Perhaps it is the only Theatre in *Europe* which can date its Excellency so far back; and with regard to the Rules of Writing, as well as the Genius and Taste of the Writers, it has proved the Model of all the Theatres that have been since erected.

Towards the Middle of the xviith Century, *Spanish* Plays took Place instead of their most perfect Dramatical Performances; and so prevailing was this universal Degeneracy of Taste, during the last fifty Years, that the best Pieces of their Ancestors, which came into their Hands, were but very little esteemed

in

in the Country. A Poetical Production, in the Manner of *Petrarch*, met with but very few Admirers, and was generally looked upon as low and infipid. The Productions for the Stage met with the fame Fate; for during all that Period, if a good Play appeared, it was received with Contempt, and a Man would have blufhed to fay that he had read it. In fhort, the Tafte for the *Spanifh* Drama, which muft be owned to have its Beauties, was carried in *Italy* to the higheft Pitch of Extravagance. The Productions in this way are very numerous in *Italy*, and moftly in the laft I have mentioned.

But the Madnefs began to abate, and towards the End of the Century, Men of Learning, Wit, and Tafte, appeared almoft thro' all the Cities of *Italy*, who by their Writings and Academical Differtations, in Seminaries or Societies of Learning, revived and eftablifhed good Senfe in every Province of Poetry. With regard to the *Drama*, Tranflations from *Racine* and *Corneille* were oppofed to the prevailing Extravagance of Tafte, and the mercenary Players, in imitation of thefe private Judges, ftruck into the Road of good Senfe; thus after a hard Struggle betwixt Truth and Error, *Tafte* again prevailed in *Italy*.

Since the Year 1700 a great Number of good Tragedies have been compofed by the

Wits

Wits of *Italy*; some upon the *French*, some upon the ancient Plan of Writing; the latter are the Productions of the finest Pens of *Italy*, who dissatisfied with the *French* Manner have, but not with all the Success that one could wish, endeavoured to revive that of the *Greeks*; we have likewise seen Comedies in both Manners appear, and all in Verse: It is true, they are so very few that the *Italian* Stage, since the Year 1700, is extremely low, if we compare it to those of *England*, *France*, and *Spain*, which every Year increased their Stock by the Accession of new Plays.

The Barrenness of the *Italian Stage* is doubtless owing to the Authors that write for it reaping no Profit from their Labours. A Man of Wit and Fortune, sometimes for his own Amusement and Satisfaction, composes a Theatrical Performance and gives it to the Players. Others, such as *Martelli* and *Gravino*, ordered their Productions of that kind to be printed before they appear upon the Stage, leaving the Players at Liberty, after they are printed, to represent them in what Manner and at what Time they please; but these Hits so seldom happen, that we have all the Reason in the World to fear, a true Taste for the Drama will be soon entirely extinguished in *Italy*.

Men of Wit and Spirit, who don't always share equally in the Gifts of Fortune as of Nature,

Nature, follow another Road for attaining their Ends. Time has infenfibly deftroyed moft Part of the Academies; and in thofe that remain, the fame Tafte does not prevail. If from time to time, and merely as the Fancy ftruck them, they take it into their Heads to compofe fome Pieces for the Theatre, they chufe rather to tranflate them from the *French* than to compofe Originals. This is the Practice in the Colleges of *Rome*, *Parma*, and almoft all the other Colleges of *Italy*. The Eafe with which the *French* Plays are tranflated debauches thofe into that Practice, who have Genius enough to compofe Originals; and *Gigli*, one of the beft Poets of his Age, after having compofed a great many original Pieces, tranflated the *Tartuff* of *Moliere* under the Title of *D' Pilone*. Hence I forefee that the *Italian* Poets will degenerate into mere Tranflators, and my Prediction is already but too much fulfilled.

Tho' in *Italy* the *Dramatic* Poets have never wrote for Money, yet we find by the *Dramaturgia* of *Alacci*, that their Number was very confiderable. According to that *Catalogue*, it amounts to no lefs than one hundred and thirty nine *Tragic* Poets, and three hundred and eleven *Comic* Poets of a correct Age, *i. e.* fince the Year 1500.

The fame Author, whofe Account reaches

no

no farther than *A. D.* 1660, gives us the Titles of the Pieces, together with the Names of the *Authors* who have wrote *Tragi-Comedies*, *Pastorals*, and *Sacred Tragedies*; and adding thefe to the Poets in my *Catalogue*, we will find that the Number of *Italian Dramatic Poets*, in the Space of one hundred and fixty Years at moft, amounts to one Thoufand two Hundred and Twelve. But this Catalogue leaves a Gap unaccounted for of no lefs than feventy fix Years back from this Date; and if, amongft that infinite Number of Performances, there were fome of them taken from the *Spanish*, or written in the Manner of that Nation, yet a fufficient Number of good ones will be found to perfuade me that if the *Italian* Theatre had been as productive of Rewards to the Poets, as the other Thearres of *Europe*, it muft have produced both better Performances, and in greater Number than any other; for when Glory and Profit meet together, they form the ruling Principle of a Genius.

As we have treated of the *Dramatic Poets* from the Year 1500 to 1660, it will be of fome Ufe to make the World acquainted with the Number of Pieces that were printed in that Time. In the Collection of the *Vatican Library* we meet with no lefs than two hundred and thirty five prophane *Tragedies*, five hundred *Comedies*, two hundred and thirty

thirty feven *Paftorals*, one hundred and
twenty *Tragi-Comedies*, and four hundred
and five *Sacred* or *Moral Tragedies*. *Alacci*
in his fixth Lift gives a Catalogue of Tragedies, Comedies, Paftorals, and other Dramas which have not yet been publifhed, but
which were written before the Year 1660;
and not contented with adding to thefe an
Hiftorical Account of them, he points out
the very Libraries and private Repofitories
where they are preferved in Manufcript:
But fince the Days of *Alacci*, not above
twelve of thefe Pieces have been
printed; in this Lift we find one hundred
and ten *Prophane Tragedies*, feventy *Sacred*
or *Moral* ones, two hundred and three *Comedies*, twenty *Paftorals*, and a great Number
of *Operas*. And in a kind of *Supplement*
which he has added, he reckons up twelve
Tragedies more, eighteen *Sacred Reprefentations*, fifteen *Comedies*, ten *Tragi-Comedies*,
two *Paftorals*, and a great Quantity of *Operas*, which ought to have been added to his
Catalogue. Upon fumming up thefe different Numbers, we fhall find that the *Italian*
Stage has produced above two thoufand
Plays; and if the Catalogue of feventy fix
Years, which intervenes betwixt this prefent
Time and the Year 1660, fhall ever appear,
I make no Queftion but that *Italy*, in the
Space of two hundred Years, has enriched
their

their Theatre with upwards of five thoufand Plays. We may advance this Fact with the greater Affurances, as the *Dramaturgia* of *Alacci* contains only a Collection of thofe Pieces that remain in the *Vatican Library*, and not thofe that were printed betwixt the Years 1500 and 1660, and which are ftill more numerous than thefe he has mentioned. I have a great Number of Tragedies and Comedies of which *Alacci* takes no Notice, and I daily find others that neither of us knew any thing of before. This makes me believe that we never fhall have a complete Collection, or even a genuine Catalogue of all the Pieces belonging to the *Italian Theatre*.

Italy, which at that Time contained almoft as many *Sovereigns* as it contains *Cities*, each of which had their particular Theatres, could not make a Collection of their Plays with the fame Eafe as the *French*, *Spaniards*, or *Englifh*. As thefe laft were all under one Sovereign, the Theatres were the fame in their feveral Capitals, and there was no great Difficulty of finding, in the fame Cities, all that was neceffary for Information on this Head in their moft ancient Regifters, or in their Libraries. But in *Italy*, a Man, whether prompted by his own Curiofity, or obliged to obey the Commands of his Prince to make fuch a Collection, muft have vifited all thefe Cities in order to collect the *Memoirs* and

and *Anecdotes* peculiar to the feveral Entertainments exhibited in every City or Palace,
and then indeed he might have left us a general Catalogue of all the Pieces belonging to
the different Theatres; therefore it is to
Chance alone that we owe a great Number
of Pieces preferved in the Libraries and Ca-
binets of the Curious.

But if true *Comedy* fhall be loft among the
Italians, they will always retain a kind of
Comedy, tho' not deferving that Appellation,
and more properly to be called *Farce*; I
mean that ancient mercenary *Comedy* which
was played *extempore*, and fucceeded to the
Latin Comedy, which at firft indeed was
low and immodeft, but afterwards was improved into greater Decency and Correctnefs.
Should the Ruin of Learning become general
in *Italy*, and fhould her *Species* of *Dramatic*
Poets ever be extinct, the Ignorance of the
People would give them a Relifh for this
kind of *Comedy* or *Farce*. It is therefore to
be prefumed, that it will continue but too
long fhould it be once introduced, but its
Reputation can never be folid, becaufe it muft
always depend upon the Abilities of the
Actors.

Thefe Farces, the Original of which is to
me unknown, and which have run thro' all
the Courts of *Europe*, have led many *French*
Writers into a Miftake, when they have been
F   fpeaking

fpeaking of their own Theatre, and have been obliged to run a Parallel betwixt it and thofe of other Nations. The Abbe *Aubignac*, the Author of the *French* Theatre, printed in 1674, whofe Name I am unacquainted with, *Moreri*, and every Author who has handled this Subject, in fpeaking of the *Italian* Theatre, have mentioned only the *extempore Farces* performed by Actors in Mafque, becaufe, in reality, this was the only Species of the *Drama* known in *France* fo late as the Reign of *Henry* the Third, which was about the Year 1578.

The *Italian* Players don't always ufe to play their Parts *extempore*; they have, as I fhall fhew by and by, fometimes learned it by heart, according to the different Ages in which they lived. But in thofe Courts-in *Europe* who are not fo well acquainted with the *Italian* Language, and where the *Italian* Players are fought after and encouraged, they have gone entirely into the *extempore* Manner, and it is under this Character that they are known over all *Germany*, and particularly in *France*. Hence arofe the Miftakes into which the *French* Authors I have named were led, in fuppofing that the *Italian* Drama confifted *formerly* entirely in thofe Sorts of Buffoonries; and upon this Suppofition, without examining further, they have pronounced the *French* Theatre to be fuperior

both

both in Tragedy and Comedy, to all the other Theatres in *Europe*. In this Opinion they are not perhaps far in the wrong; but it would not at all derogate from the Merit of the *French* Theatre, fhould their Authors examine the State of the *Italian* for an Age or two before, and upon a juft Comparifon of the Merits of both, found the Superiority which they attribute to their own Countrymen. I am pretty much convinced that the Glory of *Corneille*, *Racine*, and *Moliere*, would receive an additional Luftre by comparing them with Rivals; and not as they do, found their Triumphs upon a Conqueft, where the Forces of the Parties are by no means equal, or rather where they can have no Opportunity of a Struggle. It was in order to diffipate this Miftake which fo generally prevails in *France*, that I have given to the Public the long Catalogue of Tragedies and Comedies in my *Hiftory of the* Italian *Theatre*.

The *French* Authors have run into another Miftake with regard to *Italian* Players, in maintaining that as they only excel in the Mimic Way, they are incapable of doing Juftice to any thing that is great and pathetic. But this Notion is effectually deftroyed, not only by the *Italian* Company eftablifhed at *Paris* in the Year 1716, but by other Players of that Nation, who at different

Times have ftudied their Parts both in true Tragedy and Comedy. The Action of the Company I have mentioned, in theTragedies of *Merope* and *Andromache* in *Italian* Verfe, and in the Tragi-Comedies of *Hercules, Sampfon*, and *Life is a Dream*, and many other Pieces, have fufficiently convinced the Public that *Italian* Players are as capable as thofe, of any other People, to touch the Great and Pathetic.

Befides we find in *Italy* an Excellence not eafily to be met with amongft other Nations. No *Italian* Company ever contains more than eleven Actors or Actreffes; of whom five, including the Scaramouch, fpeak only the *Bolognefe, Venetian, Lombard*, and *Neapolitan* Dialects. Yet when they are to act a Tragedy which requires a large Number of Players, every one of them is employed; even *Harlequin* lays afide his Mafque, and they all declaim in Verfe as properly as if they were Natives of *Rome*. This Practice renders them capable of doing Juftice to the moft fublime Sentiments of Dramatic Writing, and at the fame time of agreeably imitating the moft ridiculous Oddities in Nature. This is a Merit which we may fay is peculiar to the *Italians*, fince amongft the Companies of other Nations, which generally confift of at leaft thirty Actors, every one is determined by his natural or acquired Qualifications in
the

the Choice of the Part he undertakes; and it is very rare that we meet with one or two who can fuſtain different Characters, and ſuit themſelves to every accidental Variation of Characters and Perſons.

Of

Of *the* ITALIAN OPERA.

FROM the firſt Riſe of the *Italian* Theatre, Muſic has always been inter-mixed with Action. The Method of intro-ducing it into the Drama has varied accord-ing to the ſeveral Junctures. At firſt it began by the Chorus's always being ſung, then the Prologues, Interludes in Verſe, and Epilogue. When the Theatre, by the fine Productions of a more poliſhed Age, began to improve, the Practice of intermixing Muſic with the Repreſentation of true Tragedies or Come-dies wore out in twenty or thirty Years, and both were repreſented in the Taſte and Sim-plicity of the Ancients; Tragedy having a Chorus that declaimed, and Comedy a Pro-logue that was repeated. By this ſudden Change, we may eaſily conceive that the Uſe of Muſic was quite laid aſide, becauſe incon-ſiſtent with theſe regular Repreſentations, and deſpicable, as its being one of the Parts of Farce which had been juſt aboliſhed.

Some time after, the Poets abandoned that Severity for which they had been ſo remark-able at the Beginning of their Reformation; nor does any *Italian* Writer inform us of the Reaſons. I am inclined to believe that the
Audiences

Audiences were difgufted with the dry Exactnefs of Rules, and that their Poets accommodated themfelves to the Tafte of the
People, which demanded perhaps fomething
more entertaining. After that, Tragedies
were reprefented without a Chorus, Mufic
was again admitted into the Prologue of Comedies, and by degrees they introduced Interludes which had no relation to the main
Subject; fometimes thofe Interludes were
unconnected the one with the other, and
each made an Action apart;* but very often
three or four Interludes formed a continued
Action, which was a great Embellifhment to
the principal Piece.

It will not be improper to obferve, that the
three Examples referred to in the Note are
of the noble and exalted kind, and that they
are adapted to the Nature and Genius of the
feveral Pieces to which they were fubfervient,
which are either Paftorals or Tragi-Comedies; as there are likewife Interludes of another kind, adapted to the Manner and Spirit of Comedy.

We muft likewife obferve, that at this
Time the Theatre begun infenfibly to de-
cline, and that inftead of exact Tragedy and
regular Comedy, Paftorals, Tragi-Comedies,
and Interludes were introduced, which daily

[de-

---

* *L'Aurora Ingannata*; *Glauco Schernito*; *Dafnè converfa
in Laura.*

degenerating, at laſt produced the monſtrous Births we have mention'd.

Theſe muſical Interludes, interrupted by performing the ſeveral Acts in the principal Pieces, afforded a formal and pompous Show; and if they had been ſeparated from the Paſtoral, or Tragi-Comedy, to which they were annexed, they wanted nothing but a *Name* to denounce them a Species of Repreſentations quite different from Tragedy or Comedy.

The *Italian* Writers have been at a great deal of Pains to ſettle the preciſe Time in which the Opera begun. Some maintain that the *Euridice* * of *Rinuccini*, acted at *Florence* in the Year 1600, upon Occaſion of the Marriage of *Mary de Medicis* to *Henry* the Fourth, was the firſt of this kind. Others aſcribe the Merits of its Invention to *Emilio del Cavalieri*, who, in the Year 1590, exhibited *Il Satyro* and *La Diſperazione de Fileno*, both muſical Paſtorals, at *Florence* in the Great Duke's Palace.

Without troubling myſelf to criticiſe upon their ſeveral Diſcuſſions of this Point, I ſhall take my Date from that muſical Tragedy, which the Senate and Republic cauſed to be acted in the Palace of the *Doge* before *Henry* III, when he paſſed thro' *Venice*, in his Return from *Poland* in 1574‡. All the *Italian* Princes

* *Rinuccini* : *Rime*, p. 13.

‡ *La gloria della poeſia è della muſica.* Printed at *Venice* without a Date.

Princes about this Time publickly exhibited Operas in their own Palaces. It is however univerfally agreed that the firft Opera appeared at *Venice* in the Year 1634. ‡

The Book I have quoted informs us, that during the Carnaval, in the Year 1637, the firft public Opera, called *Andromachus*, was exhibited on the Theatre of St. *Caffan*. Next Year at the fame Time, and upon the fame Theatre, a fecond was exhibited, called the *Magician Thunder-ftruck*. Thefe two firft Operas were exhibited with great Magnificence, and at the Expence both of the Poet and Muficians. In the Year 1639, the Theatre of St. *John* and St. *Paul*, on which nothing but Comedy had been acted, was rebuilt; and the firft Piece exhibited upon it was *La Delie de Jule Strozzi*, where alfo they exhibited the *Armida*, as an Entertainment during the Carnaval. The Theatre of St. *Caffan* acted at the fame the Opera of *Thetis* and *Deleus*; and in the Autumn the other Theatre exhibited that of *Adonis*, which had fo great a Run, that it was acted, without Interruption, from the Month of *October* till Lent.

In that fame Carnaval, which began the Year 1640, the old Theatre called St. *Mofes*'s, the Foundation of which is unknown, exhibited the *L' Arriane d' Octavio Rinuccini*, which many Years before had been acted in

the

‡ *Idem.*

the Palaces of fome *Italian* Princes, and which, according to the Edition in 1608, is prior, by thirty two Years, to the Reprefentation I have juft now mentioned.

I fhall not here pretend to enumerate all the different kinds of Operas which for thefe hundred Years have appeared upon the *Venetian* Stage; they would difguft the Reader, and fwell this Volume to an ufelefs Bulk: I fhall content myfelf to refer the Curious to a Book I have already quoted, which is a little Volume in Twelves, printed at *Venice*, entituled *The Glory of Poetry and Mufic*. This Book is a Catalogue containing two hundred and fixty eight Pages; the Bookfeller has added, by way of Appendix, a Lift of the Operas that have been prefented for that Year. This Book is printed without any Date, and began to appear in the Year 1730. One may eafily judge how much Operas are in Fafhion at *Venice*, when he is told that at certain Seafons they play every Day, and in fix Theatres at the fame time.

No Sovereign ever fpent fo much upon thefe Reprefentations as the *Venetians* have done, except perhaps *Ranuce Farnefe*, Duke of *Parma*, who amazed all *Italy* by the Entertainments which he prefented in the Year 1690, on Occafion of the Marriage of his Son Prince *Edward*. The World yet talks of two Operas which he prefented, the one

in

in the Night-time upon the great Stage of his Palace, and the other in the Day-time upon the great Bafon which he caufed to be built in his Gardens. It were to be wifhed that we could give an exact Detail of all the Machines which the fkilful Architects contrived on that Occafion; and of all the wonderful Reprefentations of that kind that have been executed at *Venice, Rome, Naples, Florence,* and the other Cities of *Italy.* As to the Decorations and the Machinery it may be fafely affirmed, that no Theatre in *Europe* comes up to the Magnificence of the *Venetian* Opera; fome of them will be handed down to our moft diftant Pofterity; for Inftance, the Opera entitled *The Divifion of the World,* which the Marquis *Guido Rangoni* exhibited in the Year 1675 at his own Expences, upon the Theatre of our *Holy Saviour.* In the Shepherd of *Amphife,* which was prefented twenty Years after upon the Theatre of St. *John Chryfoftome,* the Palace of *Apollo* was feen to defcend of very fine and grand Architecture, and built of Chriftals of different Colours which were always playing; the Lights which were placed behind thefe Chriftals were difpofed in fuch a Manner, that fo great a Flux of Rays played from the Machine, that the Eyes of the Spectators could fcarcely fupport its Brightnefs.

The

The two *Bebienas*, thefe eminent Architects and celebrated Painters now alive, have
convinced all *Europe*, by their grand Decorations, that a Theatre may be adorned without Machinery, not only with as much Magnificence, but with more Propriety. Machines produce a magical, or, if you will, a
marvellous Effect; and we are often obliged
to call to Mind the Contrivance of the
Theatre, and that every thing that we fee is
moved by Pulleys, Ropes, Springs, and
Weights, in order to prevent our Senfes from
being impofed upon, fo as to believe what we
fee is reprefented to be real. I fhall give one
Inftance of fuch an Illufion.

Cato of *Utica* is the Subject of an Opera
prefented upon the Theatre of St. *John
Chryfoftome* in the Year 1701. As *Cæfar*
with his Army is fuppofed not to be far from
that Scene where the Action is laid, and that
the Inhabitants of the Province had prepared
an Entertainment for him upon the Banks of
the River, the Ground of the Stage reprefents a Field, towards the Middle of which
there was hung in the Air a Globe, refembling
that of the World; this Globe was obferved by
degrees to advance towards the Front of the
Stage, to the Sound of Trumpets and other
Inftruments, and all this without the Spectators being able to difcern the Pulleys and
Machines that directed the whole. In the
Moment

Moment when it comes oppofite to *Cæfar,* it opens into three Parts, reprefenting the then three known Parts of the World. The Infide of the Globe fhines all with Gold, Precious Stones, Metals of all Colours, and contains a great Number of Muficians. Thus we fee what the Contrivance of a Theatre is capable of effecting, which is artfully to conceal the Pulleys and Springs; for by means of the firft Scaffold being built above the Stage, it is eafy to fuftain and conduct in the Air a Machine of what Weight you pleafe; and in fuch a Situation a Spectator ftands in need of his Reflection, to put him in Mind that all is purely the Effect of the Machinery and Difpofition; but in the mean time this is what the Poet and the Mufician ought to endeavour to make him forget.

Players by their Art fometimes imitate Nature fo perfectly, that they perfuade the Spectator that all they fee is real; but it is a much harder Tafk for the Mufician to attain to this, it being much more difficult for them to accommodate their Notes to the Paffions of Anger, Grief, Sorrow, and even to Death itfelf. The Poet and the Engineer, far from encreafing thefe Difficulties by unnatural Decorations, ought to reprefent to the Spectators the moft elevated Ideas only with that Art which is moft proper to render them more fufceptible of the Impreffion that is to
be

be conveyed. The principal End of the Stage is Illusion, and that End can be obtained only by keeping to what is probable.

As to the *Italian* Musics, all *Europe* agree that towards the Middle of the last Century it arrived at *Perfection*, and continued in that State to the Beginning of this. The Compositions of *Scarlati* the elder, *Bononcini*, and many other excellent Masters, are undisputable Proofs of this. But these twenty Years past, the great Reputation it had acquired among Foreigners is a good deal diminished, because the *Italian* Taste of Music is now changed. In short, at present it is all a Whim; *Strength* is fought instead of *beautiful Simplicity*; and *Harshness* and *Singularity* is substituted instead of the *Expression* and *Truth* which distinguished the former Manner. The surprizing Capacity of their Singers, it is true, begets *Admiration*, but moves no *Passion*; and Judges say justly, that it is unreasonable to force a Voice to execute what is too much even for a *Violin* or a *Hautboy*. This is the true Reason why the *Italian* Music falls so far short of Perfection in *Expression* and *Truth*, and why it is threatened with total Ruin if it shall continue to deviate from that Manner which formerly brought it to Perfection. The new Manner however has got such Footing in *Italy*, that even Masters in the Art are obliged

in

in conformity to the general Tafte, contrary to their better Judgment, to deviate from the Simplicity and Greatnefs of the ancient Manner, both in vocal and inftrumental Performances.

As to their Muficians, the *Italians*, by their Method of *manufacturing* a Voice, have always a great Number of excellent Singers both with regard to the Finenefs of the Pipe, and their Skill and Tafte in Singing; fuch as *Piftocco, Pafqualino, Siface, Mattecucio, Cortona, Luigino*, and many others, whofe Memory the Muficians of our Days will fcarcely be able to efface. The Female-Performers have at all times difputed with the Males the Excellence of Singing. We may inftance, among thefe who have excelled for half the laft Century, *Francifca Vaini*, *Santa Stella*, *Tilla, Margaretta*, *Salicoli*, *Reggiana*, with many others. But fhe who in our Days retained the true Manner of *Italian* Excellence in Mufic, was the celebrated *Cuzzoni*; every Body knows that in the Year 1724 fhe fung with univerfal Applaufe a Motet and a Pfalm compofed by *Bononcini*, in the Chapel of *Fontainbleau*. She fupported at *London*, for fix Years, the Glory of the *Italian* Nation, and was recalled thither in the Year 1734, notwithftanding the Bickerings and Divifions betwixt the *Italian* Theatres. Her Salary was about fifteen hundred Guineas a Year,

as

as was that of *Francis Bernardi*, known by the Name of *Senesino*, an excellent Musician, who never suffered himself to be carried away by the Taste for the new Music. But what is very extraordinary in *Italy*, and over all the World, he joined to the Charms of his Voice, the Merit of *Action*, and the Player was as accomplished as the Musician.

I ought not here to forget the famous *Faustina Bardoni Asse*, whose Talents and Profits were equal to those of *Cuzzoni*, whom I have mentioned. It was owing to her extraordinary Capacity and her surprising Command of Voice, that *Faustina* was obliged to invent a new manner of Singing. As she has been extremely well received all over *Europe*, many Attempts have been made to imitate her; but her Imitators having neither her Pipe nor her Art, have only spoil'd their own Manner; and it is owing to this wretched Imitation that a bad Manner both of Singing and Composition prevails now so much in *Italy*, from whence it has been communicated to all *Europe*.

I have chosen to speak of *M. Carlo-Broschi*, sirnamed *Farionelli*, last of all, both as he is the latest and youngest of the celebrated *Italian* Musicians. He sings in the Manner of *Faustina*; but it is owned by the best Judges that he infinitely outdoes her, having brought his Art to the last Degree of Perfection

fection. In the Year 1734 he was invited to *London*, where he sung three Winters with universal Applause. He arrived at *Paris* in 1736; and after he had sung in the most eminent Families, where he was received and treated with great Distinction, the King did him the Honour to hear him perform in the Queen's Chamber, and applauded him in a Manner that astonished the whole Court. The Admiration he created was so universal, that it is on all Hands agreed *Italy* never did, and perhaps never will, produce so complete a Singer. He is now in *Spain*, and kept by the King and Queen to sing in their Chamber. That Prince by his Liberality, and the large Appointments he allows him, has completed the Good-Fortune of *M. Farinelli*, who by his great Talents and personal Merits deserves all he enjoys.

Formerly, the most able and celebrated Musicians at *Venice* received only one hundred *Roman* Crowns for performing for the whole Autumn and Carnaval; and if thier Appointments reached to one hundred and twenty Crowns, or six hundred * *French* Livres, it was considered as a Mark of great Distinction and a Proof of superior Merit. But for these thirty Years past, a fine Singer,

G   either

---

* About 28l. Sterling.

either Man or Woman, has always had upwards of one hundred Golden Sequins, which is about 550 *l.* Sterling. *Sancta Stella, Fauſtina, Cuſzoni* and *Farinelli*, were all paid on this Footing; but theſe prodigious Expences have ruined all the Undertakers of the Opera at *Venice*, and drained the heavieſt Purſes in *Italy*. On this Account, and in order to raiſe the vaſt Sums that are paid to their Performers, they have for ſome Time paſt retrenched their expenſive Machinery.

Three Livres of *Venetian* Money gains Admittance into the Hall of the Opera, thirty Sols a Seat in the Pit, and the Boxes are in Proportion. If we compare theſe poor Receivings with the Expences that are neceſſary for ſupporting the Magnificence of theſe Shows, we may eaſily account for the Loſſes which the Undertakers of the Opera ſuſtain; it being impoſſible, that for the four Months, during which theſe Entertainments laſt, the Receiving ſhould equal the Outgiving; for the *Venetian* Opera begins at ſooneſt in the Middle of *November*, and continues only to the laſt Day of the Carnaval.

As it is experienced all over *Europe*, and eſpecially in *Italy*, that the beſt Performers, and the fineſt Voices cannot of themſelves procure Succeſs to an Opera, unleſs its Muſic and Drama is good; and that on the contrary,

trary, a good Drama and good Mufic, and very often the laft alone, may fucceed very well, tho' the Performance is but indifferent; therefore at *Venice*, where this is more fenfibly felt than elfewhere, they follow a Method quite different from the ancient.

Since the Opera began there, fix hundred and fifty Operas have appeared in lefs than one Century, tho' they were reprefented only in the Winter. Since the Year 1637, which is the Date of the firft Appearance of the Opera at *Venice*, to the Year 1700, we compute only three hundred and fifty feven, exclufive of five or fix, which were reacted on account of their great Succefs. It appeared furprizing, that in the Space of fixty three Years in *Venice* alone, three hundred and fifty Operas fhould appear, but that Myftery is now folved. The Undertakers, not willing to run the Rifk of Novelty, almoft every Year react the Operas which fucceeded in the preceding, nay, they fometimes act the fame Opera two Nights fucceffively; a Practice which difgufts the Spectators, and not a little blemifhes the Glory of the *Italian* Theatre, fo fertile in Novelty.

Some of the *Italian* Poets who have wrote in this way, have diftinguifhed themfelves by a noble and chafte Verfification, and others by a poetical and elevated Imagination; but

the

the greateft Part of them do not deferve mention. Formerly, the Opera comprehended all Subjects, but, fince the Machinery has been laid afide, it deals no longer in Fables, Divinities, Mufic, Paftoral, and the like, but confines itfelf entirely to Hiftory.

The old Operas that have come to our Hands, are Proofs of the *Italian* Genius in treating Hiftorical Subjects. But at prefent, a Barrennefs of Imagination feems to have fucceeded this Fertility; the *French* Tragedies being commonly pilaged, to furnifh out their Plans, their Scenes, and even their Thoughts.

All the Inconveniences we have mentioned may foon reduce the Opera into the fame Situation with the Comedy: And we may talk fome time hence of the *Italian* Opera, in the fame manner as we now do of their Comedy of a *correct Age*, by efteeming the Antients, and defpifing the Moderns.

THE

THE
SPANISH THEATRE.

BELIEVE one might venture
to affirm, that the *Spaniards* were
the firſt of any People in *Europe*
who wrote for the Stage, could it
not be proved that ever ſince the Decay of
the *Romans* the Theatre has been open
in *Italy* without Interruption. It muſt indeed be owned that Impoſtors and Mountebanks contributed not a little to its Conti-
nuation ; for they were the chief Supports
of low Comedy, if one may beſtow that
Name upon their Buffoonries, which were
Productions of a very monſtrous Kind, in
which the Laws of Dialogue were overlook'd, and the Propriety of Language diſ-
regarded. Tho' theſe Mountebanks afterwards added a Luſtre and Dignity to their

En-

Entertainments, by exhibiting them either in Courts or in the Galleries of Noblemen's Houfes, yet this is no Reafon why we fhould believe that Comedy was reduced to any Form, either in *Italy* or any other Part of *Europe*, before the Eleventh or Twelfth Century. Thefe Entertainments did at beft refemble the *extempore* Farces which the *Italian* Comedians act at this very Day; and it is even to be thought that their Form and Model were not near fo perfect and unexceptionable as that of the prefent *extempore* Farce.

I don't intend by this to deftroy what I have elfewhere faid; for I am perfwaded that in the thirteenth Century there were Comedies wrote in *Italy*; but as they never faw the Public, and were only acted privately, we cannot fix their Date with fo much Certainty as we can do that of the Comedy acted *extempore*.

The Theatre in *Spain* begun in a quite different manner: It is true, that neither the *Spaniards* nor any other Nation boafted of acting *extempore*; but they may juftly claim the Honour of renewing and eftablifhing the true Comedy. The Hiftory of *Spain* furnifhes us with very ancient Accounts of their firft Theatrical Entertainments, which were fmall Farces of one Act, called *Entremeffes* or *Jornadas*, which is the Name they

now

now bear in *Spain*. Thefe Pieces confifted of very few Scenes, and were performed by very few Actors. The Action of the Piece turned upon fome Subject that was ridiculous and common. All this was wrote down, and being filled with Touches of Wit and Satyre, made a very extravagant Medley, not unlike the Performances of the Latin *Mimes*, for both their Subjects were of the fame Nature. Thefe *Entremeffes* were exhibited and performed in Thoroughfares, and in the moft public Places of the Towns, on occafion of fome facred or profane Feaft, fuch as the Dedication of a Church, the Marriage of a Sovereign Prince, or his Acceffion to the Throne, or fome fuch Occafion. The *French* did not, till a long time after, imitate the *Spaniards* in this. If we were to judge of this fort of Performances by the modern *Entremeffes*, which the beft Dramatic Poets in *Spain* have furnifhed us with, we would have Reafon to believe that the firft of thefe were very weak and infignificant Pieces ; for fuch of them as were wrote in the time of *Calderon* are very wretched Performances, and can pretend to no greater Share of Merit than that of being *Farces*, in the loweft Senfe of the Word.

Thefe Diverfions, intended only for the Amufement of the People, were fucceeded

by

by Comedy, which was eftablifhed in the
fame manner as it was in *Greece*. It was
exhibited almoft without any Ornaments
and Decorations, and in Places not at all
fuited to the Feafts that occafioned it. Tho'
the *Spanifh* Theatres are now under better
Regulations, yet they ftill keep the old Name
of *Corrales* or *Court-yards*. But when People intend to honour them with a nobler
and more fplendid Name, they call them
Palios or great Courts. The Theatres which
are in the Palaces of Princes or great Men
are not called *Corrales* (that being a Name
too low for them) but *Colifeos*.

It is evident that the *Spaniards* have infenfibly introduced a better Sort of Comedy
inftead of thefe Farces : But it is impoffible
to fix the precife Time of this Change,
which put their Stage into its prefent Condition. It is certain, however, that they
can juftly boaft of being the firft who
carried Comedy to that Pitch of Perfection, at which we have for fome Time paft
obferved it ; and they can date this Re-
eftablifhment from the middle of the xvth
Century, whilft the *Italians* can only date
the Commencement of their regular Comedy, from the beginning of the xvith
Century ; and the *French* theirs, from about
the End of the xviith, that is to fay, from
the Days of *Moliere*.

D.

D. Lope de Rueda and *Navaro*, who were Contemporaries, begun to reduce Comedy to three Acts, which were formerly divided into four : It was ufual with the People of thofe Days to call what we term *Acts, Actos*; and the two Authors, juft now cited, ftile them *Jornadas*; which Practice has been follow'd by all the Authors who have hitherto had their Performances printed. But I judge it highly neceffary to examine the Conftruction and Contrivance of their Play-houfe, by which means we may get fome Light with regard to the Antiquity of their Comedy.

The Theatres in *Spain* are erected in a Form quite peculiar to themfelves : They are almoft fquare, and have three Stories for the Accommodation of the Audience. There are only Boxes in the firft of thefe ; and thefe Boxes are not like thofe of *France*, they being only divided by Rails. The Front Box, and which is immediately above the Door which leads to the Pit and the Theatre, is ftiled the City-Box, becaufe it is always taken up by (what they call) *Regidores*, or Lieutenants of the Police. Below this Box, in the reft of the Front, is erected a kind of Amphitheatre, which jutts out a little into the Pit, and is furnifhed with Seats. They call it *Cazuela*, and none but Women fit in it. Below the *Cazuela*, and on the

the two Sides of the Door by which they enter into the Pit, are two dark Boxes called *Aloxeros*, in one of which, an *Alcade de Corto* (who is a Royal Judge) fits, having all his Retinue before him in a small Appartment which is in the Pit. This Magiftrate, however, does not always fit here, 'tis only when the Scene is embaraffed by the Decorations; for at the fimple Comedy, which they call *de Capay Spada*, he fits in a Chair, on one of the Sides of the Theatre, with two or three of his Officers behind him.

Above the loweft Boxes on the two Sides of the Hall is a fecond Row confifting of a kind of Boxes, or little Chambers called *Banes*; in which thofe Perfons who want to be concealed from public View, chufe to fit. On the fame Line, and in all the front Appartments, is an empty Space (as large as the *Cazuela*) called the *Tertulia*, where the Monks, Priefts, and other Perfons, whofe Charaɛters oblige them to a ftrict Obfervance of the Laws of Decency, fit. On the two Sides of the Pit, are Places allotted for the Men, who fit in the fame Manner as they were wont to do in the antient Amphitheatres. Thefe Places are called *Gradas*, and the People go up to them by fmall wooden Steps. They are inclofed with a kind of Baluftrade, and joined to two Rows of Seats which are upon the Stage. At the End of
                                        thefe

thefe Steps, is another Place joined to the Theatre and as large as it. It is raifed a little above the Pit, and is called *Los Tabouretes*, or *Media Lunetta*, and refembles the Orcheftrum of the *Italian* and *French* Theatres. In the *Patio*, or Pit fronting the Theatre, are Seats joined to the loweft Steps of the two Amphitheatres we have mentioned. Formerly, the Amphitheatres had no Roof, as they now have, upon that Part of the Pit. So that the Spectators were often expofed to Rain, and to the Inclemency of the Air ‡.

This Form of Theatres which in *Spain* differs fo widely from the other Theatres of *Europe*, may be a Proof of their Antiquity; for 'tis natural to think, that if the Theatres of *Italy* had been erected before thofe of *Spain*, the *Spaniards* in the Conftruction of theirs would have copied from the *Italian* Model, as the other Nations of *Europe* have for the moft Part done. For Inftance, the Form of the Amphitheatres in *France*, which might, neverthelefs be copied from the *Cazuela*, of the Theatres of *Madrid*; as the two Rows of Seats upon the *Spanifh* Stage, may have alfo laid a Foundation for the Six erected on the *French* Theatre for the Accommodation of more Spectators.

---

‡ At prefent they have built at *Madrid* a very large and magnificent Theatre in the *Italian* Tafte, except retaining a few Parts of their ancient Form.

The

The manner of paying, for feeing a *Spanish* Play, is the fame with the *Italian.* They firft pay for their Entrance into the Hall, *Quatro quartes,* which is equivalent to two Sols and a half *French* Money, and afterwards for a Seat, they pay the fame Sum, or a little more, according to the Quality of the Seat. 'Tis ufual likewife in *Spain* to hire Boxes for a whole Year ; but this Practice is chiefly ufed by Ladies of Fortune, who are on fuch Occasions, attended only by their own Relations, or their old Servants. But they now begin to fhake off this Reftaint, and in a great many Points, act with greater Freedom. If one inclines to take only a fingle Seat in a Box, (which Men only do) he pays for it two *Reales de plata,* which mount to twenty Sols. The Tabouretes are let at the fame Price, and all the reft in proportion.

The Decorations were formerly very inconfiderable, confifting only of a wretched Curtain which concealed the Doors, at which the Actors came in and went out. This Piece of Decoration is not quite laid afide, but is chiefly ufed in the Comedies, called *Capay Efpada.*

The Habits ufed on the Stage were formerly very plain ; but Luxury has now reached the Theatre, and the Actreffes (efpecially in the Opera) are dreffed in a very fplendid

did and magnificent Manner. Their Authors make Choice of their Subjects from Fables, so as Music may bear a great Share of the Entertainment; and then indeed the Decorations, the Shiftings of the Schenes, the Habits, and all the rest of their Equipage are very sumptuous and magnificent. But when any Piece is acted in the *Salon de Palacio*, in the *Coliséo del Ritiro*, or in the House of some Man of Figure or Quality, they endeavour to vie with the *Italian* Theatre in Grandeur, Pomp, and Magnificence.

It would be hard to tell the precise Number of Dramatic Poets produced by *Spain*; but among those of the best Reputation we may justly reckon *Lopez de Vego*, *Calderon*, *Mureto*, *Solis*, *Salazar*, *Molina*, and some others. With regard to the Number of Dramatic Performances, the *Spaniards* are superior to all other Nations; and without exaggerating, one may say, that there are more *Spanish* Comedies than there are of *French* and *Italian*, from their first Date to this very Day. If any one should call in Question what I say, he needs only examine, for his Satisfaction, the Works of some of the Poets of this Nation.

Don Pedro Calderon de la Barca alone has published nine Volumes of Comedies, and six Volumes of *Autos Sacramentales*, every one

of

of which Volumes contains twelve Pieces, which in all amount to an hundred and eighty ; and it is certain, that he wrote more which have never been printed. Tho' *Augustine Mureto* published only thirty six Pieces, he certainly wrote a great many more. *Fray Gabriel Thelles* composed a great Number of Pieces, tho' we have only five Volumes printed, every one of which contains twelve Comedies. It is plain by the ancient Register, or Journals of the Theatres, that *Lopes de Vega Carpio* wrote more than one thousand five hundred Pieces, which have all been acted ; but now we can only find, and that too with Difficulty, twenty six Volumes of them, containing three hundred and twelve Comedies. If any one should dispute his Pieces which have not reached our Hands, yet he cannot controvert the 312 which have : This prodigious Number sufficiently shews that the most fertile Genius of all the Dramatic Poets, cannot, or ought not to be compared to *Lopes de Vega,* at least in Luxuriancy of Fancy, and Fruitfulness of Imagination.

Don Juan Peres de Montabalan has wrote thirty six Comedies; and twelve *Autos Sacramentales* : And among all the Authors who have wrote for the Theatres, there is scarcely one who has not been Author of twenty four Pieces, except *Antonio de Solis,* and

and *Don Auguſtine de Salazar*, who (tho'
each of them has only wrote nine Pieces)
are juſtly eſteemed amongſt the beſt Poets
of their Age. We need not be ſurprized,
that the Performances of theſe two Authors
are ſo few compared with thoſe of their
Contemporaries, if we conſider that *Solis* died
very young, and *Salazar*, when he was little
more than a Child. 'Tis reported that the
former left a Piece unfiniſhed, entitled *Amor
es Arte de Amar*, but nobody ever made an
Attempt to finiſh it. It was upon Occaſion
of *Salazar*'s Death, that *Calderon* expreſſed
himſelf thus, *Emperaba par d'Onde el Aca-
baba*, that is, he excelled all others in thoſe
Pieces which received the laſt Touch from
himſelf.

There are ſix hundred *Autos Sacramentales*
printed, beſides an infinite Number which
never appeared. Theſe *Autos Sacramentales*
are ſacred Dramas, acted at certain Seaſons
of the Year, but eſpecially at *Chriſtmas*.
We have no Reaſon to think that they bear
any Reſemblance to theſe Dramas, which
are ſo numerous in *Italy*, and which repreſent the Myſteries of our *Saviour*'s Paſſion,
or ſome remarkable Event in the Lives of
the Martyrs or Holy Virgins. No, they are
allegorical Performances, which treat indeed
of the Myſteries of Religion, but in a very
peculiar Manner. *Don Pedro Calderon* is
eſteemed

efteemed the beft of all the Poets in this way, and 'tis univerfally agreed, that he is unrivalled.

The Form of thefe Dramas is always allegorical, as we have already obferved; and the Memory, the Will, the Underftanding, Life, Judaifm, the Church, Idolatry, Apofta-cy, &c. are introduced as Perfonages. Nay, *Don Pedro Calderon* has made Perfonages of the five Senfes, but among thefe, there are very often Characters from Life, efpecially of the Comic kind; as we have already ob-ferved, the whole Action of this fort of Dra-mas turns upon the greateft Myfteries of Re-ligion, efpecially the Euchariff where the Action generally ends.

The *Autos Sacramental des las Plantes* of the fame *Calderon*, appears to me a very fin-gular Performance in this way : The Bram-ble, the Mulberry-tree, the Cedar, the Al-mond-tree, the Oak, the Olive-tree, the Spikenard, the Vine, and the Laurel, are the Actors. Two Angels appear upon the Thea-tre; and adreffing thefe Plants, they tell them that one among them ought to produce a fweet and admirable Fruit: They then in-vite them to a divine Combat for a Crown, which one of thefe Angels holds firff in his Hand, and then hanging up at a Corner of the Theatre, endows them with the Faculty of Speech, and then retires. The Trees fpeak, and

and feem to be furprized at their Trans-
formation. The *Cedar* appears upon the
Stage with a Baton in his Hand in Form
of a Crofs: The reft of the Actors are
reprefented as furprized at the Sight of
him; none of them having ever feen that
Tree before. The *Cedar* makes a long
allegorical Difcourfe upon the Creation of
the World, the Formation of Man, and the
Production of Animals and Vegetables: He
tells them, that as the feveral Species of Animals, which inhabited in the Sea, the Air,
and the Earth, had their refpective Kings,
fo the Trees ought to have theirs. He adds,
that he did not, upon account of fuperior
Merit, claim this Prerogative; but that he
would be Judge which of them has the
jufteft Title to it. He then goes off the
Stage.

The Plants which remain upon the
Stage are not a little enraged, that a ftrange
and unknown Tree fhould arrogate to
itfelf the Right of judging in Matters belonging to them: They enumerate the feveral Properties and Qualities attributed to
them by Mankind; and by thefe every one
pretends to make good his Right, and carry
the Point in his own Favour.

In the next Scene the *Cedar* propofes to
every Plant to give in a kind of Petition, in
which his Title fhould be proved; which is
H   accord-

accordingly done. Then the *Cedar* appears holding before him a Crofs, the Arms of which are twifted round with the Leaves of *Cedar*, *Cyprefs*, and *Palms*. The Plants are divided into two Factions; fome juftify, and fome condemn the Conduct of the *Cedar* in appointing himfelf their Judge. The *Bramble* is ready to burft with Rage, and afks the *Cedar*, who he is? The *Cedar* refufing to tell him fo much as his Name, the *Bramble* is more enraged, and fays, that he alone is able to root out and deftroy a Tree fo infolent, fo tyrannical, and unknown in the Country. He then advances to the *Cedar* and takes hold of him. The *Cedar* fcreams out, and complains that he tore his Body: Immediately upon this, Streams of Blood were feen to flow from the Crofs; and all the Plants groan at the difmal Sight. The *Cedar* faid, he would fprinkle all the Earth with that Blood; to receive which the *Spikenard* and the *Vine* came up to the Crofs. The *Cedar* then obferving their Compaffion and Humility, and holding the Crofs ftill before him, addreffed them in thefe Words:

> *Pues Humildes, pues Piadofos*
> *Lo dos recedib mi Cuerpo,*
> *O mi Sangre, en lo dos Solo*
> *Defde oy mi Cuerpo, y mi Sangre*
> *Sera divina teforo, &c.*

Which

Which is, *Since with Humility and Com-*
passion you both receive my Body and my Blood;
in you two alone shall my Body and Blood re-
main a divine Treasure from this Day. The
Bramble, seeing himself besmeared with the
Blood, is filled with Despair; and observing
that all the Plants fled at the Sight of him,
he breaks forth into hideous Lamentations:
Then the Cross appears in the Air, and
some of the Plants desire the *Cedar* to pronounce, who deserved the Crown. The *Ce-*
dar declares that Humility gave the best Title to it, and accordingly decreed it to the
Spikenard and the *Vine.* Then the Piece
ends. In this manner end all the *Autos*
Sacramentales, still concluding with a
Thought relating to the Mystery of the
Eucharist.

Thefe Dramas are usher'd in by a Prologue
which they call *Sacramental,* and to which
they give a particular Title that seems to
have no manner of relation to the Mystery
of the Sacrament, which nevertheless is the
chief Subject of the Piece. As for Example, *Loa Sacramental del Loco,* that is, the
sacramental Prologue of the Fool. At the
Beginning of this Prologue the People in the
Area cry, *Take Care of the Fool who has*
made his Escape. Let us run, let us run after
him. The Fool afterwards appears, desiring
those who call'd after him not to make them-

felves

felves uneafy, fince he is not now the Perfon he formerly was, and telling them that the Pleafure of being Witnefs to the Feaft had made him come forth, *&c*. Then in lefs than two hundred fmall Verfes he makes an Enumeration of all the Miracles and Myfteries in the *Old* and *New Teftament*. The Cafe is the fame with the Sacramental Prologue of the *Peafant* ; as likewife with that of the *Doublemeaners* ; the Titles of which promife quite the Reverfe of what is the Defign of the Pieces.

Befides the known Authors, there are a great many annoymous ones, who in their Title-pages affume no other Name than that of an *Ingegnio, Dos ou de tres Ingegnios*. A Bookfeller in *Madrid* has had the Curiofity to make a Collection of all the Theatrical Pieces of annoymous Authors, publifhed under the Name of *Ingegnios* ; and tho' he has not as yet been able to make up a complete Sett, yet he has got four Thoufand eight hundred. If we add to this the immenfe Number of Theatrical Pieces, printed with their Author's Names, we may eafily difcern that all the Nations in *Europe* cannot equal the Number of Plays in *Spain*. I know the Critics will object to me, that a great many of thefe Pieces do confift but of one Intrigue founded upon the Point of Honour, which has occafioned not only a great Refemblance

femblance one to another, but even made Authors tranfcribe their own Works. But we are to confider that this kind of Compofition is accommodated and adapted to the prevailing Tafte of the Nation ; that it is natural for an Author to conform himfelf, in Works of this kind, to the Turn and Humour of his Country; and that the fame may be faid of the *Italians* and the *French*, who for a long time paft have only chofe as the Subjects of their Drama, Love-Intrigues, differing very little from one another.

As this is the Cafe, we have no juft Reafon to reproach the *Spaniards* with having made Point of Honour the chief Subject of their Drama. We ought likewife to own, that it is not the only Subject their Dramatic Writers have touched upon, fince we may learn from thofe who have imitated them, what a peculiar Turn their Ideas have, and with what Eafe they not only invent their Subjects, but likewife work up their Fables into a Conformity to the National Tafte ; and notwithftanding the great Number of their Comedies, there are very few that in their Plans and Sentiments are borrowed from Writers of other Nations. The *Spaniards*, on the contrary, have furnifhed Materials for all the Dramatic Poets in *Europe*.

From the Beginning of the *Italian* Comedy, down to the Middle of the feventeenth

Century,

Century, the *Italians*, both in Tragedy and Comedy, have made the *Greeks* and *Latins* their Patterns; but for the two hundred and thirty Years following, their Dramatic Performances were for the moſt Part only Tranſlations from *Spaniſh* Originals. The *French* may be ſaid to have done the ſame. In the Infancy of their Theatre, they begun by imitating the *Greeks* and *Latins*, but afterwards tranſlated from the *Spaniards.* Tho' in the Days of *Corneille* the *French* Tragedy appeared with a quite different Face from what it formerly had, yet they even then imitated the *Spaniards*; the *Cid* of *Peter Corneille* and the *Vinceſlaus* of *Rotrou* are ſufficient Proofs of this; and even in our own Time we ſee very beautiful Tragedies almoſt entirely taken from the *Spaniſh* Language. The *Ines de Caſtro* of Mr. *Houdart de la Motte* is a Piece ſo exquiſite, that it is ſufficient to convince us, that the greateſt Genius ought not to deſpiſe ſo rich a Mine a Treaſure in which ſo many beautiful and precious Materials are hoarded up. And Experience convinces us, that a Man of Taſte may thence draw Ideas which not only pleaſe, but ſtrike with uncommon Force, provided he knows how to tell them properly.

It is not thro' Ignorance that the *Spaniards* have neglected to follow *Ariſtotle*'s Rules. *Don Lopez de Vega* tells us that *Don Lopo de*

de Rueda has obferved them with great Severity in his Plays; there are alfo feveral other
Comedies, and Tragi-Comedies in *Spain,*
which their Poets rehearfe to their Readers,
and boaft that they are compofed according
to the exacteft Rules of the Drama. *Vega*
himfelf, in writing of the Dramatic Art, tells
us, that if the *Spanifh* Poets have not fub-
jected themfelves to Rules, it is not fo much
to be imputed to their Ignorance, as the Neceffity they are under to pleafe the Tafte of
the Nation, particularly the Ladies, who in
Spain, as well as in other Countries, fix the
State of the Stage and the Language. But
notwithftanding this Negligence, Men of
Genius, in tranflating the *Spanifh* Plays into
another Language, may eafily reduce them
to all the Exactnefs which is neceffary. This
we fee has been done by the two *Corneilles,*
by *Molliere,* and many others. Thus we
may look upon the *Spanifh* Theatre as an
inexhauftible Fund, from whence all other
Nations may be fupplied.

At *Madrid* there are at prefent three famous Dramatic Writers; viz. *Don Felles de
Arebo, Don Bernerdo Jofeph de Reynofo y
Quifiones,* and *Don Jofeph de Canizares.*
The laft of thefe has the moft fertile Pen,
and the greateft Reputation: None of them
have yet publifhed any of their Pieces, becaufe
it is not ufual to publifh them one after an-
H 4   other,

other, as is done in *France* ; for there they wait until they have a complete Collection for the Theatre. If those Authors alone are as exuberant in their Fancy as their Predeceffors, they will leave more Pieces to Pofterity than all the *French* Authors their Cotemporaries.

The *Spaniards* obferve great Order in their Theatrical Reprefentations: For however they may clap or laugh, there is never any Tumult to difturb the Actors. Their Applaufes, like thofe of the Ancients and the Modern *French*, confift moftly in clapping their Hands. If the Play is ill wrote, or ill acted, they wait to the End before they give their Judgment : If it happens to pleafe, the whole Audience raife a confufed Shout, and demand it again next Night, as is done in *Italy*, and particularly at *Venice :* And to prevent Diforder, there is (as I have already obferved) always an *Alcaide de Corte* prefent with his Guards.

As the *Spanifh* Actors (who always feek after Truth in their Expreffion) faithfully imitate Nature, they are no lefs careful to do fo in their Action and Gefture, without departing from that Gravity which is peculiar to their Nation. This I am informed of by the Memoirs which I have received from them on that Subject, and which I can affure the Reader, are authentic. Tho' feveral *Spa-niards*

niards acted in *Italy* in my Time, I muſt
own that I could never thoroughly underſtand them: But having one Day met a *Spaniſh* Player, I aſked the Favour of him to repeat ſome Scenes to me; which he did in a
manner that quite ſurprized me, and affected
me ſo ſtrongly, that I ſhall never forget it.
My Surprize was ſtill increaſed becauſe his
Habit was very unfit for one that was going
to make a noble Declamation; having no
other Dreſs but a coarſe kind of Cloak, which
he had wore in a Pilgrimage to *Rome*.   As I
was commending him for his moving Action, he aſſured me he was but one of the
middling Actors of his Country, and named
ſeveral others then living, of whom he gave
me a ſurprizing Character.   Tho' I am inclined to believe him, yet, leſt I ſhould be
deceived, I ſhall be determined by thoſe who
have ſeen and underſtand the *Spaniſh* Drama.

The *Spaniſh* Farces are more upon the
Italian Taſte than thoſe of any other Nation. He that acts the principal Part is called
Gracioſo, and very much reſembles the Dreſs
and Character of our Harlequin. It is true
that the *Gracioſo* is not very lucky in the
Subjects of his Witticiſms; for on every Occaſion he ſwears by the Saints, of which the
Poet affects to chuſe the moſt unuſual
Names, in order to make his Wit more comical, if it can be called Wit.   They who
are

are curious to fee more of this, may look into the *Spanish* Plays, which are full of it. Indeed I am not furprized, in the main, that the *Graciofo* fhould fo nearly refemble the Harlequin of the *Italian* Comedy. I fuppofe the *Spanish* Theatre to be an Age older than that of *Italy:* This the *Spaniards* themfelves pretend ; but they cannot trace it back any further. However that may be, it cannot be more ancient than the *Italian Extempore* Comedy. Harlequin was introduced foon after the Decay of the Gentil Comedy, if it be true that it came directly from the *Centunculus* of the *Latins*, as I have endeavoured to prove in another * Place. The *Spaniards* in forming their Theatre followed no other Patterns but thofe of *Greece*, *Italy*, or the *Extempore* Comedy of the *Italians*, which undoubtedly prevailed during feveral Ages afterward: Thus it is but natural to fuppofe that the *Spaniards* imitated thofe ; and it is for that Reafon we find fo

great

---

* In my Hiftory of the *Italian* Theatre printed at *Paris* 1728, Page 5, *&c.* the Reader may fee that not only the Harlequin is a kind of Remnant of the *Latin Mimi*, and his Habit almoft the fame, but alfo that fince the Decay of the Gentil Theatre, the Habit and Character of thofe *Latin Mimi* in all their Parts have been continued in *Italy* down to our Times. To prove this we may confult *Cicero*, *Apulecus*, *Diamed*, *Voffius*, &c.

great a Refemblance between the Farces of the two Nations.

The *Spanish* Pieces have commonly a kind of Bawds whom they call the *Capa y Espada*: Thefe are of the fame kind with the *Dame Invifible*, or the *Efprit Folet* of the *French* Theatre, and with the *Maifon a deux portes*, a Comedy acted *extempore* on the *Italian* Theatre, all taken from *Calderon*. The *Spanish* Theatre is full of Pieces of this kind, from whence Authors of all other Nations may draw numberlefs Copies. Thofe which are of a more elevated kind, either by the Quality of the Perfons which are introduced, or the Greatnefs of the Plot and the Incidents, may ferve as a Model for Tragi-Comedy and Tragedy; and in copying after, or imitating thefe, the *Italians* and *French* have made no fmall Advantage.

From all that has been faid we may conclude, that tho' the *Spanish* Theatre is deftitute of Rules, yet if we confider the great Beauty of their Thoughts, and the prodigious Number and Variety of Dramatic Subjects peculiar to them, that their Stage has been, and is the great Source of Poetry, and the grand Model for all the Stages in *Europe*.

T H E

THE

FRENCH THEATRE.

THE Original of the *French* Theatre is not so obscure as those of *Italy* and *Spain*; for the Traces which remain of it afford us a more certain Knowledge of its Rise, than the *Spaniards* or *Italians* have been able to preserve of theirs; and several *French* Authors have fixed these Epochas, and handed them down to us. It is true we sometimes meet with some Anachronisms, but they are not of so great Consequence as to alter the Truth of Facts; and whatever Difference we may meet with in Point of *Time*, or even *Facts*, yet we are still able to account for the true Original State of the *French* Theatre. Ever since the Year 1500 we meet with *French* Authors who have written

in

in the Dramatic Way; and the Differtations on that Subject have never been difcontinued for an Age together. As I own myfelf not very well qualified to give the *complete* Hiftory of this Theatre, I fhall content myfelf with giving the Reader a Hint of what they have copied from the *Romans*, and for that Purpofe go as far back in my Refearches as I am able.

After I had ended this Treatife in 1734, a Hiftory of the *French* Theatre appeared: And as that new Work obliged me to abridge mine, the Reader I hope will pardon me to take this Opportunity of publifhing my Remarks and Obfervations thereon.

The Author of that Hiftory pretends that Comedy was re-eftablifhed in *France* by the *Troubadours* about the twelfth Age; but I don't know on what he founds his Opinion: All that he fays upon that Head only fhews us the different Changes which Comedies fuffered before it was formed into a Theatrical Reprefentation. All the Works of the *Troubadours* which he mentions, and which indeed don't deferve the Name of Comedies, only ferved to give the *French* Nation gradual and more perfect Ideas of it. With regard to its Origin, I believe we may well raife it five hundred Years higher than the Epocha given it by this new Hiftory.

In fpeaking of the *Troubadours,* that Author

thor afferts that they were the Inventors of
Comedies in *Provence*, and that among them
there were fome who were called Comics,
whom he would have us believe were Comedians. It would feem that he has mifunder-
ftood the Meaning of the Word *Comic*,
which fignifies only a *Fool* or *Buffoon*. To
prove this I need only tranfcribe that very
Paffage of *Noſtradamus* quoted by that Author with regard to *Nouez*, who died *Anno*
1220. " That Poet (fays *Noſtradamus*) was
" a *good Comic*, and went about among the
" Houfes of the Nobility finging, dancing,
" and making Geftures; by which, and by
" the other Geftures proper to a true *Comic*,
" he gained an immenfe Treafure." This
is an exact Defcription of a Buffoon : And
if in thofe Days the Buffoons met with
greater Efteem than was due to that Character, it was becaufe they added to it the
Merit of making Verfes, which they rehearfed with fome Degree of Art.

I believe he is no lefs miftaken when he
fays, that in the twelfth Century they had
Comedies and Tragedies in *Provence*, becaufe
at that Time they had Pieces of Poetry
which went under that Name : But how can
he give the Name of Comedy to thofe
Poems which by his own Confeffion (Page
13) *refembled rather Dialogues than Comedies?*
To which he afterwards adds, that by *the
Motion*

Motion of the Body and Change of the Voice,
Noſtradamus intends to deſcribe the Art
which *Nouez* had of reciting his Dialogues
alone, ſpeaking either with a Man's or Woman's Voice, or ſhifting the Place, Geſture,
or Air of his Countenance, almoſt like *Sofia*
in the Soliloquy of the Play of *Amphytrion:*
Indeed thoſe Qualities may be well taken for
thoſe of a *Comic, i. e.* a Droll, but not that
of a Comedian.

The *Trouvers,* or *Troubadours,* who compoſed thoſe different kinds of Poems, called
them *Songs, Sonnets, Sounds, Verſes, Words,*
Lays, Satyrs, Paſtorals, Comedies, &c. Now
thoſe two laſt Titles can only belong properly to Theatrical Pieces; and it is preſum-
able that theſe above-mentioned were only
Poems, or rather Dialogues, which (like ſome
others of that kind) had their Names from
their Subject: Thus, for Example, thoſe
which treated of Shepherds and rural Pleaſures, were called Paſtorals; thoſe in Verſe
full of Comical or Droll Lines, tho' rehearſed
only by one Perſon, were called Comedies.
Perhaps thoſe Authors called their Poems
Comedies for the ſame Reaſon that *Dante*
gave that Name to his Poem, (Comedy ſigni-
fying Dialogue) tho' we don't look upon it as
a Dramatic Poem. And even in the Epic, becauſe the fourth Book of the *Æneid* is almoſt
entirely Dramatic, muſt we for that Reaſon
call

call it a Tragedy? Perhaps the *Provencois* had no other Reason to call their Comical Dialogues by the Name of Comedy.

I think *Paffarol's* five Poems ought not to be admitted among the Number of Tragedies: For properly speaking, they were no more than a Collection of Tragic Verses, in which he introduced some Person who rehearsed, declaimed, imprecated, or discoursed with another, without the Form of Representation, and only by one Actor, who it is said varied his Voice and Gesture. The Plans of those pretended Tragedies mentioned by the Author of the History of the Theatres, are rather those of Historical Facts, such as that of *Joan* Queen of *Naples* having four Husbands, taken Word for Word from *Mezeray* and *Brantome*; and it is very probable that *Paffarol* composed his Satyrical Verses on those Facts, and afterwards named them Tragedies, because according to him the Subjects were tragical; and thus, as I have already observed, all the *Provencal* Poems took their Names from the Subject, as is the Custom of all other Countries at this Day.

In order to prove what I have said, I believe I may safely affirm that no Nation in *Europe* can fix the Date of their Theatrical Performances with any Certainty. And tho' St. *Thomas Aquinas*, who lived in the Beginning of the twelfth Century, doubted if

Comedy

Comedy might be acted without committing
Sin, we muſt not think that he meant written
Comedy; for in his Time, and perhaps for
ſeveral Ages after him, *Extempore* Comedy
prevailed in *Italy*. The *Spaniards* indeed pretend that their Theatre is much older than
that of *Italy* or *France*; but I have already
ſhewn that they have no ſure Ground for that
Aſſertion. In Hiſtory I think we ought to
bring *certain* Proof, and not conjecture for
what is advanced, leſt we ſhould impoſe upon
thoſe who without duly weighing Facts, take
them upon the Credit of the Hiſtorian; now
of all the Parts of Literature, we are moſt at
a Loſs for the Hiſtory of Theatres, and conſequently Authors may more eaſily impoſe
upon the Public on that Subject.

After all thoſe Reflections, it muſt be
obſerved, that from the Eſtabliſhment of the
Troubadours until the Year 1384, our Author brings no Proof that the *French* had
either Theatres or Plays. What he has hitherto called *Provencal* Comedies, are only the
Rehearſals of Songs, or Dialogues, either
Comical, Tragical, or Satyrical; and tho'
rehearſed by one Perſon in a Chamber, Court,
or any other Place, they cannot be named
Comedy, *i. e.* a Piece deſigned for a Theatre.

The Beginning of the *French* Theatre
cannot therefore be fixed before the Year
1398, at which Time the Myſtery of the
I   Paſſion

Paſſion was repreſented at St. *Maur.* By
our Author's inſerting the Order of the *Pro-
voſt* of *Paris* on that Subjeçt, he endeavours
to prove that the Repreſentation of the Myſtery was begun long before the Year 1398,
and indeed I am of his Opinion; but I cannot agree with him that thoſe ſacred Repreſentations that uſed to be made by Clergy-
men or Laics in Church Porches, or even in
Churches, can aſcertain the Date of the
French Theatre, which ought to begin from
the Confraternity of the Paſſion.

By a Quotation which our Author has
taken from the eleventh Book of the Hiſtory
of the City of *Paris*, Page 523, he ſays, that
Anno 1313 *Philip* the fair gave a magnificent Feaſt, to which he invited the King of
England; and among the other Diverſions,
the People *repreſented divers Shews, ſometimes
the Joys of the Bleſſed in Heaven, and ſometimes
the Puniſhments of the Damned.* The Author
ſays, that theſe Shews were Repreſentations
recited by way of Dialogue. This I am
willing to believe for once, and am only
ſorry that there is not one Pattern remaining
of thoſe Dialogues. In the Repreſentation
of Hell what Crying, Howling, and Lamentation ſhould we hear: On the contrary in
Paradice we ſhould behold nothing but Joy
and Adoration. In fine, I muſt beg Leave
to tell this Author that I differ from him.

In

In my Opinion all that was nothing but Reprefentations in Figures, void of Dialogue of any kind. As that Feaft was made only for the Kings of *France* and *England*, is it likely that thefe two great Kings, with their numerous Attendants, would ftand an Hour and an Half in the Street to fee thofe Reprefentations? No, certainly ; for I believe they only looked at them as they paffed, or at moft, ftopped to hear an Angel or Devil rehearfe fome Lines, till they could have a fmall Notion of the Entertainment. Thefe figurative Reprefentations will not appear fo ftrange after reading the following Examples. In the Year 1690 I was in the City of *Genoa* on *Corpus Chrifti* Day : There they had feveral Theatres erected in the Corners of the Streets through which the Proceffion of the Holy Sacrament was to pafs. On each of thefe was reprefented in living Figures a Myftery taken from the *Old* or *New Teftament.* The moft remarkable of thefe was that which had been erected without the Gate by the Fifhers of the Town: The Decoration reprefented the Sea with the Shore at a Diftance: There appeared Jefus Chrift, as he is defcribed by the Evangelifts when he ordered his Apoftles St. *Peter*, St. *John*, &c. to throw their Nets into the Sea ; and when they anfwered that they had been toiling all Night to no Purpofe, Chrift com-

manded

manded them to let fall their Nets on the other Side of the Veffel: All this was performed by Action and Gefture without Speech. The Actors chofe to delay drawing the Net till the Sacrament was paffing by the Stage; then they took them up, and found them full of a great Number of the moft delicious and rare Fifhes, which had been catched feveral Days before, and kept alive in Water for that Purpofe. In the City of *Naples*, at the Feaft of the Holy Sacrament, they alfo exhibit Shows of this kind, *viz.* Our Saviour on the Crofs on Mount *Calvary* accompanied with the bleffed Virgin, *Mary Magdalen*, the other *Mary*, and all the reft of that Myftery. To do that with the greater Propriety, they make Choice of fuch Women and young Girls as can beft reprefent the Action, and who have Habits proper for the feveral Perfonages. In moft of the Cities of *Flanders*, on certain Feftivals they have Chariots carrying Stages through the Streets; on fome of them they have Gardens and Pyramids: On thefe Theatres they have Actors who perform all in dumb Shew. The Subject is commonly taken from the *Old* or *New Teftament*, or allegorical Objects of Piety. Thefe Feafts they call *Carmeffes*.

I was affured by a Gentleman of that Country, that on *Chriftmas-Day* he had feen

a

a Toilet fet where the Proceffion of the
Sacrament was to ftop firft: Before it was
placed a fine Lady adorned with Jewels and
Precious-ftones; fhe fat adjufting her Drefs,
and putting on her Patches until the Hoft
refted: After that, fhe rofe up all of a fudden, pufhed away the Toilet, and kneeled
down before the Sacrament. When it was
taken up again, fhe followed it, beating her
Breaft until the fecond Reft, where fhe alfo
fell down upon her Knees with great Com-
punction, fhewing all the Signs of true Re-
pentance; fhe next pulled off all her Jewels
and Drefs, and remained in the Habit of a
Penitent. In that Condition fhe followed
the Proceffion, fetching heavy Sighs and
Groans, and fhedding Tears in fuch a manner as drew them alfo from all thofe who
faw her. Is not this one Action followed
through all its Forms?

In an Electoral City of *Germany* they
commonly erect a Theatre in the Cathedral
Church on one of the Days of the holy
Week, reprefenting the Garden of Olives,
where Chrift after returning from Prayer
found his Difciples afleep. All this is done
by living Perfons: And he that reprefents
Chrift, goes three times and awakes the
Apoftles, and as often returns to Prayer: In
a word, we may there fee a *complete* Image
of what happened in the Garden of Olives.

I 3   All

All this Action is performed in Dumb Shew and Pantomime. After thefe Examples, I think I had Reafon to affirm, that the Reprefentation of Heaven and Hell, which I have mentioned, was but figured Reprefentations, and executed in the fame manner with thofe I have been relating.

If we believe the Author of this Hiftory, the firft Comedies that were acted in *France* were thofe of *Provence*, and begun *Anno* 1198; if (I fay) we believe him, how is it poffible that 200 Years afterwards, when the Myfteries of the Paffion were firft reprefented at *St. Maur*, there fhould be fo much Simplicity and Ignorance in thofe Theatrical Reprefentations ? Indeed it is highly improbable, as I have already obferved, that at the Diftance of two Ages after the Reprefentation of the * *Provencal* Comedy, the fame Ignorance fhould continue fo long without the leaft Improvement either in *Provence* or *Paris*. For furely if it were true that the *Troubadours* had acted Comedy, and *Paffarol* Tragedy, we fhould not have

---

* In the Reprefentation of the *Myfteries*, the Theatre reprefented Paradice, Hell, Heaven, and Earth all at once; and tho' the Action varied, there was no Change of the Decorations. After an Actor had performed his Part he did not go off the Stage, but retired to a Corner of it, and fat there in full View of all the Spectators.

have been fo much at a Lofs concerning the
Origin of the *French* Theatre.

I would not however infer from thence
that Dramatic Poems began to appear in
France only in that Year wherein the Myfteries of the Paffion were exhibited at *St.
Maur*; on the contrary I am perfuaded, that
thofe Myfteries, fuch as they were then reprefented, void of all kind of *Order* or Principle
in the Compofition, could not be the firft
which were reprefented at *Paris*. They
muft at leaft for fome time before have reprefented either facred or prophane Plays in particular Places, Crofs-ways, *&c.* but thofe
Actions (if we confider their Nature) can
never be fufficient to eftablifh the Epocha of
the *French* Theatre. However that may be,
the Myfteries reprefented at *St. Maur* (I repeat the Affertion) will be found to be the
firft Exhibition of that kind that appeared in
France. I know no Author who gives us
the leaft Hint of any older Theatre, and
every other Method we fhall ufe to afcertain
it, muft be vain, ill-founded, and conjectural.

With regard to the Origin of Comedy in
France, I think we may believe their Hiftorians, who tell us, that feveral Writers erected
Theatres whereon they acted Pieces of their
own. We have alfo Authorities which prove,
that in the Reign of *Charles* the Great, the
Councils of *Mayence*, *Tours*, *Rheims* and

Chalons,

Chalons, prohibited the Clergy from affisting at † Farce-Plays, and the King ratified the Order of the Council by an Edict which was published in the Year 813. Hence we know that the Comedy which had been difufed among the *Romans*, had been renewed in *France* and *Italy* by Strollers and Farce-Players, who acted in the Streets and other public Places. We fee that to thofe Shows which by an Edict of *Charles* the Great were declared ‡ obfcene and infamous, fucceeded the *Troubadours*, *Jongleurs*, and others who rehearfed, or rather fung Scraps of Hiftory, Gallantry, and Satyr: And after thofe *Troubadours* had fallen into Contempt, and were even banifhed the Court of ‖ *Philip Auguftus*, they found Means to eftablifh themfelves again in that very Reign, and obtained Apartments in one particular Street of the City, which from them was called *La Rue de Jongleurs*, now *Menetriers*. From that Time they only were paid at Feafts and Affemblies. But we learn by two Orders of the Provoft of *Paris*, from the Year 1341 to 1395, that they were prohibited from fpeaking,

---

† The Farce Players were even then held to be infamous Perfons, and none were allowed to bring them before a Court of Juftice. See *Marre*'s Treatife of Policy, Vol. I, Page 433, &c.

‡ *Hiftrionum turpium & obfcenorum infolentias jocorum*, &c.

‖ *Rigor de Geft*. Philip. *Aug.*

fpeaking, finging, or acting in public Places, or otherwife, any thing that might give Scandal or Offence. Not content with thofe Reftrictions, they changed their Manner of Action, and applied themfelves to exhibit furprizing Poftures and dangerous Combats with naked Swords, which gave Occafion to their being called *Battaleurs*, or Prize-fighters, a Name they have retained ever fince.

If the Progrefs of thofe Farce-players had not been obftructed by Orders of the Councils, and the Edicts of the King which I have mentioned, perhaps the *French* had continued to encourage them. We may even venture to fay, that the fuppreffing of thofe Farce-players gave Rife to the Buffoonries of the *Troubadours*, who afterwards degenerated into Farce-players no lefs fcandalous than the firft, and who were alfo fuppreffed under the Reign of *Philip* the Auguft, as I have before obferved. From thefe two Epochas fo remarkable, it is probable that the firft Farce-players, in the Time of *Charlemagne*, were the Remainder of the *Roman Mimi*, who acted in the Streets and public Places as they do now in *Italy*; and there is good Reafon to believe that by this Progrefs they would have been led by Degrees to build Theatres, if they had been fuffered to act without Interruption, as is done in *Italy*.

About the Year 1370, in the Reign of
Charles

Charles V, we may eafily obferve the Origin of Tragic Declamation in thofe long Repetitions of hero c Verfes which were often taken from the Myfteries of Religion, with a kind of Apoftrophe to the Prince to whom they were dedicated, which at times they called the § *Royal Song.* Hence proceeded thofe myfterious Dialogues which perhaps were acted in particular Places and without any Ornament, and were firft reprefented on a Theatre in the Village of *St. Maur*, but were prohibited by the Provoft of *Paris* by an Order dated the 3d of *June*, whereby he *forbids all the Inhabitants,* &c. *to act or reprefent any Play by Perfons, either the Lives of the Saints or otherwife, without Leave from the King, on Pain of,* &c. *

The Actors in thofe Reprefentations formed a Part of the Royal Houfhold, and in order to make themfelves more agreeable to the Public, erected their Society into a Fraternity by the Name of *The Actors of our Saviour's Paffion. Charles* VI. went to fee thofe Shows, and was fo well pleafed with them, that he granted the Actors Letterspatent dated the 4th of *December* 1402, which are printed at length in Mr. *De Marre's* Treatife of Policy, Page 437. They alfo

---

§ See *Pafquier*, B. 7. of the Memoirs of *France.* **Chap.**
V.   * Treatife of Policy by *Marre*, T. I.

alfo built the Theatre of the Hofpital of the Holy Trinity, on which, during the Space of almoſt one hundred and fifty Years, they acted the Myſteries, or other Pieces of Piety and Morality under the common Title of *Moralities*. In the Year 1518 *Francis* I. confirmed all the Privileges of the Fraternity by his Letters-Patents, dated in the Month of *January* that Year.

At laſt the People, tired with theſe ſerious Repreſentations, forced the Fraternity to join prophane and burleſque Farces, which pleaſed them ſo much that they ran in Crowds to ſee them acted. But this Mixture of Morality and Buffoonry diſpleaſed the better Sort, who began to reflect that thoſe devout Subjects, which the Simplicity of diſtant Times had brought upon the Stage, were rather a Profanation of the principal Myſteries of Religion than Shews, and that they ought no longer to be tolerated. About that Time an Epidemical Diſeaſe prevailed in *Paris*, which obliged the Parliament to augment the Number of Hoſpitals, and to order by an *Arret*, dated the 30th of *July* 1347, in the Reign of *Henry* II. that the Houſe of the Trinity ſhould from hence-forth be only uſed as an Hoſpital, which obliged the Fraternity to demoliſh their Theatre. But as they were then grown rich, they purchaſed the Scite of the Duke

of

of *Burgundy's* old Houfe, and there built a new Theatre. That Eftablifhment was confirmed by an Arret of Parliament dated the 19th of *November* 1548, which permitted them to act, *but always on this Condition,* (thefe are the Words of the Act) *that they shall meddle with none but prophane Subjects, such as are lawful and honeft, and not to reprefent any facred Myfteries.* And by confirming all their Privileges to them, all others are prohibited to act in the City or Suburbs, except in the Name, and for Account of the Fraternity, &c. This Privilege was further confirmed by Letters-patent from *Henry* II. in the Month of *November* 1559, and of *Charles* IX, 1563. Thus the Fraternity remained in peaceable Poffeffion of their Theatre; and in order to fhew that they were the fole Proprietors, they had their Coat of Arms cut on Stone (*viz* a Scutcheon fupported by two Angels, on which was reprefented a Crofs and other Inftruments of the Paffion) fixed in the Front of the Houfe towards the *French* Street. This was the ancient Device of the Fraternity, who, now that their new Theatre was finifhed, and that they were prohibited from acting divine Myfteries or the Lives of the Saints, acted only prophane Pieces. They who are of another Opinion are miftaken: The Stone with the Coat of Arms which I have mentioned, being only an Infcription,

can

can never be a fufficient Foundation for their Affertion. All the Meaning of it was to fhew that they were fole Mafters and Proprietors of the Privileges of acting, or caufing to be acted either prophane Comedies or Tragedies within the City of *Paris:* And all the moral Pieces that have been acted fince, except by the Fraternity, have only been in private Houfes, or upon Scaffolds.

In Confequence of the Order of Parliament in 1548, and the Letters-patents of *Henry* II. and *Charles* IX. confirming that Privilege, they continued for a long time to act upon their new Stage under the Name and Authority of the *Fraternity of the Paf-fion.* I fay under their Name and their Authority: For after the Opening of that Theatre, the Fraternity did not act *all* the Plays that were exhibited upon the Stage. They thought it was below the Dignity of their Name to mount the Stage only to act prophane Comedies, and immediately gave a Leafe of their Houfe and Theatre to a Company of Comedians who were formed into a Body for that Purpofe, referving only two Rooms to themfelves, in which they acted as long as their Privilege lafted.

We have neither the Names or Characters of thofe Pieces which were acted at the Opening of this Theatre, and they only quote the old Farce written by *Pathelin,*

acted

acted in the Reign of *Henry* II. The Reafon given by the Writers of this Age for not tranfmitting them to Pofterity, is, that the Pieces were fo worthlefs, and the Authors fo mean, that they were not worth recording. They only mention one *M. Jodelle* who wrote the firft Tragedy after the Opening of the *Burgundian* Theatre.

Here we may obferve that the *French* have copied the *Italians* in one Miftake, *viz.* they have always reckoned *Jodelle* the firft Tragic Writer, tho' he was not; for there were feveral before him, as *The Deftruction of Troy the Great*, printed at *Lyons* in 1485. *The Iphegenia of Euripides* by *T. J.* printed in 1550. *The Hecuba of Euripides* by *Boucherella*, and another by *John Antoine Baif*, one in the Year 1537, the other in 1550; and the *Electra*, or *Revenge of Agamemnon*, tranflated literally from *Sophocles* by *Lazarus de Baif*, Mafter of the Requefts, and *F. Anthony Baif*, printed in 1537. But as thofe Tragedies were only Tranflations from the *Greek*, and *Jodelle* wrote two, *viz.* *Cleopatra* and *Dido*, which were neither Tranflations nor Imitations of the Ancients, there is fome Reafon to allow him the firft Place among the Tragic-Writers, and to fix the Epocha of Tragedy from his Works. Perhaps it may be fufpected that *Jodelle* imitated the *Italian* Tragedies of *Cleopatra*

and

and *Dido*, written and printed long before
he wrote, while the *Italian* Stage flourished:
But as I examined and compared them
together, I can assure the Reader they are
very different. Not but that there were
many Translations from *Italian* Plays in
those Days, as we may learn from *Du Verdier*'s *French Bibliotheque*, who in speaking
of the Comedy of that Time, has the following Words: " A very elegant Comedy,
" in which are contained the Loves of
" *Eroftratus* the Son of *Phelogonus* of *Cata-
" nia*, and of *Polymnefta*, the Daughter of
" *Damon*, taken from the *Italian* and put
" into *French* Rhyme. Printed at *Paris* by
" *Herom Marnef* in 1545, the Author un-
" certain."

This Passage of *Du Verdier* naturally leads
us to make one Observation which is mentioned by the greatest Part of his Contemporaries, concerning the Establishment of
Comedy in *France*. They pretend that as
soon as the *Burgundian* Theatre was opened,
and for several Years after, no Plays were
acted worthy of Notice: And of all the
Pieces that were represented in *France* in
those Days, they have only mentioned a
Farce written by *Pathelin*, the *Eugene* of
Jodelle, the *Taillebras*, imitated from the
Miles Gloriofus of *Plautus*, and the *Eunuch*
of *Terence* by *M. Baif* in the Year 1567;
but

but at the fame time they obferve that all the Plays before thefe were only forry Farces or Buffoonries. But according to *Du Verdier*, the Tranflation of that *Italian* Comedy which he commends fo much appeared in 1545, and confequently before the Opening of the *Burgundian* Theatre, together with the *Andrian* of *Bonaventure de Periers*, which appeared in 1537. Thus we may reafonably conclude, that while the *Moralities* and Myfteries of the Trinity were reprefented upon the Theatre, Tragedies and prophane Comedies were alfo acted at *Paris*; and if that was not done publickly and on the Theatre, the Fraternity had obtained that Liberty by the Letters-patent with all other kinds of Reprefentation.

As foon as the *Burgundian* Theatre was finifhed, the Fraternity of the Paffion let it to fome Players, who (according to the Hiftorian) immediately formed themfelves into a Company. But if at that Time they had no Actors at *Paris* who had been bred to the Theatre, how could the Company of Comedians be formed immediately? For tho' that be none of the moft difficult Profeffions, yet it requires Time and Application to be Mafter of it. We may therefore conclude, that tho' Comedy was acted in feveral Places of *Paris*, there were alfo Comical and Tragical

gical Pieces invented or imitated long before the Establishment of the *Burgundian* Theatre.

Nay, it is certain that the *Bazoch, i. e.* the Clerks of the Attorneys of Parliament acted Comedies long before this Establishment: And we have all the Reason in the World to believe that they acted in Public on Scaffolds, or else on Theatres erected in private Houses. By a Petition of *Marot*, to the King for the *Bazoch*, we learn that his Majesty sometimes was present at those Representations. The Pieces which were acted by the *Bazoch* were commonly Satyrical, and *Lewis* XII. was the Subject of some of these. But he laught at them, and told the Fraternity, that if from henceforth they endeavoured to break their Jokes upon any Person that belonged to him, he would cause them all to be hang'd.

The Fraternity of the Passion were not therefore the only Theatrical Actors: And the Mysteries which from their first Institution had been represented in Churches, in the *Flemish* Palace, on Highways, public Places, and cross Streets of the City, at Feasts, and public Rejoicings, consequently must have employed several Persons in the Art of Acting. After this, it is easy to imagine that the Fraternity would, without much Difficulty, soon find a Band of Comedians to take

K   a

a Leafe of their Theatre, in order to act profane Pieces.

From all that has been faid on this Head,
I think we may venture to affirm, that the
Author of the * Theatrical Library has not
fufficiently examined what he has advanced
on this Subject. In his Remark, under the
Letter *A*, on the *Andrian*, he fays, " It was
" the firft Tranflation from *Terence*, that had
" appeared upon the *French* Theatre, becaufe
" the *Eunuch*, which was tranflated by *M.*
" *Baif* in the Reign of *Charles* IX, was not
" acted, there being then no Comedians at
" *Paris*." This he repeats again under the
Article of the *Eunuch*, without remember-
ing that in the Catalogue of Additions and
Corrections at the End of the Book, he fays,
" That to the *Andrian* we muft add the
" *Bonaventure* of *M. Periers*, *Anno* 1537."
Therefore the *Andrian* which appeared in
1704, was not the firft *French* Tranflation
from *Terence*. The fame may alfo be faid of
the *Eunuch* tranflated by *Baif* about the
Year 1560.

Charles IX. who began his Reign about
that Time, found the *Burgundian* Theatre
fettled and furnifhed with a Company of
Comedians; for it was opened *Anno* 1548
or 49, the 2d of the Reign of *Henry* II.
There muft therefore be fome other Reafon
which hindered the *Eunuch* of *M. Baif*

* Printed at *Paris, Anno* 1733.　　　　from

from being reprefented ; and the moft probable one is, that when the Myfteries were
reprefented upon the Theatre of the Trinity,
and before Plays were acted at the Palace of
Burgundy, they played Tranflations from the
Claffics upon private Stages only ; for it is agreed
that the *French* Stage was then very lame and
poor, tho' afterwards it came to make a confiderable Figure. A celebrated *Italian* Writer
tells us a Story of the *French* Theatre, which
is not to be met with in any other Author :
I mean *Girolamo Rufcelli*, who in his Collection of the beft *Italian* Plays, printed in
1554 with Notes at the End, fpeaking of
Caffandra, a Comedy written by *Bibiena*,
fays, " That in his Time they had a kind
" of dumb Farces in *France*, in which the
" Actors, without fpeaking one Word,
" were furprizingly underftood by their
" Geftures." He adds, " that the Action
" was fo agreeable, and fo taking with the
" Spectators, that he was much pleafed with
" it. I am furprized (fays he) that this
" Method has never been brought into
" *Italy*."

So candid a Relation from a Stranger,
who tells us he faw thofe Farces, is of un-
queftionable Authority ; and I know not
why no *French* Writer (at leaft that I have
ever feen) has thought fit to give us the leaft
Information concerning thefe Farces. From

the

the Defcription of *Rufcelli*, thefe Pantomimes
muft have been an excellent Show, and
a true Imitation of the Mimes of the Ancients. Admitting this Fact as certain, how
comes it to pafs that an Art, in which none
of the Moderns have made any great Progrefs, yet was perfectly well known in *France*
in thofe Days, fhould be fo much loft as that
the fmalleft Traces of it are not remaining?
We muft not imagine that the Farces, which
about twenty four Years ago were acted at
Paris by Labels, are of that kind: For as I
have been twenty Years in *France*, and have
once feen a Farce performed by Labels, I am
thereby enabled to judge of the Difference.

Thefe Farces which were acted with
Labels are a very pretty Invention of their
kind: Every one knows that the Actors
appear upon the Stage without fpeaking:
That as foon as they appear, the Labels fall
down fucceffively from the Ceiling upon
their Heads; thefe are filled with Couplets of
Songs written in large Characters, the Tunes
of which are played by Mufic, and the
Words read and fung by the Pit. The Actors, during that Time, are making Geftures
agreeable to the Meaning of the Words, but
in thofe there is very little Diverfion or Pleafure: All the Pleafure confifts in the odd
Cuftom of making the Dialogues of the Actors to be fung by the Spectators. That is
indeed

indeed quite a modern Invention, and yet was not the Effect of Choice, but Necessity. As the King's Company of Comedians and the Opera were possessed of very extensive Privileges, they would not allow the Companies of the two Fairs of *St. Lawrence* and *St. German* to act either by Singing or Speaking. These Strollers invented the Labels in order to keep up their Theatre, and at first drew up a great Number of People to be Spectators, which was a great Loss to the privileged Theatres. There is therefore no Reason to believe that those Farces which were acted with Labels, were taken from the dumb Farces above-mentioned, much less that they were any thing like the pantomime Dances that were in Use in *England* and *France* about twelve Years ago; for *Ruscelli* informs us, that these Farces passed in dumb Shew; and if this Action had been carried on by the Assistance of Dancing and Music, (which bear some Analogy to Language) our *Italian* Author would not have neglected to acquaint us with this Circumstance, which I believe he himself would not have been so much surprized at. And 'tis stranger still, during an hundred and fifty Years there was nothing preserved in *Paris* which could so much as furnish us with the faintest Ideas of these Pantomimes mentioned by *Ruscelli*.

These Shows, which were exhibited at

K 3 *Paris*

Paris even about the Middle of the sixteenth Century, would induce me to think that they were the Remains of the before-mentioned Representations of the *Pains of the Damned, and the Glory of the Blessed*, exhibited in the Year 1313 under the Reign of *Philip* the Beautiful, and which I have asserted were not wrought up into Dialogue, but only represented in dumb Shew. Two Ages after they were exhibited at *Paris*; and because Time gradually perfects every thing of this Nature, they were perhaps in the Year 1550 arrived at that Degree of Perfection mentioned by *Ruscelli*. I must again express my Surprize that this Art should be lost, and the very Traces of it undiscoverable in *France*.

It is indeed astonishing that the *French* Theatre should have remained so wretchedly bad (as we find it to be, not only by its printed Production, but by the Accounts of so many Authors) till the Year 1650, and even in the Time of *Corneille*. They who have spoke of this make no other Apology for it than the Ignorance of the Times when it was in its *Infancy*; for so they chuse to call its first Beginnings. But did not this Infancy last too long? Sure it did; for an hundred Years passed between the Opening of the Theatre of *Bourgogne* and the Days of *Corneille* and *Moliere*, the former born in 1606, and the latter in 1621. Had not their Au-

thors

thors (during that Age of pretended Ignorance) the Aids of the *Italian* Theatre,
which at that Time flourished? The Pieces
which had been acted on the Stage of *Italy*
were not then unknown in *France*; for many
of them were translated into that Language.

Here I shall only mention the Titles of
these Pieces, the Times in which they were
printed, and the Names of some of those
translating Authors. " *Josias*, a Tragedy
" translated from the *Italian* of *Messer Pi-*
" *lone* into *French* Verse, by *Louis des Mazu-*
" *res de Tournay*, in 8vo. in the Year 1556.
" *The Sophonisba* of *Claude Mermet*, tran-
" slated from *Trissimo* in 1584. *The Cartha-*
" *ginian* of *Montchretien*, of which the
" Machinery and Scenes are the same with
" those of *Trissimo* in 1619. *The Two Pro-*
" *stitutes* of *Hierome d' Avost de la Val*, tran-
" slated from *Domenichi*. *The Counterfeits*,
" a Comedy translated from the *Ariosto* in
" 1552. *The Necromancer*, a Comedy
" translated from the *Ariosto* in Prose, by the
" *Sieur de la Taile de Bondaroy* in 1568.
" *The Emilia* of *Lewis Groto, the blind Man*
" *of Hadria*, in 1608. *The Bravadoes of*
" *Captain Spavante* by *Francis Andreini*, a
" Comedy translated by *John de Fonteney* in
" 1608. *Solyman, Emperor of the Turks*,
" a Tragedy translated from *Bonorelli* by
" *D' Alibras* in 1637." These Transla-

tions

tions were made by thofe who were either
fenfible of a Barrennefs of Genius for Invention, or were unwilling to put themfelves to
that Trouble.

All thefe Tranflations from the *Italian*
were brought into *France* either by Chance,
or by the Caprice of fome Writers; for the
Source of the *French* Imitation was *Spain*,
which for a Century paft has been the fole
Model for their Theatre. *Corneille* and *Moliere* have in the *Spanifh* Drama found excellent Ideas for Tragedy and Comedy; and
even the Authors of the prefent Age do now,
and always may find the fame, fince (as I
have elfewhere obferved) the *Spanifh* Theatre
is an unexhauftible Source for the Drama.
But the *Spanifh* Theatre, notwithftanding
the Abundance of its Subjects, and the Variety of its Intrigues, did not at firft contribute
to the Eftablifhment of a good Tafte on the
French Theatre, and it was neceffary that fuperior Geniufes fhould point out the Ufe that
was to be made of thefe Subjects and Intrigues.

At the Time when *Peter Corneille* diftinguifhed himfelf above all his Cotemporaries,
by treading (if I may fo fpeak) in the right
Path, the *Cid*, the *Horace*, the *Cinna*, and
all the other Tragedies of that great Man
did not all of a fudden correct the reigning
Tafte of the Theatre, but by degrees opened
the

the Eyes of the Spectators, who at length came to the Knowledge of true Beauty in Dramatic Performances.

This however did not hinder the Dramatic Poets from going still on in their old Road; and some Tragedies in the Year 1660 were so defective and repugnant to good Sense, that one could never believe them to have been wrote in the Days of *Corneille.* The Example of *Rotrou,* a Tragic Poet, is not only worthy of Admiration, but ought to be a Direction to those whom Genius prompts to write for the Stage. After he had wrote one and thirty Pieces, all composed in the *Spanish* Taste, the Applauses with which the *Cid* of *Peter Corneille* was received made him change his Method, and he wrote *Vinceslas,* a Piece indeed drawn from the *Spanish,* but wrought up in a manner quite different from those he had formerly wrote upon foreign Models. His *Cosroes* which afterwards appeared, does not deviate from the new Path into which he had struck; and here we may observe that a great many are deceived, when they ascribe to *Vinceslas* the Change of *Corneille's* Manner. *Racine,* who found the Road paved to him, did not scruple to tread it; and one may say that, without imitating his Predecessor, he has established the Model of good Tragedy in *France.* These two Authors have no longer
left

left the Dramatic Poets in doubt of the best Manner of Writing, and all of them have since endeavoured to imitate the sublime of *Corneille*, or the natural and easy Manner of *Racine*.

As for Comedy, it, as well as Tragedy, stood in need of Alterations and Amendments in order to bring it to Perfection; it did not find the Genius of the two *Corneilles* thoroughly adapted to its proper Character, tho' by their Means it had appeared under a Form less despicable, and more decent than it had under their Predecessors. But to perfect Comedy, a *Moliere* was still wanting, who, destined to be the Restorer of the Theatre and of the true Comic Taste, appeared at *Paris* in the Year 1658. He was first taken Notice of on Account of his two Comedies entitled *L' Etourdi* and *Le Depit Amoreux*, which were the first Essays of his Muse while he was in the Country. A Year after, he published his *Precieuses Ridicules*, which was soon followed by his *Cocu Imaginaire* and his *Ecole des Maris*. These Pieces, which bore no Resemblance to any Works either of the Ancients, or of the Moderns, justly got him the Reputation of an excellent Comic-Poet, which he has ever since kept, and to which I can add nothing by here repeating the Sentiments of Esteem and Admiration, which through the whole of of my Writings I have teſtified for that great Man; and I think it my Duty to confeſs, that during my five and forty Years Practice on the Stage, I have ſtudied this Author, and never failed, upon every Review of his Excellence, to find ſome new Beauty, which till then had eſcaped me.

As to the Dramatic Works and Authors appearing in *France* from the Year 1450 till 1500, we have only an Account of three of them, the Subjects of which are the Myſteries of Religion: The Pieces of this kind which now remain, have been confounded with the Impreſſions made ſince 1500. From the Year 1500 till the Year 1600, we may count eighty three Authors, and a hundred and forty ſeven Pieces of a Comical, a Tragical, a Farcical, or a Moral Nature. From that Period to the Year 1700 we find two hundred and ſeventy eight Authors for the Stage, and eleven hundred and eighty eight Dramatical Performances of all kinds: Tho' that Age appears ſo fertile of theſe Productions, yet it is but mere Show; for three Fourths of them are defective, and almoſt unknown to the World; and we may even add that moſt Authors who preceded *Corneille*, *Racine*, and *Moliere*, and even ſome of their Cotemporaries, wrote upon that Model which prevailed in the Infancy of the *French* Theatre. From the Year 1700 to this

Time

Time † we have had feventy Authors and three hundred and fifty Plays, including thofe under the Name of the Comical Opera. It appears therefore from this Detail, that from the Year 1450 to 1730, or thereabouts, the *French* have had four hundred and thirty one Authors, who were Fathers of one thoufand fix hundred and fifty five Dramatical Productions, including the Operas of the Academy of Mufic, which we fhall mention afterwards.

Tho' the *Italians* in an hundred and fifty Years produced twice as many Dramatical Performances as the *French* did in two hundred and eighty Years, yet we are not on that Account to give the Preference to *Italy*. The greateft Dramatic Excellence of the *Italians* during that Period, falls fhort of what *France* can fhew in feventy Years. All the Nations in *Europe* ought to yeild this to ‡ *France*, fince their Productions, however numerous, are miferably defective and lame. The *French* Theatre, by a Succeffion of excellent Works, is a Proof of the Character and Genius of her Dramatic Poets, who for

the

---

† Viz. 1737.

‡ The Author, by not being acquainted with the *Englifh* Stage, has here been very partial to *France*; for it is certain *England* has produced a greater Number of beautiful Tragedies and Comedies than any Nation, and perhaps fewer faulty ones.

the laft hundred Years have compofed in a right Manner.

Above all, we may remark how much the *French* Drama has improved in Truth, in Tafte, and in Wit within thefe forty or fifty Years; and I can almoft venture to affirm, that many of the Theatrical Pieces which were not acted in *France* within that Time, would have fucceeded in any other Country and have been Stock-plays. As a Proof of this, amongft all that vaft Number of *French* Tragedies tranflated into *Italian,* and acted with Succefs in *Italy,* a great many of them were never played above once or twice at *Paris.*

There is a ftrong Probability that in the Infancy of their Stage, and even towards the Middle of the laft Century, the Actors both in Comedy and Tragedy were generally maf-qued. This I can prove by a Remark of a *French* Author, who fays, in fpeaking of *Hugues Guerru,* furnamed *Flechelles,* and *Gautier Garguille:* " *This Man who was fo*
" *diverting in Farces, fometimes acted the*
" *King very well in ferious Pieces, and even*
" *hit his Gravity and Majefty with the help*
" *of a Mafque and a Night-gown, which*
" *concealed his Legs and thin Make."*

In *France* they highly commend four Co-medians, or rather Players of Farces, who, before the Year 1600, rofe from Booths into
the

the Theatre of *Burgundy*, where they acted with Applause. Their Names were *Turlupin, Gautier Garguille, Big William*, and *Guillot Gorgu*: These were all masqued except *Big William*, who instead of a Masque bedaubed his Face with Flower, and had an Art, by the Motion of his Lips, to make it fly upon the Actor who played along with him. All that is told of those excellent Farce-players, proves only that they were Strollers so low, and so childish in their Profession, that their Reputation was entirely owing to the Ignorance of their Age. But if Authors, from the Comedies of *Moliere*, have learned what Truth and Excellence is, the Players, who since the Death of that great Man have acted his Works, know how to afford Diversion to People of Sense and Quality.

At present no masqued Actors appear on the *French* Stage; they don't so much as wear false Beards, except when it is absolutely necessary in playing the Part of an old Man; nor does any peculiar Habit prevail in Comedy, except that of *Crispin*, which is not very old: The Footmen wear Livery, and the Aged are cloathed agreeably to their Years and Character: They are forced indeed to preserve the Habits peculiar to the Characters of *Moliere* in the same Fashion they were in his Time; and when they make

any

any Alteration in this refpect, the Actors make a like Alteration in the Verfes that allude to the Drefs, or leave them entirely out.

The Actors who play Tragedy furnifh their Theatrical Habits out of their own Pockets. Thefe Habits which are commonly in the *Greek* or the *Roman* Fafhion, are very expenfive, being all finely embroidered with Gold and Silver: Thofe of the Women efpecially, coft vaft Sums. The Players of Comedy are obliged to do the fame, but the Expences among them are very unequal. The Footmen, the Bawds, and the old Men have Dreffes agreeable to their Characters, and which are not very expenfive. But it is different with thofe Players who act the Parts of Lovers, and reprefent diftinguifhed Characters in Comedy; thefe are often obliged to have new Dreffes, commonly very magnificent and fafhionable; nay, thefe Actors often invent new Fafhions of their own, which are foon followed by the Town. The *Andrians*, and many other Dreffes arofe from the Stage. There are fome Habits defigned for *particular Characters* or Difguifes, which being very extraordinary, are paid out of the Purfe-ftock, efpecially when there are fome Diverfions extraordinary in the Entertainment.

In *France* the Spectators (I mean thofe in the

rhe Pit) have always behaved in a turbulent Manner. We see by a Regulation of the Civil Magiftrate, made on the 5th of *February* 1596, That *every Perfon is prohibited from doing any Violence in the Play-houfe of* Burgundy *during the Time any Piece is performing, as likewife from throwing Stones, Duft, or any other thing which may put the Audience into an Uproar, or create any Tumult,* &c.

Lewis XIV. refolved to eftablifh Decency and Tranquillity in public Shews: For this effect (befides the old Guard kept by the Crown) he ordered every Perfon who difturbed the Shew, either by whiftling, or making any other Noife, to be kept in Prifon for a Year and a Day. This Law is ftill in being, and is now and then reinforced by the Lieutenant of the Police.

The Theatres of *France* are built almoft in the fame Form with thofe of *Italy,* which were the Models of all the reft in *Europe,* except that beyond the Pit, there is a Place a little elevated, called the Amphitheatre. This Amphitheatre has Seats, and is funk a little lower than the firft Row of Boxes, that all the Spectators may have the fame free and open View of the Stage. There is alfo at the Foot of the Theatre a kind of Area, called the Orcheftrum, which was formerly defigned for the Mufic, but by contracting

their

their Accommodation, the Spectators may now
have Seats there. The Entry to it is below
the Theatre, and it accommodates about forty
or fifty Perfons, who pay the fame Price with
the Stage; and when the Houfe is thronged,
the Women fit in it on little Seats without
Backs, juft as they do on the Amphitheatre.
The Theatres here are very fmall, having
only three Ranges of Boxes. There are not
here (as in *Italy*) five or fix Rows of Boxes;
and the largeft Pit in *France* contains no
more than five or fix hundred Perfons ftanding, and very much crowded.

This Cuftom of ftanding in the Pit is not
very ancient in *Franee*, for it is evident that
the Spectators had formerly Seats in it, as
may be feen by a Book wrote by *M. M. D.
P.* printed at *Paris* in 1668, entitled *Ideas
of the new Shews*. In this Piece fome Ad-
vices are given with regard to certain Ufages
that needed Reformation; and in fpeaking
of the Time immediately before a Play, the
Author advifes (in favour of the Citizens, and
efpecially the Ladies) *to have fome regard to
their own Conveniency, and to take their Seats
in the Pit*, which would be a fure and eafy
Expedient for preventing Tumult and Diforder, fince People ftand a far better Chance of
being diftinguifhed when they fit than when
they ftand in a Crowd. This Cuftom has
been followed in the Theatres lately erected

in

in the Fares of *St. Germain* and *St. Laurence*, where both Women and Men have Seats; only that in thefe two Theatres they are fo modeft as to call that the *Parquet* which in othr Theatres is called the *Pit*.

As for the Hour of drawing the Curtain it has not always been the fame; for on the 12th of *November* 1609, the Civil Magiftrate, with the Advice of the King's Procurator, made a Regulation, by which *the Comedians were ordered (from St.* Martin'*s Day till the* 15th *of* February*) to open their Doors at one o'Clock, to begin the Entertainment with fuch Perfons as fhould be prefent at Two in the Afternoon, and to put an End to it at half an Hour after Four at moft**. But it appears by the Book above cited, that this Regulation was not obferved in 1668; for the Author advifes the Comedians, for their own Advantage, to open their Doors in Winter half an Hour after Three, and in Summer half an Hour after Four, from which we may conclude that the Entertainments of his Days did not begin till fix o'Clock. The fame Author complains of the Cuftom the Spectators had of placing themfelves on the Theatre, which by the bye ftill continues; and tho' it be vaftly prejudicial to Action, in *France* they take no Exception at it, fo much is it the Cuftom.

As to the Admittance-Money, the Regu-

* *La Marr*'s Treatife of Policy.   lation

lation of the Civil Magiftrate in 1609, of which we have already fpoke, (in order to prevent the Comedians augmenting it at their Pleafure) fixes it in thefe Terms: *Comedians are hereby prohibited from taking more than five for the Pit, and ten Sols for the Boxes and Galleries,* &c. But this Price was augmented in proportion as Money rofe in its Value. Under the Reign of *Lewis* XIV. the firft Boxes on the Theatre and the Orcheftrum could not be had under three Livres. The fecond Boxes and the Amphitheatre not under thirty Sols. The Pit not under fifteen Sols; and the third Row of Boxes not under twenty. For about thirty Years under the fame Reign, the Entrance-Money for Plays was raifed a fourth for the Benefit of Hofpitals; fo that at prefent the Places in the firft Boxes of the Stage, the Amphitheatre, and the Orcheftrum coft four Livres: The Amphitheatre within thefe few Years is the fame Price with the Stage, becaufe in reality it contains the beft Seats in the Houfe. The fecond Row of Boxes coft forty Sols; the third thirty, and the Pit twenty.

The Play-houfe has two Street-doors, one leading to the Pit only, the other to all the other Divifions of the Houfe. On one Side of thefe Entrances there is a Place with Bars, thro' which the Spectator receives a Ticket that introduces him either to the Pit or the other Places, and the Ticket is commonly marked with the Name of the Seat that is paid for. The Receiver of this, upon delivering it at the Inner-Door of the Playhoufe, gets another there, marked *Countermarque*, with the Name of the Place he is entitled to. Thefe Tickets are again delivered to the People who are placed to open the Boxes, to fee the Company feated in them, and then to fhut them up as foon as they contain eight Perfons, that is, four upon the fore, and four upon the back Seat. Thus eight may be in one Box, Men and Women, and none of them know one another. But the Truth is, that fometimes it is very troublefome Sitting there on account of the Lady's Hoops; therefore to avoid the Inconveniency, the Ladies commonly fend in the Morning, or the Night before, to befpeak a Box for themfelves. Each firft Box is equivalent to eight Places, and amounts to thirty two Livres, and they who hire it referve it wholly to themfelves. The fecond Row pays in proportion fixteen Livres, and with regard to the third, as they are upon a level with the Gallery, no Place can be kept there, but by fending a Servant without Livery to keep one, as is done on the Stage and Orcheftrum, &c.

The firft Front-Box on the right-hand is called the King's Box; and all the Range on

that

that Side to the Bottom of the Play-houfe is
called the King's Side. The firft Front-Box
on the left-hand is called the Queen's Box,
and all the Range on that Side is called the
Queen's Side; and indeed thefe Boxes are
fet afide for the King and Queen, whenever
their Majefties honour the Play-houfe with
their Prefenee, which happens very feldom,
becaufe there is a Play-houfe at Court where
the Players act as often as they receive Orders.

If the Princes and Princeffes of the Blood
come to the Play-houfe, their Birth entitles
them to the principal Boxes, even tho' they
may be hired by private People, who are in
that Cafe obliged to take up with inferior
Boxes. The Princes of the Blood commonly
fit upon the Stage, and then the Players make
a Paufe in the Action, and all the Spectators
rife out of Refpect, and the Princes place
themfelves in the firft Seat, which is yielded
by whoever poffeffes it; and when the Play
is done, the Player who gives out the next
Play makes a profound Reverence to them,
and with all due refpect craves their Permif-
fion to give it out.

Formerly when a new Play had a Run,
they acted it every Day for two or three
Months fucceffively, which fatigued the Actors and Audience, efpecially Strangers, who
for that Time were obliged to take up with a
dull Repetition of the fame Play. This

Incon-

Inconveniency is remarked by the Author of a little Book, entitled *New Diverſions*; but at preſent the new Plays are acted only every other Day, ſo that during the Run, the Spectators are entertained with other Plays.

The firſt Opera ſung in *Paris* was in 1645, the Cardinal *Mazarine* having cauſed Muſicians, an Architect, and all neceſſary Workmen to come on purpoſe from *Italy*; and it was exhibited in the *Little Bourbon*, where, by Order of the ſame Cardinal, others were exhibited for ſeveral Years following with greater Magnificence, but they were all *Italian*. The firſt was called *La Treſta Teatrale della Trinta Pazza di giulo Strozzi*, which had appeared in *Italy* for ſome Years before.

As to the firſt *French* Opera, Mr. *De la Marr* places it in the Year 1672, and the Author of the *Dramatic Library* places it in the ſame Year in which the Abbe *Perine* received the Royal Privilege, which was in 1671, and which the Year afterwards reverted to Mr. *Lully*. Theſe firſt Operas were like thoſe in *Italy*, eſpecially in the Machinery; but ſince the *Italians* have left that off, it is diſuſed in all Places except in *France*, and eſpecially at *Paris*, where that Taſte ſtill prevails. It is true, it has never yet been brought to that Pitch of Perfection as it was in *Italy*; but ſtill it gives a great Pleaſure to the

the Spectators who love Machinery, which
they do the more as it is to be met with
almoſt in no other Part of *Europe* but there.
As *France* had no other Model from which
ſhe could take her Opera but that of *Italy*,
I was tempted to think that *Quinault* had copied from them in his Opera. That of *Proſer-*
pine was exhibited in *Venice* in the Year 1644,
and the *Proſerpine* of *Quinault* in 1680:
That of *Perſeus* was acted at *Venice* in the
Year 1665, and that of *Quinault* at *Paris* in
1682. In the Year 1639 the Opera of
Armida was exhibited at *Venice*, and the
ſame of *Quinault* was exhibited at *Paris* in
1686. It is very probable that theſe Subjects
ſerved as a Model in ſome meaſure to the
French Opera. I have not indeed examined
theſe *Italian* Operas, having never ſeen them
acted, therefore I can ſay no more on that
Subject: But I am led into that way of
thinking, becauſe in the Infancy of the *Ita-*
lian Opera, it often conſiſted of very ſerious
Tragedies, in which were introduced the
Characters of old Women, Bawds, and comical Serving-men; a Method intirely copied
by *Quinault* in his firſt Operas.

No Spectators ſit upon the Stage in the
Opera, becauſe that would be a great hinder-
ance to the Execution of the Machinery, the
Choruſes, and the Dancing, the Stage of the
Opera being in its Contrivance nothing diffe-

rent

rent from that of the Play-houfe. With regard to the Price it is double that of any other Entertainment, in proportion to the Preference of Places.

From the Year 1671 to the Year 1737 inclufively, we reckon one hundred and thirty two Operas, comprehending *Caftor* and *Pollux*, and the two *Italian* Operas acted at *Paris*, and including all that either had or had not Succefs.

The Opera is furprizingly magnificent in the Number and Quality of its Dreffes; the Embroidery is but Tinfel, yet it is of an excellent Tafte, and makes as fine a Shew as the beft Dreffes in the Play-houfe. The Diverfity and Gallantry of the Dancing-Dreffes is very magnificent and peculiar to *France*, and all is provided at the Expence of the Undertakers.

The Decorations of the Stage of the Opera are very handfome, but not to be compared with thofe of *Italy*, the Smallnefs of the Stage not admitting of their being either fo large or fo magnificent as thofe of the vaft Theatres of *Venice*, *Milan*, &c. But their Dancing makes up for all their Deficiency in Point of Decoration.

All *Europe* knows what a Capacity and Genius the *French* have for Dancing, and how univerfally it is admired and followed; however the World is divided on that Subject at prefent,

prefent, fome People pretend that true and graceful Dancing is loft, and they condemn high Dancing, efpecially in Women; others prefer this to the fmooth Dancing and the Beauty of an Attitude. I fhall decide nothing upon this Subject, only I fhall lay before the Readers a Reflection I have made.

Formerly all the Dancers of the Opera in *Germany* and other Countries were brought from *Paris*; in a certain Term of Years they commonly returned to *France* without leaving any Pupils who were capable to eftablifh in their Country a Tafte for *French* Dancing, except for the Minuet, the Bouree, and Courant, &c. they were therefore ftill obliged to recal the *French* Dancers; but at prefent the *Italian* Nobility who travel, and who formerly were enchanted with the Dancing in the Opera at *Paris*, are not only no longer furprized, but pretend that their own Country can boaft a Preference in this Science. This appears to me fo much the more unreafonable, becaufe when they are afked in what the Excellency of their Dancing confifts, they anfwer, that for one top Dancer at *Paris*, they have a Dozen in *Italy* of equal Excellency; from whence I conclude, that the prefent Method of Dancing is neither the beft nor the moft difficult, as it can be fo eafily imitated by Strangers, who never could have done it, had it been more fimple and full of native Graces. PARALLEL

PARALLEL

Between the

Italian, Spanish, and *French* THEATRE.

THESE three Theatres, of which I
have given a short History, were without Dispute the first that *Europe* saw. The
Original of the Stage in *Spain* and in *Italy*
is, as I have already remarked, wrapt up in
so thick a Veil of Obscurity, that to dissipate
it seems to me next to impossible, or to decide, for Certainty, which of them gave a
Model to the other. On the one hand, the
old *Italian* Plays leave us in the dark as to
the Time in which they appeared; on the
other, no *Spanish* Play which I have met
with bears Date before the Year 1500, which
would induce me to believe it to be later
than the other, did not the *Spaniards* assert
the contrary, tho' without advancing one
Proof to support their Assertion. We shall
therefore leave to these two Nations the Pleasure

fure of contending for the Antiquity of their Stages.

The *Italians* in their firſt Theatrical Performances imitated, perhaps too ſervily, *Plautus* and *Terence*: They however laid aſide in their Plays the Cuſtoms and Manners of the ancient *Romans*, which agreed not at all with the Age they lived in. The Amours of the young Gentlemen with the Slaves, or with the Ladies of Pleaſure, were commonly the Subjects of the *Latin* Pieces. The *Italians* copying after them, and thinking Licentiouſneſs to be a neceſſary Quality in Comedy, ſubſtituted Intrigues with married Women, Tricks of Monks, Traffics of Procurers, and in ſhort the moſt ſcandalous and criminal Acts of corrupted Manners. In this they committed an inexcuſable Fault. In vain do they pretend that they aim at correcting Licentiouſneſs, for when it is repreſented on the Stage, that Gayneſs and Looſneſs, with which it is accompanied, is apt to debauch the Minds of the Spectators; and even the Heart that is leaſt corrupted is highly offended at it; for which Reaſon Prudence ought to prevail with the Dramatic Writers to expoſe and cenſure only the *Ridiculous*, the Images of Vice being too dangerous. When the *Italian* Stage amended as to Scandal, it ſunk in Genius and Taſte, which makes it neceſſary, in reading their

Comedies,

Comedies in that Language, to be acquainted with these licentious Pieces.

The *Spaniards*, on the contrary, represented nothing in their Comedies but honourable Love between unmarried People. The Customs, by Jealousy, introduced into *Spain*, afford room for Intrigue in these sort of Subjects, which in another would produce a Play so uniform, as to be for the most Part void of any Action, The romantic Point of Honour, by which the *Spanish* Nation may be characterised, fills up great Part of their Theatrical Works. Their Servants speak not so freely by far, as in *Italy*; but to make up for that, it is not unusual to hear them imprecating and swearing by the whole Catalogue of Saints. The Mixture of the Sacred and Prophane is very frequent in the *Los Autos Sacramentales*, of which I have spoken. There is one in particular, entitled *Le Chevalier de St. Sacrement*. In this Comedy we see a Church on Fire, so as they despair of extinguishing it. A Chevalier runs into the Flames, and returns with the Host in his Hand. This Action, which elsewhere would perhaps be condemned, passes in *Spain* for a most respectful Mark of Zeal, and the Spectators are at once edified and affected. In these Sort of Entertainments, Farce has its Share, which must be disagreeable to every Man of Sense: But, to

take

take it in the whole, the *Spanish* Stage is that which with the moft Eafe may be chaftifed into the pureft Decency.

As to *France*, if fhe did not produce Works for the Theatre fo early as the other Countries, fhe was not very flow in following them, but much more late in arriving at Perfection. Tragedy itfelf was not exempted from Licentioufnefs. *Rotrou* began the Reformation, which was accomplifhed foon after by *Corneille*. * *Moliere* is the firft that brought *Good Manners* upon the Stage, tho' imperfectly. They who immediately fucceeded him have been more loofe than he. But during the Space of thirty Years, the *French* Stage has inceffantly refined itfelf from that Fault, the Praife of which is due to the Audiences at *Paris*: It is owing to them that their Poets are checked, by denying their Applaufe to every thing that bears an Air of Indecency. We fee Rife given to Theatrical Reprefentations of a new Kind, the Traces of a Model of which we may difcern in the *Spanish* Theatre, and fome few in the *Italians*, but both very imperfect. There are Characters in the World of too

low

---

* We don't know if a difcerning Reader will agree with our Author in this Criticifm, fince it is certain that as to Decency of Character *Moliere* has been improved upon by few of his Succeffors.

low a Station for Tragedy, and yet too high
to defcend to that kind of Drollery required
by Comedy. They accommodate an Action
fuitable to thefe Characters, and work it up
with moving Circumftances, which occafion
an agreeable Entertainment; and in its Con-
fequences this kind of Comedy may a
good deal injure Tragedy, but it carries the
Cataftrophe infenfibly to that Point where
Religion and Decency requires it fhould
terminate.

This Kind, as it had its Beginning but
lately, is as yet imperfect; for when the
Circumftances of the Piece are as moving as
thofe of Tragedy, the Mixture of low Humour which interpofes, drives from our
Minds that Concern which we are ready to indulge. But it is eafy to amend
this Deficiency, and fome bright Genius will
doubtlefs raife this new kind of Writing to
Perfection †.

In the moft affecting Subjects we may
fuftain

---

† My Work was finifh'd when *L'Ecole des Amis*, wrote by
Mr. *De la Chauffeé*, one of the Members of the *French* A-
cademy appear'd. That Piece may ferve as a Model for
Productions of this kind. Some however have fo far miftaken it, as to pronounce it a Comedy writ in the Manner of
the incomparable *Moliere*; and not finding his comical Turn
in it, (which indeed ought to have no Place in a Work of
its kind) have fpoke too contemptibly of it, and by that
means have brought a greater Slur upon their own Judgments than upon the Piece itfelf.

suſtain a Dignity of Humour which may ariſe from the Subject itſelf; but this is a Perfection only attainable by a fertile Genius. The modern Authors will, without doubt, endeavour to perfect this Species of Comedy, fearing left they be reproached by the World, of having embraced this Kind, out of Deſpair of attaining to the Sublime of *Corneille*, or the Humour and Wit of *Moliere*.

In ſhort the *French* Theatre will ſuſtain its Glory, and every Day increaſe it, becauſe it produces Entertainments of a new Sort, when the Audience are tired with a Repetition of the old ones.

T H E

THE

ENGLISH THEATRE.

IF the Commencement of the *English* Theatre was not so early as the others, it seems to have followed soon after. The Origin of the first Dramatic Reprefentations in *England* had the fame Rife with thofe of *Italy*, *Spain*, and *France*; I may venture to fay that they copied from the *Mimi* of the *Latins*, while like Vagabonds they travelled up and down the Country without Referve and without Shame.

In the Reign of *Edward* III, which began in 1015, and ended in 1038, it is faid in a Book printed at *London*, that that good King ordained by Act of Parliament, *that a Company of Men called Vagrants, who had made Mafquerades throughout the whole City, fhould be whipt out of* London, *becaufe they reprefented fcandalous Things in the little Alehoufes,*

and

and other Places where the Populace assembled.

There is good Reason, tho' no Certainty, for believing that these scandalous Amusements were of long standing in the City of *London*, but were over-looked by all preceding Kings. The same happened in *France* in the Time of *Charlemagne*; and the Statutes published by these two good Kings conceal the Original of the Drama in these two Nations.

After so positive and rigorous a Decree in *England*, nothing that had the least Resemblance of a *Play* could appear in *London*, or the rest of the Kingdom, unless disguised beneath the Veil of Religion. It was therefore by these sacred Representations that the Theatre began to form itself in *London*, as before it had done in *Paris*.

We find in a Book called *The* * *Antiquities of London*, that under *Richard* II, who reigned in the Year 1378, the Clergy and the Scholars of St. *Paul*'s School presented a Petition to the King, praying his Majesty, *To prohibit a Company of unexpert People from presenting the History of the* Old Testament, *to the great Prejudice of the said Clergy, who have been at great Charge and Expence, in order to represent it publickly at* Christmas.

M   It

* * S T O W's.*

It is therefore in thefe Times that we can fix an Epocha for the Moral Reprefentations of the *Old Teftament* in the City of *London.* We cannot fay, however, that they began precifely in that Year when the Petition, we mentioned before, was prefented. They might perhaps have been introduced a long time before; I am led to think thus by thefe Words made ufe of in the Petition, *A Company of unexpert People.* Had not the Clergy and the Boys of St. *Paul's* School been long exercifed in Affairs of this Nature, and ufed to give fuch Reprefentations to the People, they would not have ftiled Perfons, who undertook to reprefent the like, *unexpert.* But as no *Englifh* Hiftorian, or other learned Perfon have treated this Subject *ex profeffo,* it is not poffible to clear it from that Obfcurity in which it is left. We muft therefore content ourfelves with eftablifhing its Epocha in the Year 1378, and faying, that the Ufe of thefe holy Reprefentations infenfibly led them to the prophane Theatre.

Richard II reigned twenty two Years, till the Year 1399. Suppofing that the Boys of St. *Paul's* School prefented their Petition the fame Year that the King died, yet the fame Petition lets us know, that the Boys had played thefe Myfteries fome time before, and that for Money. And we know the *Fraternity of the Paffion* did not begin to act

at

at *St. Maur* before 1398. It is therefore
evident that the Eſtabliſhment of a public
Theatre in *England* was before that in
France. I do not believe that the *Engliſh*
preceded the *French* in the acting of Myſteries, which were in *France* many Years before the Repreſentation at *St. Maur*; and
much leſs Ground have we for diſputing
with the *Engliſh* their being the firſt that
expoſed their Entertainments publickly, and
for Money.

The *Engliſh* Chronicles ſpeak of a prophane Repreſentation, which is commonly
in that Country ſaid to be the firſt they had.
Theſe * Chronicles ſay, that

The 7th Day of May 1520, *the King
cauſed a Maſquerade to be prepared, and ordered a Stage to be raiſed in the Great Hall at*
Greenwich, *&c. The King, Queen, and
Nobility came there to the Repreſentation of a
good Comedy of* Plautus.

We are therefore to believe that from the
Year 1378 to 1520, no prophane Farces
appeared at *London* either mixt with the *ſacred,* or diſtinct from it, as happened in
France. And if really that *Good Comedy of*
Plautus was the firſt that appeared, we
muſt yield to the *Engliſh* the Merit of having opened their Stage with a GOOD *prophane
Piece,* whilſt the other Nations in *Europe*
began theirs with the moſt *wretched Farces.*

The

* *Hollingſhed.*

The fame thing may be faid with regard to Tragedy, the firft of which was played before Queen *Elizabeth*; and we find in the Appendix to the Lives of the *Englifh* Dramatic Poets, that

" The Lord *Buckhurft*, afterwards Earl
" of *Dorfet*, writ, in Conjunction with Mr.
" *Norton*, a Tragedy, valued in thofe Days,
" of which there were three Impreffions.
" The Title to the firft Edition is FORREX
" and PORREX printed in 8vo. at *London* in
" 1565 by G. G."

The fecond Edition was printed by Confent of the Authors with this Title, " The
" Tragedy of *Forrex* and *Porrex* without
" Augmentation or Diminution, as it was
" acted before the Queen nine Years ago,"
that is, on the 18th of *January* 1565, by the Gentlemen of the *Inner-Temple*, printed in 8vo. at *London*.

The Title of the third Edition is, " The
" Tragedy of *Gorbeduc*, of which three Acts
" are written by *Thomas Norton*, and the
" other two by *Thomas Sackville*, publifhed
" as it was prefented before the Queen in
" the *Inner-Temple*, printed in 4to. in *Lon-*
" *don* 1590." In this laft Edition † the *Englifh* Writer lets us know that they changed
the

---

† A Miftake: For *Buckhurft* was called *Sackville*.

the Title and the Name of one of the Authors : I can't imagine for what Reason.

Thus we fee the firft perfect Comedy and the firft perfect Tragedy of the *Englifh*, which gives not a little Glory to that Nation. The Perfection of the Comedy is not to be queftioned, feeing it was one of the *good* Comedies of *Plautus*. But as to the Tragedy I don't know, if upon the fole Report of that Writer, who fpeaks in its Praife, and is influenced by *its great Reputation*, if we may form the fame Opinion of it, and implicitely rely upon the Judgment of that Age. It was the firft Tragedy that had appeared in that Country. The *French*, their Neighbours, could fhew them no Original fit to copy after, becaufe what they had were very low. And *Italy*, whofe Theatre had attained to the higheft Pitch of its Glory, was at too great a Diftance for *England* to imitate. We may therefore doubt of the Perfection of this firft *Englifh* Tragedy ; and altho' in that Age it might have been accounted excellent, yet might it not be fo in reality : We fhall form a better Judgment of this in profecuting the Hiftory of their Theatre.

In the Life of *Shakefpear* prefixed to his Works, we read that " in the Year 1590 there were profeffed Comedians in *London*, but they had no eftablifhed Theatre, and played no

Tragedies,

Tragedies, for then they had no Idea of them in *London*." Tho' this is speaking very positively, yet it appears to be false, because Tragedy was known in the former Part of that Reign, if that, of which we have given an Account, was acted. It is not to be thought that in the Space of twenty five Years which had passed since *Gorbeduc* appeared, all Remembrance of it could be effaced; the three Editions which I have mentioned were certainly sufficient to preserve its Memory. Wherefore I think that to judge rightly of this, we should conclude that Tragedy was unknown in *England*, because *Gorbeduc* was the only one, and it not having been acted in Public, but confined to the Court, the common Players not having a Relish for it, perhaps this kind of Dramatic Poetry was unknown till *Shakespear's* Time.

William Shakespear for a small Trip of Youth was obliged to leave the Country and come up to *London*, where he commenced Player. He was blessed with Genius and Capacity; and wrote a ‡ Comedy much liked by Queen *Elizabeth*. She, to express her Regard for *Shakespear*, granted a Patent to the Comedians, declared them her Servants, and formed them into a Company, with proper

‡ The Merry Wives of Windsor.

per Appointments, and the Ufe of a Theatre.

In the Year 1596 *Shakefpear*, at the Age of thirty three, gave the World his firft Tragedy of *Romeo* and *Juliet*; and the Year after he produced *Richard* II.

James I, who fucceeded Queen *Elizabeth*, by a Licence confirmed the Privileges of that Company of Comedians: He named nine new Actors, and ftiled them his Servants. This Licence is conceived in Terms, Part of which I think neceffary to repeat ; it fays towards the End, " And we permit them to " perform the faid Plays, Tragedies, Inter- " ludes, Moral Pieces, Paftorals, Stage- " Plays, and fuch like in Public, and for " their greater Advantage, (when the Infection " of the Plague fhall ceafe) as well in our " Houfe called the *Globe*, in our County of " *Surry*, as in the Cities, Halls, Public " Places, or any other privileged Place, and " in any Borough of our faid Kingdom."

In this Licence of *James* I. two Things are remarkable. In 1603, when it was pub-lifhed by the King, the *Englifh* Comedians performed all thefe feveral kind of Theatrical Reprefentations, that we find mentioned in their Charter: This Theatre therefore muft have been of long ftanding, fince all the different kinds of Dramatic Poems were then known, which could not be expected in the

Practice

Practice of twenty or thirty Years. Mention in the Licence is likewise made of public Places, and which lets us fee that in *England*, as well as in *France*, they ufed upon Scaffolds to play as well moral as prophane Plays. Plays being twice mentioned, firft fingly, and a little lower with the Addition of Stage-Plays, leads us to know that two Species of Comedy are fpoken of : Thus making apparent Diftinction between thofe that were played in public Places, and thofe played on an eftablifhed Theatre. We are therefore forced to conjecture, that during the two hundred Years from 1378, moral Reprefentations and prophane Farces had been performed, and that they were at leaft tolerated by the Kings, tho' not licenced by their Authority.

Before *Shakefpear* embraced the Profeffion of a Player, there was a Theatre in *London*, that is to fay, Dramatic Performances had been exhibited there for a long time. It is true that little Mention is made of it, only in the Life of that Poet we read, that to him we owe *Ben. Johnfon*, who by his Encouragement writ his Comedies. Thus by thefe two Poets, the greateft that their Age or Country ever produced, *England* is enabled to fix the Epocha of her Theatre.

It is furprifing that Tragedy firft rofe in *England* by every Horror that human Imagination

gination can fuggeft, and that the Tafte for it ftill remains, notwithftanding the Attempts of fome Authors, who have endeavoured to give it another Turn. I have examined into the Reafon of it, and tho' I may be miftaken, yet fhall I always fpeak what I think.

It ought not to be queftioned that the chief Aim of a Dramatic Writer is to pleafe the Spectators, and that to do this, he muft be acquainted with the Bent of their Inclinations. When the Poet fancies he has attained to that Knowledge, he ftudies to fet before them Images and Actions fuitable to the Tafte of that Nation for which he writes.

When that is fuppofed, it muft be granted that Theatrical Pieces let us into the general Character of their feveral Countries, and that without any other Light than what is ftruck out of the ancient and modern Plays, we might judge that the *Grecians* were violent and given to Pleafure ; that the *Romans* were fenfual, but always with an Air of Grandeur ; With the *Romans* we may rank the *Italians,* with fome little Difference ; we may fay that the Quality of the *Spaniards* is a noble Bravenefs, that they are punctilious, and myfterious ; and the *French,* on the other hand, are witty, airy, and gay to Excefs : And of all thefe different Characters, I don't know if any is far diftant from Truth. One there-

therefore might be tempted to believe from *Shakefpear*'s prefenting to them the moft horrible Objects, that the *Englifh* are cruel, inexorable, and next to inhuman, whereas indeed nothing is lefs true. The *Englifh* are gentle, humane, extremely polite, but generally penfive to Excefs. It is this laft Quality that forms their general Character, as their own Writers agree. Let us proceed.

The *Englifh* Dramatic Poets have, beyond Imagination, ftained their Stage with Blood; of this I fhall give you two Examples only. In the Tragedy of *Hamlet*, five principal Characters die violent Deaths during the Action. About the middle of the Play we fee the Funeral of a Princefs; the Grave is dug on the Stage, out of which are thrown Bones and Skulls: A Prince comes then and takes up a Skull in his Hand, which the Grave-digger informs him was the Skull of the late King's Jefter; he makes a moral Differtation upon the Skull of the Jefter, which is reckoned a Mafter-piece: The Audience liften with Admiration, and applaud with Tranfport: And it is for that Scene that the major Part of the Spectators refort to the Play-houfe when *Hamlet* is performed. In the Tragedy of the *Moor of Venice*, among other Things, the *Moor* inflamed with Jealoufy, goes to fearch for his Wife, who lies awake in Bed; he fpeaks with her, and after ftrong Conflicts
between

between Love and Rage, he refolves to be revenged, and ftrangles her before the Eyes of the Spectators. Were I to give a Detail of every thing horrible that is to be found in *Englifh* Tragedy, it would be hard to be per-fuaded of the *Englifh* being fo very gentle and humane, as I have painted them, and as they are in Effect: We fhould rather be in-duced to think, that the Poet prefented for the Entertainment of his Countrymen, what was moft agreeable to their Cruelty and Ferocity. If that was not his Motive, why did he entertain the Nation with Objects fo terrible? After all thefe Reflections, I will venture to give my Opinion.

The principal Character of the *Englifh* is, that they are to be plunged in Contemplation, as I obferved before. It is owing to this their penfive Mood, that the Sciences of the moft fublime Nature are by the Writers of that Nation handled with much Penetration, and that Arts are carried to that Pitch of Perfection which they are now arrived at; becaufe their native Melancholy fupplies them with that Patience and Exactnefs which other Countries have not.

To purfue my Reafoning; I believe that were there to be exhibited on their Stage, Tra-gedies of a more refined Tafte, that is, ftript of thofe Horrors that fully the Stage with Blood, the Audience would perhaps fall afleep.

afleep. The Experience which their earlieft Dramatic Writers had of this Truth, led them to eftablifh this Species of Tragedy, to raife them out of their contemplative Moods, by fuch bold Strokes as might awaken them.

For the fame Reafon, the *Englifh* Comedies are crowded with Incidents, infomuch that having adapted to their Stage fome *French* Plays, the Authors have doubled the Intrigue, or they have joined them with another Plot to keep the Spectator in Breath, and not allow him Time to wander with his Thoughts. The Mifer of *Moliere* among others, which in the Original is perhaps too full of Intrigue, has much more in the *Englifh* Tranflations. *Harpagon's* Miftrefs, in order to raife his Averfion, making great Expence at the Charge of the old Fellow, occafions an additional Intrigue to that Play, which increafes the Plot beyond meafure.

I have faid that the *Englifh* Poets, with Defign to make lively Impreffions on the Imaginations of the Spectators, fill their Tragedies with Horror, and over-charge their Comedies with Incidents; with regard to the latter we may add that they have form'd Scenes and Dialogues obfcene to Excefs. It is not my Defign to particularife any Comedy of that Sort which I have feen acted at *London*, but I fhall refer to Mr. *Collier's* Criticifm on the *Englifh* Stage. He reproaches
the

the Poets of his Country with their Licentioufnefs; and by comparing the ancient Stage
with the modern, he fhews them that no
Inftance of Licentioufnefs on that Stage was
ever equal to what appears on the *Englifh*
Theatre: But the Obfcenities and the Com-
plication of Events in Comedy, have at leaft
as much Force to move the Audience, as the
Horror in their Tragedy has Power to
touch them. It is, perhaps, by Defign that
the Authors have written in the Tafte which
we now have remarked. It were to be
wifhed that thefe Spectators, as well as the
Poets, were once well convinced of the true
Object of Dramatic Pieces; for the Terror
which ought to be infpired by Tragedy, confifts not in the Effufion of Blood, and the
Reprefentation of Death.

In fhort *Oedipus* who tore out his Eyes,
and *Jocafta* who hang'd herfelf, do not fo
much touch the Audience, as the Reflection
of *Oedipus* on being guilty of Inceft and Parri-
cide. Had *Athaliah* actually perpetrated the
Maffacre of the High Prieft and *Levites*, as
fhe threatned, we fhould not be fo fenfibly
touched, as by her Converfation with young
Joas, with Defign to carry him away and
deftroy him. Does not every one tremble in
Iphigenia, thro' the Fear of feeing the Daughter facrificed by her Father? Are we not
affected in the fame manner in *Phocas*, who
feveral

several times is upon the Point of causing
his Son to be killed without knowing him.
The Horror which reigns in these two *English* Tragedies that I have named, and in all
the others, has not such Force to affect
and touch the Spectators, as the real Terror
of which I have given some Instances.

I can't tell what Hopes to entertain of the
Reformation of the *English* Theatre, but we
have Proofs to believe it will not be sudden.
It is now twenty five Years since Mr. *Addison's Cato* appeared at *London* with the universal Applause of the whole Nation. Without entering into the Merits of that Tragedy,
let us only observe with what Judgment the
Poet chose a Subject in which both the Parties of the Nation were at the same Time
interested, and he conducted it in such a Manner, that both were equally pleased.

It is Mr. *Addison* who has with admirable
Art put in Execution the grand Point of
which I have spoken, to study well the Inclinations of the Spectators, in order to please
them. One would imagine that this Tragedy would have new-modelled the *English*
Stage: But the new Tragedies since that
Time writ in the ancient Taste, and particularly one of the latest, entitled *George Barn-
well*, which met with great Success, leave us
no Ground to presume that ever there will be
a Change at all. They say, however, that
they

they have begun to exhibit some Things in the refined Taste, which met with no bad Reception from the Public. Was this successful Beginning prosecuted to Advantage; were the *English* Poets guided by Reason and Truth, the Spectators might improve, and the *French* Stage in a little Time meet with a formidable Rival. No Force or Beauty is wanting in the *English* Language, to express the noble Sentiments and sublime Thoughts with which their Tragedies are filled. Nor has it less Elegance for Wit and Humour in Comedy, which is often set off with more Spirit than in the Plays of other Countries.

Amongst the Crowd of *English* Poets, Mr. *Congreve* is most esteemed for Comedy. He was perfectly acquainted with Nature; and was living in 1727, when I was in *London*; I conversed with him more than once, and found in him Taste joined with great Learning. It is rare to find many Dramatic Poets of his Stamp. The Architecture of their Play-house is beautiful and commodious. All the Pit is in Form of an Amphitheatre, where both Sexes sit promiscuously, which afford a very agreeable Sight. There is but one Row of Boxes, and above are two Galleries with Benches one above another, where People sit. It is about forty Years since the *English* Nobility went into the Taste of
Italian

Italian Operas, which they support with great Magnificence, and at an astonishing Expence. They draw to *London* the best Singers in *Italy*, who leave their Country without any Regret, tho' there Music meets with very great Encouragement. The Prices for Admission into the House are much the same as at *Paris*.

There are commonly two Theatres for acting Comedies and Tragedies, which are nobly ornamented with Decorations and Dresses. As to the Actors, if after forty five Years Experience I may be intitled to give my Opinion, I dare advance that the best Actors in *Italy* and *France* come far short of those in *England*. The *Italian* and *French* Players, far from endeavouring at that happy Imitation of Nature and Justness which forms the Beauty of Action, affect a forced, stiff Manner of Acting, which never fails to mislead the Audience. To form the better Judgment of both, let us compare them impartially. The *English* Authors copy Truth, and are at great Pains not to flag on the Stage. As for me, I have always thought, nor have I been singular in my Opinion, that pure simple Nature would be cold upon the Stage. This I have experienced in several Comedians. Wherefore the Action should be heightned a little, and without straying too far from Nature, some Art added in the Speaking.

Speaking. As a Statue to be placed at a Diftance fhould be bigger than the Life, that,
notwithftanding the Diftance, it may appear
in due Proportion to the Spectators, fo the
Englifh Actors have the Art, if I may ufe
the Expreffion, to heighten Nature, fo as it
ought to be fhown at a Diftance, to let us
fee that it is pure Nature which they reprefent. When I was at *London* a thing happened, which, for its fingularity, deferves
Notice. At the Theatre in *Lincoln's Inn-
Fields* I happened to be at the Acting of a
Comedy, the principal Plot of which I was
a Stranger to, but with Eafe could underftand an Epifode, which the Author without doubt had placed in the Intrigue: It is
that Scene which we have fo often feen in
Crifpin Medecine. The fole Alteration that
is made therein, is the introducing an old
Man in Place of a Footman, who by his
Buftle excites the Laughter of the Audience,
while he places himfelf in the room of a
dead Body which the Phyfician is to diffect.
The Scene was thus difpofed; the amorous
old Gentleman entertains himfelf with a
Footman belonging to his Miftrefs's Houfe;
the Footman either hears, or pretends to
hear, a Noife, and defires the old Fellow to
hide himfelf; all the Doors being locked, he
advifes him to place himfelf on the Board on
which the Body is laid. After fome Diffi-
N culties

culties made, the old Man confents to it, and does precifely what *Crifpin* does in the *French* Comedy: But to give it the greater Air of Truth, the Footman makes the old Man ftrip to his Shirt; the Operator comes; Chirurgical Inftruments are brought; he puts himfelf in order to begin the Diffection; the old Man cries out, and the Trick is difcovered.

He who acted the old Man executed it to the niceft Perfection, which one could expect in no Player who had not forty Years Exercife and Experience. I was not at all aftonifhed in one refpect, but I was charmed now to find another Mr. *Guerin*, that excellent Comedian, Mafter of the Company at *Paris*, which had the Misfortune to lofe him in our Time. I was miftaken in my Opinion that a whole Age would not produce fuch another, when, in our own Time, I found his Match in *England*, with the fame Art, and with Talents as fingular. As he played the Part of an old Man, I made no manner of doubt of his being an old Comedian, who, inftructed by long Experience, and at the fame time affifted by the Weight of his Years, had performed it fo naturally. But how great was my Surprife, when I learn'd that he was a young Man of about twenty fix! I could not believe it; but I own'd that it might be poffible, had he only ufed a trembling and
broken

broken Voice, and had only an extreme Weaknefs poffeffed his Body, becaufe I conceived
it poffible for a young Actor, by the Help
of Art, to imitate that Debility of Nature to
fuch a Pitch of Exactnefs; but the Wrin-
kles of his Face, his funk Eyes, and his loofe
and yellow Cheeks, the moft certain Marks of
a great old Age, were inconteftable Proofs
againft what they faid to me. Notwithftanding all this I was forced to fubmit to
Truth, becaufe I knew for certain that the
Actor, to fit himfelf for the Part of the old
Man, fpent an Hour in dreffing himfelf, and
that with the Affiftance of feveral Pencils he
difguifed his Face fo nicely, and painted fo
artificially a Part of his Eye-brows and Eye-
lids, that at the Diftance of fix Paces it was
impoffible not to be deceived. I was defi-
rous to be a Witnefs of this myfelf, but Pride
hindered me; fo knowing that I muft be
afhamed, I was fatisfied with a Confirmation
of it from the other Actors. *Mademoifelle
Salle,* among others who then fhone upon
that Stage, confeffed to me, that the firft time
fhe faw him perform fhe durft not go into a
Paffage where he was, fearing left fhe fhould
throw him down fhould fhe happen to touch
him in paffing by.

I flatter myfelf that this Digreffion will
not be altogether ufelefs; it may let us know
to what an Exactnefs the *Englifh* Comedians
carry

carry the Imitation of Nature, and may ferve for a Proof of all that I have advanced of the Actors on the *Englifh* Theatre.

Reafon alone fketched out the firft Rules of the Theatre in the *Grecian* Tragedies: *Ariftotle* eftablifhed an Art, and made the Laws for us; the *Latins* adopted them, and Moderns have confirmed them by the Heaps of Poems, by the fo great Number of Dramas, which the *Italians*, and, ftill more, the *French* have already, and yet continue to fupply us inceffantly with. One therefore can't ftep afide from thefe Rules without incurring the Cenfure of the whole World. Otherwife nothing can be objected to the *Englifh* Poets, but their having received a particular Maxim, which differs from thofe of other Countries, and which does not want its Defenders to fupport it. In fuch a general Agreement of Opinions authorized by Good-Senfe, I am perfuaded that the Men of Learning in *England* are fenfible of the Irregularity of their Stage, and that (like the *Spaniards*) they are the firft who take Notice of it. Were it permitted to depart from thefe Rules, which Reafon itfelf hath dictated, the *Englifh* Theatre would be able to balance in Reputation both the Ancient and the Modern. The Excellence of the *Englifh* excels all the Beauties which the other Theatres in *Europe* can fhew us; and if

fome

some time or other the *English* Poets would submit themselves to the three Unities of the Theatre, and not expose Blood and Murder before the Eyes of the Audience, they would at least partake of that Glory which the other more perfect modern Theatres enjoy.

THE

THE

FLEMISH *and* DUTCH THEATRES.

HE *Flemiſh* and *Dutch* Theatres ought to be conſidered but as one and the ſame, ſince they uſe one common Idiom: For the *Flemiſh* Language being no other than the *Dutch* Tongue corrupted by the Neighbourhood of the *Walloons* and *Picards*, thoſe who have wrote in *Flanders* made Uſe of the *Dutch* Idiom as the nobleſt and fulleſt of Energy, and which approached nearest to the Mother-Tongue, which is the *German*. They both went under the Name of the *Flemiſh* Theatre, when the two Nations were under the Government of the ſame Maſter, and their Sovereigns reſided in *Flanders*; but ſince the diſmembering of the United Provinces, we muſt ſpeak of them ſeparately. It was from the

the Reprefentations of *Myfteries*, that the
Theatre of *Flanders* had its Rife, as the
others had, with this Difference however,
that as foon as the *French* Nation grew po-
lifhed, it perceived the Indecency which the
Simplicity of thefe firft *Reprefentations* concealed, and by degrees they gave Place to
Shows better underftood and more regular :
But *Flanders* had not had the fame Advantage, for Theatrical Shows having ceafed in
that Country, the Simplicity, void of all Po-
litenefs and Tafte, remained in its original
State. I could even be tempted to believe,
that the *Flemifh* as well as the *Dutch* took
for their Model, at their firft fetting out, the
Englifh Theatre rather than the *French*, feeing
that they followed the fame Method, and
did not adopt the *French* Theatre but fince
Corneille. At the Time when the *Flemifh*
Theatre might have been brought to Perfection (after the Example of other Nations)
their Sovereigns changed the Place of their
Refidence, and ever fince that Period we may
fay it has ceafed entirely. They have been
now a long time without a Theatre ; and all
that they preferve, is the Reprefentation of the
Paffion, in the fame Simplicity and Groffnefs
with which it began, and which is acted
at certain Times of the Year by Societies of
Burghers, who act alfo fometimes paltry
Tranflations of *French* Comedies. In fhort,

we

we may ſay that ſince the Year 1566, from the Time of the Civil Wars, the *Flemiſh* Theatre has not ſubſiſted: It was not ſo in *Holland*, where it has been cultivated; and I ſhall ſpeak of their Theatre alone, in the Sequel. The *Dutch* Theatre had its Original from what they call in that Country *Reden Ryckers Kameren*, Companies or Societies of Rhetoricians and Poets, who may be compared to the firſt *Troubadours* of *Provence*, as I ſhall ſhew more fully in the Deſcription of the *German* Theatre. Theſe *Companies* took their Origin from the * natural Poetical Genius of the Nation, (which is ſo great, that even their moſt ancient Chronicles are in Verſe) and the Eagerneſs of the People for Shows.

Theſe *Societies* were alſo common in *Brabant*: They had fourteen at *Antwerp*; that of the *Gilli-Flower*, and that of the *Olive-Branch* were the moſt diſtinguiſhed: There were † nineteen at *Ghent*; they had them in

Holland

---

* This Genius is ſtill the ſame, but better regulated. If any Perſon of Diſtinction is married, dies, is promoted, &c. the Poets immediately take the Field, and ten, fifteen, or twenty Epithalamiums, Elegies, or Panegyrics appear, all which are printed in the ſame manner as the *Theſes* at *Paris*.

† This may be proved by a Collection of Allegorical Pieces *(Zinneſpel)* repreſented by the nineteen Chambers of *Ghent.*

Holland in almoſt every City, as *Harlem,*
Gouda, Schiedam, Alcmaar, Leyden, Ulaer-
dinge, Rotterdam, ‡ &c.   This Cuſtom did
not prevail in the Cities alone, but alſo in
many Villages.   In the Year 1708 they had
ſtill one in the Village of *Voorſchootten* near
Leyden, and another in the Village of *Looſ-*
duynen near the *Hague;* and there is now
actually one of them in the great Village of
Waſſenaar near *Leyden.*

The Members of theſe *Societies* were the
Wits of the Place, who were applied to
for Epithalamiums, for Elegies, for Panegyrics, or Compliments, when any one was
preferred to an Office, as I have ſaid before.
The ſame compoſed Theatrical Pieces,
which they acted in the *Society-Room* (thus
they are entitled *Kamerſpel,* that is, *Society-*
Plays) and very often in the Country
in the Time of Fairs *(Kermis)* in public
upon Scaffolds.   Seldom had they any Women ;

Ghent, printed in 1539.   And by another Collection of fifty
Pieces, Allegories, Prologues (Voeorſpel) or Farces (Naſpel)
repreſented by the fourteen Chambers of *Anvers.*   Printed
by *Silvius* at *Anvers* in 1562.

‡ *Konſtonende Juweel,* or the Jewel of Art, is a Proof of
this.   It is a Collection of fourteen Allegorical Pieces, compoſed and repreſented by ſeveral Chambers of Orators at
Harlem, printed at *Zwol* in 1607 ; and *Ulaerdinge Rederykſberg*
(the *Parnaſſus* of *Ulaerdinge*) or a Collection of ſixteen Pieces
of the Orators of the Chambers in *Ulaerdinge,* printed in
1617, &c.

men; they were Men who perfonated the Characters. Oftentimes thefe *Reden Ryckers* (Poets) of one Village went to perform their Pieces at the Fair of another Village, which in its Turn did the like to the other; or thefe *Societies* tranfported themfelves in a Body to affift at certain Feafts and Reprefentations in another Town or Village ; and this they did with Ceremonies, almoft the fame with thofe they obferve in *France*, when the Companies of the *Arquebufe* (Gunfmiths) of one Town go to fhoot for the Prize in another ; and fometimes there were Societies, who even performed from one Town to another, and difputed the Prize of Wit, and after the Performance was over, the Wits of the Company recited Extempore Pieces, or Madrigals, Sonnets, *&c.* Such was the Origin of the *Dutch* Theatre, of which it would be difficult to fix the Epocha, fince that poetical Genius, and that Paffion for Shows, Dancing, and Songs, are as ancient as the Nation itfelf : However it is probable that thefe *Societies* were eftablifhed before the *Burgundy* Family reigned in the Country.

The moft ancient Piece of the *Dutch* Theatre is *De Spiegel der Minne* (the Mirror of Love) by *Colin Van Ryffele*, printed at *Haerlem* in 1561, in 8vo. In the ancient Tragedies they reprefent the Action juft as it happened : Thus in the Story of *Egmond*
and

and *Horn,* they cut off the Heads of thefe
two Earls upon the Stage; in another Piece
the Hero ftabs himfelf, and falls down dead,
after having deluged the Stage with the Blood
contained in a Bladder which he had under
his Arm: *Haman* in his Tragedy is hanged,
and *Mordecai* makes the Tour of the Thea-
atre mounted on a *Rofinante.* In *Tamerlane,*
that Prince appears on Horfeback with *Ba-
jazet:* In fhort, in the Death of *Conradin*
King of *Naples,* an Officer goes to take him
out of his Dungeon, to lead him to the
Scaffold, whither he is accompanied by two
Priefts, one habited like a Bifhop, the other
like a Cardinal. Another Singularity of
their ancient Theatre is, that which they call
Vertoning (the Reprefentation); they let down
the Curtain in the midft of an Act, and
range the Actors upon the Stage, fo that they
reprefent, after the Manner of Pantomimes,
fome principal Action of the Subject. Thus
in *Gyfbrecht van Aemftel,* they lift up the
Curtain, and on the Stage are reprefented the
Soldiers of *Egmond,* Enemy to *Gyfbrecht,*
who fack a Convent of Nuns, where
every Soldier has one, whom he ufes at his
Difcretion: The Abbefs is ftretched out in
the midft of the Theatre, holding on her
Knees the venerable *Gofwin,* the exiled Bifhop
of *Utrecht,* maffacred in his Pontifical Robes,
his Mitre on his Head, and the Crofs in his
Hand,

Hand. At the End of the Siege of *Leyden* there are eight or ten living Emblems to repreſent the Weight of the *Spaniſh* Tyranny, the Valour of the *Dutch*, Religion triumphant, Acts re-eſtabliſhed, *&c.* There are upon the Stage upwards of three hundred Perſons, and an Actreſs, with a Wand in her Hand, explains them to the Spectators, who appear aſtoniſhed: We may ſay that really this makes a beautiful Show.

The *Dutch* Spectators, beſides the Maſſacres and Blood, have adopted, and have a Taſte for, the *Marvellous* and *Extraordinary:* For Example, they act a Tragedy, where we ſee a Princeſs who has before her on a Plate her Lover's Head cut off; ſhe ſets herſelf down to write, and addreſſes her Words to the Head, who anſwers her. In another Tragedy, *Circe* deſigning to deſtroy the Confident of *Ulyſſes*, with whom ſhe was diſpleaſed, orders a Proceſs to be begun againſt him: The Criminal is brought before the Court which *Circe* had conſtituted for that Purpoſe: The Lyon is the Preſident, the Monkey the Regiſter, the Wolf, the Fox, and other Animals are Counſellors, and the Bear is the Hangman. They condemn the Confident of *Ulyſſes*, and hang him immediately without letting him go off the Stage: After the Execution, all the Members of him that was hanged, fall Piece by Piece into a Well,

which

which is beneath the Gallows. *Ulysses* comes
upon the Stage and complains to *Circe*, who,
touched at his Grief, makes him that was
hanged come forth from the Well alive and
entire as he was before.   They are very curious about their Machines and their Flights.
When a Man is to fly, a Rope is hung down
with a Stirrup at the End of it; the Actor
puts one Foot in it, takes hold of it with one
Hand, and then comes down from the
Height of the Theatre.

Their Theatre becomes every Day more
exact, and they banish all these ancient Pieces,
excepting some few, which are as it were
consecrated by long Custom.   For Example,
the *Siege of Leyden* is acted every Year on
the 3d of *October*, *Gysbrecht van Aemstel* on
Christmas-Eve; and each of these Pieces is
played every Year five or six times running,
to satisfy the greedy Curiosity of Peasants,
inferior Burghers, old People, Servants, and
Children.

From the Year 1561, which is the Epocha
of their most ancient Comedy, until the
Year 1638, the Nation counts forty Poets.
He who first wrote with any Regularity for
the Theatre was *Peter Cornelius Hooft*, Son
to a Burgo-Master of *Amsterdam*, a learned
Man, distinguished by the Name which they
give him of the *Dutch Tacitus*, Author of
a History of the Republic, and of the Hi-

ſtory of *Henry* IV, which was liked ſo much at that Time, that *Lewis* XIII. ennobled him, and gave him the Order of St. *Michael*. *Hooft* had Talents for Poetry, he was a Member of the Society of *Rhetoricians* at *Amſterdam*. His Hiſtorian *Brandt* remarks that he improved that Society very much; and giving himſelf wholly up to Poetry before he wrote his Hiſtory, he compoſed many Pieces, very regular for that Time. We have of him four Tragedies and three Comedies. The firſt, which is *Achilles and Polyxena*, is dated in the Year 1620; and thus he preceded by above fifteen Years the famous *Vondel*, of whom I ſhall now ſpeak.

Vondel, ſurnamed the *Dutch Virgil and Seneca*, began to write for the Theatre in 1638, when he gave a Tragi-Comedy, intitled *Paſcha*. His Theatrical Pieces are printed in two Volumes 4to. which contain thirty Tragedies; the firſt Volume has ſixteen on ſacred Subjects, and the ſecond fourteen prophane ones, five of which have been corrected ſince the Year 1700, according to the Taſte of the modern Theatre. The *Palamede* of *Vondel* paſſes for a Maſterpiece: It is an allegorical Piece, which couches a Satire on the Stadtholderſhip of Prince *Maurice*, and a Panegyric on *Barnevelt*, whom that Prince brought to the
Scaffold,

Scaffold, altho' it was to him he owed all his Dignities.

Before the Reign of *Lewis* XIV. we find in the *Dutch* Theatre very few foreign Pieces imitated, excepting ſome taken from the *Spaniſh*, and which they received from *Brabant*: But ſince they have approved of *Corneille*, *Racine*, and the other celebrated Tragedians, they have tranſlated their good Performances with all the Energy the *Dutch* Tongue is capable of, infomuch that they ſay confidently in their Country, that they have many Pieces of theſe Authors as good as the Originals, and ſome that exceed them: For their Language, as they pretend, is infinitely more expreſſive of the *Serious and Tragic*, than the *French* Tongue is: They pretend that one *Dutch* Word has more Force in that kind of Writing, than a Period in *French*; but I cannot judge of this, being entirely ignorant of that Language. Their Theatrical Pieces are always in Verſe, and they follow the ſame Rule they do in *France*; they ſeldom write in Blank Verſe. The Tragedies are generally in five Acts, and ſometimes in three. As for the Rhime, I am of Opinion that it is the Nature of their Language which cauſes them to follow Verſification ſo much, for their Rhimes are excellent. Their Verſe rhimes like the *Italian*, always by the two laſt Syllables: This makes

a

a Harmony ſo juſt and ſo ſonorous, that all
thoſe who are able to taſte the *Italian*
Poetry aſſure us, that, for the ſame Reaſons,
they cannot help being affeӕed with the
Dutch Rhimes.

However, notwithſtanding theſe Advantages of the Rhime in the *Dutch* Language,
I imagine that there is an Inconvenience in
it. Before I explain my Thought, I would
call to mind the Criticiſm which a *French*
Author made, *a propos*, on the *Italian* Language, becauſe it appears to me to be of the
ſame Nature with the Remark I have made
on the *Dutch* Tongue. The *French* Critic
advanced that the greateſt Part of the *Italian* Words ended with an *a* or an *o*, and
ſaid that, that continual, Monotony rendered
the Language very defeӕive. The *Italians*
who anſwered him, made him ſenſible, that
if he had been but in the leaſt able to ſpeak
the *Italian* Language, he would not have
advanced ſuch an Obſervation; but that
having judged of it only by the Eye, he
eaſily fell into the Error *. This probably
may be my Caſe, notwithſtanding all the
Precautions I have taken. The *Dutch* Poets
have

---

* The Marquis of *Orſi*, in his Letters upon *The Manner
of Thinking well*, and Mr. *Mauratori* in his *Perfetta poeſia,*
furniſh us with as many Inſtances and Examples of this kind
as can be deſired.

have imitated the *Alexandrian* Verſe in all its Parts, and I believe that their Language ought not to follow the Quality of the maſculine and feminine Rhimes of the *French* Poetry. It ſeems to me that the *Dutch* feminine Rhime is faulty in the Article of Monotony : It terminates always in the Syllable *en*, and that perpetual Sound appears to me very troubleſome. I know very well that the Pronounciation can diverſify, in ſome meaſure, the Sound of that Syllable *en*, according as it is preceeded by a long, or a ſhort, or a double Vowel, *&c.* but this cannot perſuade me that the Inconvenience of the Monotony does not preſent itſelf continually. I do not underſtand the *Dutch* Language ; but after having judged of it by my Eyes, and by Reflection I was willing alſo to judge of it by my Ears : I cauſed a *Dutchman* to pronounce to me ſome Words choſen out of feminine Rhimes, and I perceived that the Syllable *en* ſounded continually in my Ears, notwithſtanding the different Sound that every Word bears ; that it never changes its Sound, and that it is always pronounced. They aſſure me, that in familiar Diſcourſe it is ſometimes almoſt mute, or at leaſt ſoftened ; but that on the Theatre, and in the Pulpit, they pronounce it always ſtrong.

I make another Reflection : The *French*
have

have been obliged to eſtabliſh two Rhimes
which they have named maſculine and feminine, by the Nature of their Language,
the half of whoſe Words terminate in a
mute *e*; and I conceive that the *Dutch*
Tongue was neceſſitated to the ſame, having
alſo half of its Words terminating in *en*.
But I obſerve the Advantage which the
French has over the *Dutch* Tongue: In the
one we but very rarely perceive that the feminine Rhimes terminate in *e*; and in the
other we hear plainly that they all terminate
in *en*. In effect, *Image, Jalouſie, Chimere,
Sacrifice, Perfide, Adore, Colere,* &c. and an
infinite Number of Words of *French* feminine Rhimes, do not appear to end in *e*, and
each has a different Sound. But in the
Dutch Tongue, theſe Words *Leden, Voren,
Tirannen, Wonden, Gebroken, Zoonen, Barba-
aren,* and in all the reſt of their feminine
Rhimes, the Syllable *en* ſounds continually,
and conſequently the Monotony is inevitable.
I have had the Curioſity to examine, on this
Head, the *Dutch* Tragedy of *The Death of
the Prince of Orange,* which is one of the
beſt of their Theatre: The firſt Act has
800 Lines, 400 of which are feminine
Rhimes; of which there are 324 that terminate in the Syllable *en*; and twenty that
have a different Termination; and this confirms to me, that the Diſpoſition of their
Language

Language is not at all lucky, in regard to this Article, of the feminine Rhimes they have adopted; perhaps indeed they cannot difpofe any otherwife, but they never fail to be a remarkable Inconvenience *.

Their Theatre now becomes every Day more exact: They have banifhed all the ancient Pieces, and act none but new ones, which make their Theatre entirely of a *French* Tafte. Generally they perform a Tragedy or a Comedy of five Acts, followed by a fmall Piece which they call *Klugtfpel*. Many of thefe they have tranflated from *D'Ancourt* and *Le Grand*, and other *French* Authors; but thofe which are in the natural Tafte of the Country, infinitely exceed the foreign Pieces; befides that, the Authors are ignorant of the Spirit of the *French* Performances, which renders thefe Tranflations very infipid: But they perform Wonders in

O 2 Tra-

---

* The *Dutch* and *Germans* are the only Nations who have imitated the *French* in making Ufe of Rhime in Tragedy and Comedy. The *Italians* and the *Englifh* have never put them into Rhime; and if the *Spaniards* have fometimes done it, they have put the Rhimes correfponding to one another at a confiderable Diftance, and by that Means avoided the difagreeable Monotony of the *Alexandrine* Verfe. I don't think however, that they are to be followed as Models in that Particular.

From this Note of our Author's it is plain that there are a great many Englifh *Dramatic Performances, which never came to his Hands, and which he never heard of.*

Tragedy, which they recite nobly and naturally, the *Dutch* being generally averse to the Tragic Declamation of the *French* Theatre, which they regard as a Rant foreign to Nature.

The Play-houses of *Amsterdam*, of the *Hague*, and of *Leyden*, have had good Authors †; but they have but few so good Actresses, as Madam *Benjamine*, &c. They say that they would yet have better Actors and Actresses, if they were paid as in *France*; for there are great Numbers who have the Gifts of the Theatre, Memory, Taste, Presence, and good Speech; but their ‡ best Performers have not above 600 Florins a Year; so that, not being able to live by the Theatre alone, they all have Trades. *Punt* is an excellent Engraver. *Duym* is a Bookseller, *&c.*. Besides this, their Players must be sober and modest, because being almost all Burgers and Burgers Wives, they would be ashamed to appear upon the Stage with an Actor whose Virtue was suspected: On this Account the Managers of their Theatres, who are eight Persons of Distinction, were obliged

---

† *Van Sermes, Ryndorp, Noseman, Brinkhuyse, Benjamine Koning, Jan Tambour, Vander Sluys. Bor, Boekhurst, Vander Ramp, Duym, Punt,* have distinguished themselves.

‡ *Benjamine Brinkhuyse, Noseman, Rigo, Waehtendorp, Bor, Duym, Jordaan, Maze.*

obliged to diſmiſs their beſt Actreſs, becauſe
an Accident which had happened to her,
hindered her Companions to perform along
with her: However, ſome Time after ſhe
was readmitted.

Their Play-houſes are a Demi-oval, of
which, the Side of the Stage makes the
ſmall Diameter: Near to the Stage is the
Orcheſtre, conſiſting at the moſt of two
Bands of Muſicians: Behind this, two
Thirds of the Space form what they call
Bac, which is a Pit with Benches covered
with Cuſhions or Carpets: The other Third-
part, which is about two or three Foot
higher, is a Place where they ſtand up:
There is, all round the Room, a Row of Boxes
which are higher than the loweſt Part of
the Stage by five or ſix Feet. At *Amſterdam*
there is a ſecond Row of Boxes, in form of
an Amphitheatre.

They pay Twenty-pence for the Pit,
Thirty-pence for the Boxes, for the Standing-
Places Six-pence, and for the Amphitheatre
above (where there is one) Ten-pence. The
Revenue of the Theatre, (Actors paid, and all
Expences defray'd) is ſet aſide for the Support
of two Hoſpitals, which have ſometimes from
twenty to five and twenty thouſand Florins
a Year. In all the other Cities, the Performance is carried on with Tranquillity
enough: As between the Acts they lower the

Cur-

Curtain in order to fnuff the Candles, the meaner Sort of People take that Opportunity to drink, taking Care to bring a Stock along with them; but at *Amfterdam*, where the People are more forward and impudent, the Amphitheatre, above the firft Boxes, is very troublefome: They talk there very loud; they call to one another from one End to the other; they crack Nuts during the whole Performance; they are perpetually throwing Bottles up and down between Acts, infomuch that they make a terrible Noife, which is very difagreeable. If the Actors difpleafe the Amphitheatre, they plague them; they call them Nick-names, and cry aloud to them to retire, or to hold their Peace, &c. Their Play-houfes are well illuminated: Befides five or fix Sconces which hang from the Middle down on the Edge of the Stage, there are generally between the Boxes Eranched-Candlefticks with Lights in them. They boaft extremely of the Theatre of *Amfterdam*, and it is current in thefe Parts, that it is one of the moft beautiful in *Europe*; but this I can't affirm for Truth, becaufe I never faw it: It is of great Extent both in Length and Breadth: Its Decorations are magnificent: There is a Gallery of the famous *Laireffe*, which is a Mafter-piece; and a Saloon of *Trooft*, which is grand.

I muft obferve that their Tafte for Poetry

is

is not at all diminiſhed, altho' the *Reden-Ryck-ers-Kamers* do not ſubſiſt any more: They have ſubſtituted in their room Poetical-Socie-ties, and diſtinguiſhed every one by a De-vice. They count in *Amſterdam* ſo many as thirty, the moſt ancient of which have for Devices, the one *In magnis voluiſſe ſat eſt*; and the other, *Latet quoq; utilitas.* Theſe two Societies, from the Year 1680 to 1698, have produced twenty four Pieces. Another, which has for its Motto, *Nil volentibus ardu-um*, has given twenty ſix from the Year 1704 to 1717: That which has for its Device, *L' Application fait fleurir les Arts*, has pro-duced twenty five Pieces from 1700 to 1718, inſomuch that the Collection of the Thea-trical Pieces of theſe Societies amounts to near two hundred.

The Catalogue of the Pieces of the *Dutch* Theatre printed in the Year 1727, contains two hundred ſixty eight Authors, thirty Socie-ties, and four hundred ninety eight Trage-dies, three hundred ſeventy one Comedies, ſeventy ſix Tragi-Comedies, twenty three Paſtorals, two hundred ſeventy Farces, and eight Operas, which make in all one thou-ſand two hundred forty ſix Theatrical Pieces. As for Habits, they have followed the Taſte of the Times: At preſent they uſe the ſame they do at *Paris*, excepting this, that their *Roman* Habits are with Helmets, which are

O 4   yet

yet better than Hats: The Oriental Pieces are performed in a long Dress, like the *Turkish*; the rest in Dresses according to the Fashion: The whole is magnificent, and the *Roman* Habits are embroidered curiously: Their Warehouse furnishes all.

The principal Actors are at present Mr. *Duym*, whom they call their *Baron*, and *Punt*, their *Quinault*. Madams *Maze* and *Bruyn*, and some young People who form themselves on the Instructions of the old *Bor*, who will become, as they hope, excellent Actors.

T H E

THE

GERMAN THEATRE.

A L L the Capital Cities of *Europe* have applied themselves earneftly to revive Shows. In effect, as foon as Tragedy and Comedy appeared fince the Time of the *Romans,* we may obferve, that the feveral Nations took but little Time after one another, in re-eftablifhing their Theatres. In Truth, the *German* Theatre has been the lateft; and for this Reafon it is, that it is eafier to trace its Origin and Progrefs, than of the others.

Ancient *Germany* has its *Bards,* who in Quality of Poets compofed and fung the Elogies of their Heroes. Hence it is that the Word *Bar* comes, which fignifies a *Song.* Since *Charlemagne,* we have feen fucceed to thefe *Bards* another kind of Poets, called *Mafter-Langer,* that is to fay *Mafter-Singers,* who

who may be fix hundred Years ftanding. They bring all fort of Proofs to evince that they were famous even in the Days of *Otho* the Great, who had given them confiderable Privileges, confirmed by his Succeffors, efpecially *Maximilian* I. Different Societies and Clubs of thefe *Mafter-Singers* were formed in the principal Cities of *Germany*; at *Mentz*, *Strafbourg*, *Nurembourg*, and *Augfbourg*. They had a Right to write Poetry at Tournaments, public Meetings, and other folemn Ceremonies. That at *Strafbourg* is actually fubfifting yet, and enjoys certain Revenues, eftablifhed many Ages ago in favour of this Company; which is compofed of Tradefmen, Workmen, Taylors, Shoemakers, Weavers, Millers, *&c.* who perform in a confpicuous Place, or a common Hall of Tradefmen, publickly at certain Times in the Year, having their old and their chief Men, who are Judges of the Verfification and Song, and who diftribute the inftituted Prize, according to their Rules and Cuftoms; thefe ignorant Workmen, who have no Notion of Poetry, nor of the Rules of Mufic, give befides fometimes an Entertainment to amufe the By-ftanders.

It is from thefe *Singers* that we muft draw the Origin of the *German* Theatre; but they did not apply to this till late, giving themfelves up generally to compofe Verfes on Subjects

jects taken from facred and prophane Hiftory, which they recite in their public Room.
The *Royal Song* of the *French*, under the
Reign of *Charles* about the Year 1370, of
which we have fpoken in its proper Place,
has all the Appearance of being the fame
thing. I would not undertake to fearch and
determine which Nation firft fung Verfes on
Paffages of Hiftory; any learned Man, who
is curious about it, may decide it; but as for
me, I neglect that Search, as a Thing which
is not at all neceffary to my Subject.

Before the fifteenth Age, we find no Signs
of Shows reprefented by thefe *German Singers*. About the Middle of the fixteenth Age
they were frequent, efpecially at *Nuremburgh*,
where a Shoemaker named *Haanffachs*, who
was not without a Genius, had compofed
many *German* Dramatic Pieces, of which
there are feveral Volumes in Folio and Quar-
to, without reckoning the Manufcripts which
are yet extant in great Number. The Author performed them himfelf in public
Houfes, where thefe Tradefmen had their
common Meetings. Thefe firft Dramatic
Pieces were taken moftly from facred Hiftory,
like thofe which they had feen at that Time
in *France*, where they had appeared an Age
before.

It feems that they acted them *gratis*, or
at leaft their Recompence was but trifling:
They

They alfo have made them on purpofe, to amufe or inftruct their Princes. *Maffenius* tells us, that they had one which hinted at the Affairs of Religion in thefe Times, and that this was to fhew to *Charles* V. the Faults which he had committed. Some Bodies of Tradefmen in the great Towns of *Germany* making fometimes folemn Proceffions, had a Cuftom, from Time immemorial, to act Comedies and Farces. By degrees was introduced alfo into public Schools the Cuftom of Shows, but generally in the *Latin* Tongue. You will find at the End of my Book a fmall Catalogue of certain *German* Theatrical Pieces, compofed originally in that Language; for they have a great many *French* ones, and many ancient *Latin* ones, which have been tranflated into *German* by different Authors at different Times.

From the Year 1516 to 1628 or 30, their facred and profane Tragedies were but wretched; and during that Time the infipid Comedies of *Hannffachs*, and the other *Mafter-Singers*, who wrote in his Manner, poffeffed the *German* Theatre. In the Year 1626 a Company of *Dutch* Players went to *Hamburgh*, and the *German* Theatre altered its Manner, by borrowing from them the Models of a better Drama both in Tragedy and Comedy. About the Year 1627 or 28, a Company of Players was formed, which gave

gave Rife to many others; and thefe writing
Plays in the Tafte of the *Dutch*, by degrees
deftroyed the Theatre of the *Mafter-Singers*,
by turning them into Burlefque and Ridicule.
Towards the Year 1630, or at moft 35, the
German Theatre was in its Perfection; and
then their Poets wrote regular Tragedies and
Comedies in a correct Verfification, as I fhall
fhew, after I have given the Reader a general
Notion of this Theatre.

The Players however ftill retained their
Dutch Tafte of the Drama, and intermixt
true Tragedy with their ordinary Plays,
which in the main were as wretched as the
Drama of the *Singers*. Since the Year 1680,
the *German* Players being inftructed by the
Italian Companies which were invited to
German Courts, attempted to play Extempore Comedies; thefe *Italians* gave them
the Ground-plat, and thefe were pirated in
Writing during the Reprefentation.

At prefent the *German* Drama is compofed
of good Tragedies and Comedies; of Plays
written in the firft Tafte of the *Dutch*; of
great Numbers tranflated; and of the *Italian* Comedies adapted to their Idiom, and
played *extempore*.

We muft obferve that the *Germans* are
the only People in *Europe* who, in Imitation
of the *Italians*, have attempted to act *extempore*: I don't know however if they
ought

ought to boaſt much of their Succeſs; for tho' their Theatre were perfect, this Method of *extempore* is enough to debauch and ruin it. The true *Italian* Drama, wrote and played in Academies about the Year 1500, was a Reformation of the Hireling Comedy which many Ages before was played *extempore*, as we have ſeen above. But the *Germans* having begun their Drama by written, tho' wretched, Tragedies and Comedies, and their Theatre being afterwards poliſhed into a better Taſte, there is great Reaſon to fear that the *extempore* Manner, which has been ſince introduced, may occaſion the entire Ruin of the *German* Theatre.

The firſt Company that was formed in *Germany* after the Year 1626, was compoſed of young Students of good Families, and their Chief was one *Charles Paul*, the Son of a Lieutenant-Colonel. Theſe were ſoon followed by others, who, like them, choſe their Actors from among the Students of the beſt Education and Families. The Head of the fourth Company, which was formed during the Infancy of their Theatre, was *John Welten*, a Profeſſor of Philoſophy, and Son to the Profeſſor of Divinity in the Univerſity of *Jena* in *Saxony*. This able Player choſe his Company from among the Flower of the noble Scholars of *Jena* and *Leipſic* in *Saxony*. He wrote Tragedies of his own Invention.

The

The Elector of *Saxony* took them all into his Service, where they ended their Days in great Efteem. The other Companies which fucceeded, kept up the great Reputation of their Predeceffors; fome of them by their Talents and Birth have been honoured with the Laurel, and declared Poets-Laureat by the Emperor; fome of them, having left the Stage, attained to great Dignities in the Church, and to other Pofts of Power and Profit, which they could not have filled, had there not met in their Perfons the higheft Quality with the moft diftinguifhed Capacity. Some of thefe Gentlemen ftill live in great Employments, tho' it may not be decent to name them, becaufe in our Days the Profeffion of a Player in all Countries is a Blemifh upon his natural Accomplifhments.

The *German* Tragedies and Comedies, which originally were no other than Imitations of the *Dutch*, have to this Day preferved the Gloominefs of their original Models. I fhall not mention the Punifhments nor the Torments of Martyrs, nor the Racks of *Ruffians*, it is enough to fay that they never fail to bring them all upon the Stage. In their Tragedies are commonly heard horrible Voices; Spectres and Phantoms are feen with bloody Swords in their Hands, or fticking in their Breafts, together with black flam-

ing

ing Torches, Tombs, and every Object that can moſt effectually excite Terror.

As I obſerved before, about a hundred Years ago, they attempted firſt to chaſtiſe and reform their Theatre upon the Models of Antiquity; to obſerve Rules, to write in a correct Stile, elegant and ſublime at the ſame time, to poliſh their Rhimes and Numbers, ſo as to give their Plays their juſteſt Perfection and trueſt Beauty. The *Sileſians* had the Honour to be the firſt who cultivated this barren Spot. *John Opitz*, *Andrew Gryphius*, and *Gaſper de Lohenſtein*, are the three moſt able *German* Poets who have given the greateſt Beauty both to the Poetry and Stage of their Country. The firſt of theſe has wrote a *German* Proſody, where he lays down for his Countrymen excellent Rules for the Drama. The Dramatic Compoſitions of theſe Authors, which are almoſt all Tragedies, eſpecially *Gryphius* who is the *Corneille* of *Germany*, have merited the Eſteem of the Public, and their Reputation continues to this Day. The *Saxons* have only followed or imitated theſe with regard either to *Taſte*, Purity, or Elegance of Stile, or the Force of Expreſſion. No *German* Poet ſince the Time of *Gryphius* has preſumed to diſpute with him the firſt Place in Tragedy. He was likewiſe Author of ſome very pretty diverting Farces, which contained a

very

very fine and agreeable Ridicule upon the Comedies that had till then been played by the Singers whom we have already mentioned, and by the Strollers of those Days.

At prefent they have no Poets who attempt to give the Public any original Compofitions in their manner; they having adopted the Dramatic Compofitions of *foreign* Theatres to their own. Some time fince, they began to tranflate from the *French* Theatre, then from the *Spanifh*, the *Italian*, the *Englifh*, &c. without however leaving out their old *Pieces*, which ftill are the Ground-work of their Drama, tho' very wretched Stuff. If any Pieces in a quite new Manner appeared, whether Tranflations or Imitations, they for the moft part never fold one Impreffion; the Reafon of this is fingular and worthy to be accounted for.

In all their Companies there are Poets who write Plays. If any Poet who is *foreign* to their Profeffion fhall offer them a Play, he expects no Copy-Money, nor any Reward, but makes a Prefent of it to fome Actor or Actrefs; and the Proprietor enjoys all the Profits of the Author, or a certain Sum which is agreed to be paid by the Company every time it is acted, tho' it run for an Age; and thus a Play is as it were an Eftate entailed, which goes by Defcent in a Family. It is the fame with the Pieces of their *Acting*

P   Authors:

Authors: But as soon as one of their Pieces appears in Print, the Company immediately make themselves Masters of it, and give no future Confideration to the Player, who is either Proprietor or Author. For this Reason most of their new Pieces are only known by their being acted, and never appear in Print. Intereft prevents the Acting Authors or Proprietors from relishing the Benefit which the Public must receive from seeing these Performances in Print, since it must thereby be enabled to judge of the Progress or Declenfion of their Stage, which would not fail to give Rise to Differtations and Criticisms always productive of good Effects, either by confirming the Public in their Tafte when good, or expofing it when bad.

I am fensible that on the other hand a great many People, especially Players, approve of this Method, because they know that as soon as a Piece is in Print their Houses grow very thin, and the Curiofity of the Public abates by reading it. When the Pieces are not printed, they still have Novelty to recommend them; and after a ten Years Intermiffion of representing them, the Curiofity of the Public will make as crowded a House, as on the first Night of their Reprefentation. Could the Poetical Inheritance at *Paris* be brought under the like Regulation, it would be of vaft Advantage to the Players, especially

cially as the Authors are to have no Confideration whatfoever; but few Poets write
for bare Glory, and moft of them want to
make a Penny of their Works. For my own
Part I own that I am a great Stickler for an
Author's being paid, for fometimes the Sweets
of the Gain engage Perfons who excel in
the Drama, to draw their Pens in that Species of Writing, who perhaps otherwife never
would have dreamed of commencing Authors. If this Practice of rewarding Authors
was introduced by Players, the State is very
much obliged to them, for it has produced
many illuftrious Authors who have done
Honour to the *French* Nation.

With regard to the Reprefentation of
Holy Myfteries upon the Stage, it is not
above thirty Years fince the Paffion of our
Lord was reprefented at *Vienna* in *Auftria*,
but prohibited afterwards by the Predeceffor
of the prefent Archbifhop on account of the
Indecencies and Profanenefs introduced by
the Actors in the Reprefentation. In the
Exhibition of this Piece, which confifted of
five Acts, we faw the Terreftial Paradice, the
Creation of *Adam* and *Eve*, their Fall, the
Death of *Abel*, *Mofes* in the Defart, the
Travels of *Mary*, *Jofeph*, and the Child
Jefus into *Ægypt*, which laft, by the bye, is
reprefented in the Habit of a full-grown Lad,
and is fed with Spoon-meat upon the Stage.

We

We then fee the Difputation of *Chrift* with the Elders in the Temple ; his Prayer in the Garden ; his Seizing ; all his Paffion ; his Death upon the Crofs, and his Burial, which clofes the Reprefentation. Other Reprefentations of the Paffion are more agreeable to the Rules of Good-Senfe; but this is moft frequently exhibited, it being, by reafon of its fingular Decorations, the favourite Entertainment of the Public.

At *Vienna*, and all the Courts of the *German* Princes, as well as the principal Cities of the Empire, their Halls are magnificent, built by *Italian* Architects, and embellifhed by *Italian* Painters; as to the Expences of feeing a Play, they are pretty much upon the fame Footing as in *France*.

At *Hamburgh* there is an Opera where they fing in the *Italian* Manner, which is generally followed and practifed all over *Germany :* The Recitative is in their own Language, but the Airs generally in the *Italian :* They have three different Operas in one Week. I don't know if the Muficians in the Opera at *Hamburgh* are upon the fame Regulations they were forty Years ago; but I am affured that they are all Tradefmen or Handicrafts; and your Shoemaker was often the firft Performer on the Stage; and you might have bought Confections and Fruits from the fame Girls whom the Night before you

you faw in the Character of *Armida* or *Semi-ramis*. But I am perfuaded, that in Imitation of the other People of *Europe* they have exalted this Entertainment.

There are fix *German* Companies of Comedians, whereof *Sweden* has one, *Livonia* another, and the reft ftroll about as they pleafe from Town to Town. Moft of the *German* Courts have *French* Companies, fometimes *Italian*, whom they hire to refide with them; and they have likewife Operas which coft them prodigious Sums. At *Vienna* in *Auftria* there is every Year an Opera, becaufe all the Emperor's Band of Mufic are *Italians*; whence we may readily infer, that the *German* Company of Players are not very well received over that Country.

In reflecting upon the Manners of all the Theatres we have as yet defcribed, we may I believe reafonably prefume, that all of them, more or lefs, fall fhort of that Severity of Manners and Diction which Men of Virtue require, and that there is great room for a Reformation. The Cities of *Rome* and *Paris* have given very ftrong Proofs of the Defire which their Governments have to put their Stages on a better Footing in this refpect.

Lewis XIV. ordered that every new Play before it was acted fhould be approved and figned by the Lieutenant-General of the Police. This is a very wife Inftitution, and

P 3   feems

seems calculated to put it out of the Power of
any Poet to exhibit to the Public any thing
that is lewd or scandalous, in which Case
tho' a Prohibition might be put upon it
from appearing ever after, and the Impression
might be stifled, yet still that could not prevent Modesty's receiving some Shock by the
first Representation. But by a severe Examination of Dramatic Performances, Religion,
Morals, and Politics are always safe.

At *Rome* the same End is sought after by
quite different Means. The *Italian* Theatre
is no longer in the Taste of their Ancestors;
the Extempore Comedy remains Mistress in
the Field, which their Dramatic Poets
in the Year 1500 had seized upon, by introducing the Method of acting Tragedies and
Comedies written in Verse and Prose. The
Italian Theatre therefore depends upon ancient and modern Sketches which are impossible to be criticised; for the most exact and the
chastest Outlines may produce a very scandalous Comedy, especially if the masqued Actors are not People of Virtue. The Liberty
of speaking whatever comes uppermost may
sometimes seduce the most cautious Players;
Criticism would therefore be useless; for that
Reason perhaps at *Rome* these Pieces pass no
Examination: They therefore go another
way to work. They have taken Care to put
a kind of Interdict upon Women's going to
the

the Play-houfe, as being moſt liable to be corrupted; and under the Pontificate of *Innocent* XI. they were prohibited both the Comedy and the Opera.

The Women, even ſuppoſing them to be wiſe, might be a Nuſance upon the Stage. This Inconveniency is prevented ſo far as regards the City of *Rome*; but it can't be ſaid that this Reformation alone has extended to all the Stages in *Italy*. I don't know but the different Methods of *Rome* and *Paris* joined together, might have the deſigned Effect.

An Extract *from the* GERMAN.

BEFORE I proceed to the Extract I propoſe, I muſt explain my Motives of giving it. A *German* Tragedy happened to fall into my Hands with a long Preface, and at the End was annex'd a *Critique*, with an Anſwer. Tho' I don't underſtand that Language, yet in running this Performance over with my Eye, I could perceive the Names of a great many *French* Authors mentioned, and therefore was curious to know what was the Author's Meaning. I therefore put the Tragedy into the Hands of a Perſon who made an Extract from it, and I believed it would be no diſagreeable Entertainment to

the

the Public to communicate to it what the
Author has said in this Preface; for besides
that it gives us an excellent and indisputable
Notion of their Stage, I don't think his Ideas
in Writing at all contemptible. His Preface,
his Criticisms, and his Answers to them,
will enable us to judge of the Manner of
Thinking which Men of Learning in *Germany* entertain of the Stage, and may perhaps disabuse a great Number of People,
who think that in that Country they have
neither the Practice, the Knowledge, or a
Taste of Dramatic Poetry.

E X T R A C T.

The Death of C A T O, *by* JOHN CHRISTOPHER GOTTSEHED, *a Tragedy, with
the Sentiments of Mr.* de Fenelon *on Tragedy; to which are added a Critique, and an
Answer;* the Second Edition, *printed at*
Leipsic *in the Year* 1735.

The P R E F A C E.

I INTEND to publish a Tragedy in
Verse, when such Pieces after being forgot for more than thirty Years, have just renewed

newed their Appearance upon our Theatre. Three Years ago, in my *Treatife upon Criticifm*, I did my beſt to encourage our Nation to cultivate Dramatic Poetry, but I would not venture upon an Attempt of that kind myſelf, for fear of preventing others by my Example. I waited with Impatience to ſee whether any of our Poets would undertake this Taſk for the Honour of *Germany*. It muſt be owned that we don't want great Geniuſes, who ſeem to have a Talent for Dramatic Poetry, provided they knew its Rules, with the Faults and the Beauties of the *German* Theatre, and thoſe of *France, England,* and *Italy*.

Before I acquaint the Reader with my Motive for publiſhing this Tragedy, it will be neceſſary to inform him, what gave me ſo ſtrong a Bent to the Drama, and prevailed with me to write in that way.

Fifteen or ſixteen Years ago, I read one of the Tragedies of *Lohenſtein* *, which gave me a very odd Notion of Tragedy. Tho' I heard that Poet highly extolled by People of Taſte, I could never reliſh the Beauties of his Works, but durſt not frankly declare my Sentiments. I was equally diſtaſted with *The Antigona of Sophocles*, tranſlated into the

Ger-

---

* This Poet has wrote five Tragedies. See the Catalogue at the End.

German Language by *Opitz* †; and tho' I highly relished the other Productions of that Father of our Poetry, yet I could not endure the Harshness of this Translation, which likewise to me appeared a little forced and unnatural. Thus I remained in a kind of Indifference, or even Ignorance, with regard to the Drama, till the Works of *Boileau* fell into my Hands. The Satire addressed to *Moliere*, and the Encomiums and Criticisms upon Dramatic Works, with which it is interspersed, excited my Curiosity to know the rest of that Author's Pieces. I read the Works of *Moliere*, which gave me a strong Inclination to see some Tragedy or Comedy acted. In the Year 1724, I found at *Leipsic* the privileged Company of Comedians belonging to the Court of *Saxony*, who come up thither only in the Time of the Fair. Here I had an Opportunity of satisfying my Curiosity; I saw every Play, but I soon perceived that little Regularity was observed on that Theatre; for they represented great Actions of Kings and Affairs of State intermingled with the Tricks of *Harlequin*, romantic Adventures, Farces, and Buffoonries. The only good Piece acted there, was *The Combat of Honour and Love*; or, *Roderigue and Chimene*, translated into blank Verse.

---

† *Opitz* has wrote four Tragedies.

Verſe. It is eaſy to conceive that this Piece not only pleaſed me more than the other Plays, but likewiſe made me ſenſible of the vaſt Difference between a regular Tragedy, and the Exhibition of that fantaſtical Medley I have juſt now mentioned.

I became acquainted with the then Maſter of the Company. I talked to him of a better Order upon his Theatre. I aſked him eſpecially why he did not act the Tragedies of *Griphius,* as alſo his *Horribilicribrifax* *. He anſwered me, that he had formerly play'd the firſt of his Tragedies, but that at preſent ſuch Pieees did not take, becauſe they were too ſerious, and had no comical Characters in them. I adviſed him to try a new Piece in Verſe, and promiſed to write it myſelf. Thus, tho' entirely ignorant of the Rules, nay, tho' I knew not ſo much as whether there were any Rules to be obſerved in Performances of this Nature, I tranſlated the *Endymion* of *Fontenelle,* which I cauſed to be printed with the Addition of ſome comical Scenes that made up a kind of Interlude, entirely independent of the principal Action. By good Fortune I did not then venture to ſhew my Tranſlation, for *Endymion* was more ſuited to the Nature of an Opera †, than of a Comedy.

---

* See the ſmall Catalogue at the End.
† *Endymion* itſelf is in reality an Opera.

In thefe Days, the bad Pieces which I faw acted, occafioned me to make feveral Reflections; and tho' I was ignorant of the Rules, I did not find in them that eafy Turn, and ftrict Imitation of Nature, which is the peculiar Beauty, and the chief Perfection of Dramatic Performances; I became folicitous and uneafy, to know the Rules of the Drama, for I could not imagine that a Piece of Poetry, fo grand and auguft, could fubfift without Rules, fince I obferved that all the other kinds of Poetry had ftated ones peculiar to themfelves. But I have met with none of them in our Writers, exeept in *Rothen*'s *Defcription of German Poetry*, printed at *Leipfic*, in the Year 1688.

Menantes, in his Dramatic *Poetry*, gives but little Infight and imperfect Directions with regard to the *Operas*. Tho' *Rothen*'s Thoughts upon this Subject are none of the worft, yet, inftead of giving me full Satisfaction, he only opened my Eyes to a new Light, by the Encomiums he beftowed upon *Ariftotle*'s *Art of Poetry*. By means of thefe uncommon Applaufes given it by this Writer, my Curiofity led me to read it, which I did for the firft time, in Mr. *Dacier*'s *French* Tranflation. *Caufabon on the Satyr of the Greeks, Rappolts Ariftotle*'s *Art of Poetry, Heinfius de Tragediæ Conftitutione, The Abbot Aubignac*'s *Practice of the Theatre*, and other Writers

Writers amongſt the Moderns, gave me all the Satisfaction I could wiſh for. My reading the Dramas of *Corneille, Racine, Moliere, La Mothe Danchet,* and *Voltaire,* together with their *Prefaces,* and the critical Diſſertations ſubjoined, contributed not a little to my Information. But the Authors to whom I was more obliged than to all the reſt were *Father Brumoy, in his Theatre of the Greeks,* and *Riccoboni in his Italian Theatre.*

The more I knew of the Regulations of foreign Theatres, the more I was diſguſted at the Diſorder and Confuſion of the *German* Stage; but it happened that the Comedians of the Court of *Dreſden* changed their Maſter, whoſe Succeſſor, as well as his Wife, (who has a fine Genius for the Stage, and equals the moſt accompliſhed Actreſs either of *France* or *England*) had a ſtrong Inclination to aboliſh the wild Confuſion which had till then debaſed our Theatre, and to put the *German* Stage on the ſame Footing with that of the *French.* Long before this, while he was at the Court of *Brunſwick,* Attempts had been made to tranſlate the beſt *French* Tragedies into *German* Verſe, and Copies of a great many of them ſent to him for effectuating the ſame Purpoſe. And tho' they begun with the *Regulus of Pradon,* who was none of the beſt Writers of *French* Tragedy, and tranſlated very harſhly by *Breſſand,* a

Poet refiding at the Court of that Prince, yet it had fuch a Run that they were thereby encouraged to act *Brutus* and *Alexander*, tranflated by the fame Hand. Some Time after *the Cid of Corneille* appeared, tranflated by a better Hand, and met with greater Applaufes than any of the Pieces formerly played.

That I might contribute all I could to the Reformation of our Theatre, I propofed to act *Cinna*, tranflated by a Perfon of Diftinction, a Member of the Counfel of *Nuremberg*. This Mafterpiece of *Corneille* is in the Collection entitled *Vefta and Flora*, and met with the Succefs it deferved. At laft I myfelf tranflated *the Iphiginia of Racine*; and two of my Friends tranflated the fecond Part of the *Cid*, called the *Mourning*, or *Mourning Year of Chimene*, and *Racine's Bernice*, which were all three acted with Applaufe; thus we had even at that Time eight regular Tragedies acted upon our Theatre.

After having given this fhort Account of the Rife to a Reformation on our Theatre, it is neceffary I fhould fpeak of my own *Cato*, and give a particular Account of its Nature and Conduct.

Cato of *Utica*, has in all Ages of the World been looked upon as the Pattern of Stoical Refolution, as a thorough Patriot, and a true Republican. Poets and Orators, Hiftorians

ftorians and Philofophers, have celebrated him in their Works; and even under the Defpotic Government of the *Roman* Emperors who fucceeded *Cæfar*, the greateft Men praifed his Zeal and Warmth in defending the Republic. *Virgil and Horace*, under the Reign of *Auguftus*, *Lucan* and *Seneca*, under that of *Claudius* and *Nero*, have fung his Praifes. The Poet *Maternus* (as we fee by that ancient Dialogue of the Orators upon the Caufe of the Decay of Eloquence) wrote a Tragedy on *Cato*; and that Poet in all probability expreffed his Averfion to Monarchy in Terms fo full of Strength and Force, that his Friends thought the Piece not only too farcaftical, but even dangerous; a Circumftance which gives us fufficient Light with regard to the Original of that Poem.

Cato killed himfelf in *Utica*, and this Cataftrophe has rendered the Action a fit Subject for a Tragedy; it is then no Wonder that the Poets of all Nations have made Choice of it for that Purpofe.

In the Year 1712 Mr. *Addifon*, an *Englifh* Poet, publifhed his *Cato*; it is impoffible to conceive how highly this Piece was valued by the *Englifh*, and perhaps their Love of Liberty contributed not a little to its Succefs. It is however certain that this Tragedy contains fo many real Beauties, that it muft pleafe not only the *Englifh*, but all
other

other Spectators: In it the Characters and Manners are strictly preserved, and the Thoughts are suited to the different Turn and Genius of the Personages introduced. *Cato* is represented as a thorough Republican: But this Tragedy having already met with sufficient Applause on the Continent, especially in a Translation of it into *French* Prose, needs no Encomiums from me.

Soon after Mr. *Deschamps* published his *Cato*, which was printed at the *Hague* in the Year 1715. I don't believe that that Poet knew any thing of Mr. *Addison*'s Tragedy, for the two do not resemble one another in their Conduct; the Table, the Personages, and the Incidents are quite different. And in the *English Cato* even Facts and Incidents are handled in a quite different Manner. The Character of *Cato* is indeed the same in both, and perfectly, equally, and well sustained; excepting when he is killed, and thro' all the fifth Act, for as I shall prove, the *English Cato* has something excellent in this Circumstance to balance the Merit of the *French*, which indeed is preferable in Point of Regularity.

If the Subject of *Sophonisba* has been handled by the *Italians*, the *French*, the *English*, and the *Germans*, it is not surprizing if that of *Cato* has had the same Fate; but I am sorry that it falls to my Weakness to undertake

undertake this Subject in the *German* Language. But confcious of my Inability to plan out the Action of a Fable, I have made Ufe of the two Originals juft now mentioned, fo that one may fay of me what on another Occafion was faid of *Terence.*

Quæ convenere in Andriam ex Perinthia,
Fatetur tranftuliffe, atq; Ufum pro fuis.

Who confeffed, " That he took from *Perin-* " *thia,* and ufed as his own, fuch Things as " beft fuited his Purpofe in compofing his " *Andria.*"

My Imitation in this Particular is ftill farther authorized by the Example of another Poet:

Habet Bonorum exemplum; quo exemplo fibi
Licere id facere, quod illi fecerunt putat.

Who thought, " when he had the Example " of good Authors to imitate, he might " warrantably do what they on the like " Occafions did."

But without having recourfe to the Example of *Terence,* who has borrowed whole Plays from *Menander,* with but a few Alterations or Additions of his own, I may juftify myfelf by the Example of the beft Writers

Q   of

of *French* Tragedy, who have imitated, tranflated, or altered *Sophocles* and *Euripides.*

I was at firft advifed, literally to tranflate *Addifon's Cato* ; but as I was refolved to ftick to the Rules of the Drama, I found he fell far fhort in Regularity to the *French* Tragedy. The *Englifh* are indeed great Mafters both of Thought and Expreffion ; they know wonderfully well how to fuftain a Character, and enter furprifingly into the Heart of Man; but as to the Conduct of the Fable, they are very carelefs, as appears from all their Dramatic Compofitions; and it would have given me great Pain had the *German* Stage been always liable to the Reproach of being irregular. This prevailed with me to alter my firft Purpofe, and write a *Cato* different from that of Mr. *Addifon's.*

It would be ufelefs for me to prove that the Tragedy of Mr. *Defchamps* is exactly according to the Rules of *Ariftotle.* This fufficiently appears from the Criticifm annexed to it, and confirms me in the Defects of the *Englifh Cato.* In reality Mr. *Addifon* joined three Actions in one, tho' each of them was entirely diftinct from the other, independent of the main Plot, and often ferving to make the Spectators lofe Sight of it. The Action is as follows: *Cato* with his Party, which is not very numerous, is blocked up in *Utica.* *Cæfar* offers him Terms, which he refufes ; upon

upon which *Cæsar* orders his Troops to advance, but *Cato* finding himself too weak to make Head against him, runs himself thro' the Body with his Sword. Mr. *Addison*, in order to extend this Action, has inserted two Episodes, or rather two Plots, quite foreign to the main Action. *Portius* and *Marcus*, the two Sons of *Cato*, are in Love with *Lucia*, the Daughter of a *Roman* Senator. *Portius*, whom his Brother makes his Confident, acts like a wife Youth, and conceals his own Passion: *Marcus* dies, and his Brother wins *Lucia*. On the other hand *Juba* falls in Love with *Marcia*, the Daughter of *Cato*, but meets with a Rival in the Person of *Sempronius*, a *Roman* Senator, who, disguised like a *Numidian* that he might carry off *Marcia*, is surprized and killed by that Prince who gains his Mistress.

These two Episodes are quite foreign to the principal Plot, and, in reality, destroy the Principle of the Unity of Action. Besides the Improbability in the Hurry and Confusion then at *Utica*, so much Time should have been spent in Intrigues of Gallantry, the Disguise of *Sempronius* to me seems too low and trivial for Tragedy. Even *Cato* in the first Act, to me does not sustain a proper Grandeur, nor is so great as when he appeases the Tumult, and bewails the Death of his Son. All the rest of the Play is quite fo-

reign

reign to the main Action. In the *English*
Tragedy the Scenes are very ill connected
together; the Actors go and come without
any apparent Reason; sometimes the Stage
is quite empty; and the Entrances and
Exits are equally defective, which never happens in the *French* Drama. In short, I did
not think it very much in Character, that
when *Cato* was dying, he should trouble himself so much about the two Marriages. The
Moderns have made it an indispensable Duty,
and as it were a Rule, to finish all Dramatic
Representations by a Marriage, which has
long given me great Disgust. The Ancients
did it very rarely, and I wanted to try if a
Tragedy could succeed without a Marriage,
an Attempt in which I hope I have not been
unsuccessful.

If I am asked why I have not entirely
translated the *French Cato*, I answer, It was
because the Plot in the Beginning was laid
down with Good-Sense and Probability;
and *Cato* is there represented as great, as in
the last Act his Character to me appears
weak and languishing; the Death of that
great Man being not so much in the Character of a Philosopher as a Bravaoe. A
Mutiny is raised in *Utica*, where *Cæsar* then
was; his Army, who lay without the City
being uneasy about the Safety of their General, furiously run into it, and kill all the Inhabitants.

bitants. Upon this *Cato* refolves to kill himfelf; but alas the Matter is over-done! and I
can't allow myfelf to think that any one
can approve of fuch a Deviation from hiftorical Truth, and altering fo much the Character of *Cato*, which was that of a Philofopher.

Befides, *Cato* is faid to have had no Sons;
but the Speech which the *Englifh* Poet puts
into his Mouth, when he fees one of his Sons
dead, and infpires the other with a Hatred at
Tyranny, appears to me too fublime not to
merit a Place in my Tragedy. I have therefore preferved the Character of *Porcius*, tho'
I have dreffed it up in a quite different Light
from what it appears in the two foreign Tragedies. I have not brought *Marcus* on the
Stage till after his Death, that he may be
viewed by *Cato* as the *French* Poet had done
before me. This I could not difpenfe with,
fince I had ftruck out the *Englifh* Characters
of *Sempronius* and *Syphax*. As for the laft
Act of Mr. *Addifon*, I have preferved it almoft entire, having only changed the Perfons,
and cut off the Marriages of *Porcius* and of
Juba. I have likewife put another Speech
in *Cato*'s Mouth before his Death, which I
took from Mr. *Defchamps*.

It is likewife evident that the Marriage of
Arfene with *Pharnaces* is only intended, and
not actually celebrated: Mr. *Defchamps* in
his

his Preface has sufficiently justified himself in this Point. To tell the Truth, the Death of *Cato* is an Historical Fact which does not furnish sufficient Matter for a Tragic Action, without the Help of some Episode, and this one, in my Opinion, is very properly connected with the principal Action; for by Means of it, one has an Opportunity of comparing the Vices of one with the Virtues of another, a Thing as necessary for representing Virtue in her most amiable Colours, as Shades in Painting are for heightning the Effects of the Lights.

The same is the Case with regard to *Cæsar*. He did not really enter into *Utica*, as the Poet only supposes him to have done, and thereby he has an Opportunity of drawing the Parallel betwixt these two *Roman* Heroes. By comparing their two Characters, one is enabled to distinguish false from true Grandeur, and to see that Vice, when prosperous, may sometimes assume the Appearances of Virtue. The Conversation between *Cato* and *Cæsar* have not a little contributed to the Preference I have given the *French* to the *English* Poet in this Particular.

Cato was a Hero whose Character was suited to Tragedy, and comes within the Definition of *Aristotle:* His Virtue was great, yet not complete, or unstai ed with some small Mixture of Vice; for his Love of
Liberty

Liberty degenerates into a confirmed Obftinacy; his Death is bewailed, and his Rafh-
nefs condemned.

Tho' my *Cato* had a great Run when
acted, and read very well, yet I muft refer
myfelf to the learned Readers, to whom, if it
is agreeable, I flatter myfelf, that I have not
fpoilt what is good either in the *French* or in
the *Englifh* Performance; for I frankly acknowledge, that all the Beauties of my *Cato*
are drawn from *Addifon* and *Defchamps,* and
all its Blemifhes are to be afcribed to myfelf
and my little Practice in Dramatic Writings.

Extract of the TRAGEDY, *called*
DYING CATO.

Dramatis Perſonæ.

CATO.

ARSENE, *or* PORCIA.

PHENICE, *her Attendant.*

PHOCAS, *a Friend of* CATO.

PHARNACES *King of* Pontus.

FELIX, *his Confident.*

CÆSAR.

DOMITIUS, *his Confident.*

ARTABAN.

Attendants of CATO.

Attendants of CÆSAR.

The

The Scene of Action is a Hall in the Castle of
Utica.
The Action commences about 12 *o'Clock, and*
ends about Sun-set.

ACT I. SCENE I.

Arsene and *Phenice.*

Arsene comes to wait on *Cato*, from whom
she hopes Comfort and Relief in her Misfortunes, and Shelter from the Calamities
which yet threaten her. She talks of the
common Report of the Death of her Father
Arsaces, King of the *Parthians*, and of the
Arrival of *Pharnaces*, King of *Pontus*; and
she is afraid of being more misfortunate than
ever. *Phenice* asks her if she would ever
accept of *Pharnaces* for her Husband. *Arsene* declares to her, that that would never
happen, and opening her Love to her, tells
her, that she could now speak as a Queen,
her Father being dead. She bids her call to
Mind that *Roman* whom *Cæsar* sent to her
Father to gain him over to his Interests.
Phenice runs out in his Praises; and *Arsene*
confesses that she has been in Love with him
since the first Moment she saw him. *Phenice* asks her his Name. *Arsene* replies, She
does not know it; and seeing *Cato* approach,
she praises him. SCENE

S C E N E II.

To Them, *Cato.*

Cato condoles with *Arfene,* and confirms the News of her Father's Death. He afks her if, now that the *Parthians* had proclaimed her Queen, fhe would continue that Alliance and Fidelity which her Father had fwore to him; this *Arfene* promifes to do, only afks the Favour that he would not protect *Pharnaces.* She tells him that in the Civil Wars of her Kingdom *Pharnaces,* in a Battle, affaffinated her only Brother *Pacorus :* That a Peace being concluded, he came to her Father's Court to demand her in Marriage: That they fent her to *Rome* to folemnize the Nuptials: That *Pharnaces* could not leave his Kingdom becaufe of the Civil Wars of the *Romans:* That at *Rome* fhe had refided with *Cato,* and that fhe had followed his Fortune. She adds, that *Pharnaces* himfelf had but a Day before confeffed his murdering her Brother; and that befides her Averfion to this Marriage, his Guilt added to the Horror fhe had at fuch an Alliance. *Cato* promifes her all poffible Safety in *Utica.* *Arfene* goes of; *Cato* remains alone; and as he had faid before in the Scene that fhe had a *Roman Soul,* he is now aftonifhed at
the

the Sentiments he feels for her, and takes
Notice of the great Refemblance betwixt
her and *Porcia*, his deceafed Daughter. Laft
of all he declares the Arrival of *Phocas*.

SCENE III.

Phocas, *Artaban*, and *Cato*.

Phocas tells *Cato* of a great Reinforcement
that was coming up to him. He brings to
his Remembrance that when his Wife died,
fhe left him a Daughter, who was brought
up by the Wife of *Craffus*, and who was
along with him when the *Romans* were routed
by the *Parthians*, on which Occafion fhe
was flain. *Phocas* tells him that his Daughter *Porcia* was ftill alive, and prefents *Artaban* to him as the Perfon to whom her Safety
was owing. *Artaban* gives him an Account
of the Victory which the *Parthians* gained
over *Craffus*, and tells him that *Porcia* becoming his Prifoner of War, he made a Prefent
of her to *Arfaces*, who having loft his Daughter *Arfene*, for Reafons of State, adopted her.
He fhews him a Deed which King *Arfaces*
had made before his Death, and entrufted to
him, that he might fhew to *Cato*. *Cato* reads
it; and *Arfaces* in it intreats him not to deprive his Daughter *Porcia* of a Throne.
Cato deplores his Misfortune, and inclines
that

that his Daughter fhould abdicate the Crown. *Phocas* advifes him to allow her ftill to pof-fefs her Kingdom, becaufe the Aids fhe could afford might prove the Means of faving *Rome*. *Cato* for good Reafons rejects this Advice, and taking his Leave of them both, orders them not to fpeak any thing of the Matter to his Daughter, whom he himfelf wanted to inform of this Affair.

S C E N E IV.

Cato and *Pharnaces*.

After fome Difcourfe upon the prefent Juncture of Affairs, *Pharnaces* preffes his Marriage with *Arfene*. *Cato* tells him that he muft no longer think of that, fince he ought to look upon her as a *Roman* Lady. *Pharnaces* is furprized at his Anfwer, and defires him to explain himfelf. *Cato* pro-mifes to him very foon to reveal a great Secret publickly before all the City. *Pharnaces* tells him that he ought to think maturely of the Affair; that he had loft his Dominions, but that his Marriage with *Arfene* would render him Mafter of a powerful Kingdom, and that if he gave over Thoughts of that, he could no longer expect his Service; and laft of all he entreats him to take Care of his Interefts, his Liberty, and his Life. *Cato*
.defpifes

despises him; orders him to withdraw; tells him they could defeat the Enemy without his Assistance, and in fine lets him know, that *Rome* was yet free, and spoke in his Language, and that she would never truckle either to him or to Men of his Character.

S C E N E V.

To Them, *Felix.*

Felix informs *Cato* that the Plains are covered with *Cæsar*'s Troops, and that *Utica* had Reason to be afraid of Slavery. *Cato* says he is going to march forth against the Enemy, and again requests *Pharnaces* to be gone and join the Troops of *Cæsar*; on which he goes off.

S C E N E VI.

Pharnaces and *Felix.*

Pharnaces boasts that he will be revenged for the Contempt shewn him by *Cato*; that in Spite of him, he shall have both the Hand and the Kingdom of *Arsene*, and that *Cato* shall fall a Victim to him. He discovers his Design of sending *Cato*'s Head to *Cæsar* by *Timon* and *Arbates*. That in Recompence he will demand to be restored to his Kingdom,

and

and *Arſene* in Marriage: Then with Maxims
ſuitable to his Deſigns he quits the Stage, and
the firſt Act ends.

ACT II.   SCENE I.

Domitius and *Phocas.*

Domitius informs *Phocas* that *Cæſar* was
very ſoon to be in the Town of *Utica. Phocas* aſks if his Arrival did not give them
Hopes of Peace. *Domitius* is ſilent upon
that Point, and only deſires him to inform
Arſene that *Pallas* had come into the City
along with him, and that he had ſomething
of Conſequence to impart to her. *Phocas*
goes off the Stage. *Domitius* ſtays alone for
a ſhort while, and ſays that *Cæſar,* notwithſtanding his brave and warlike Soul, is never-
theleſs in Love with *Arſene.* He ſees *Cato*
approach him, whoſe Preſence ſtrikes him
with Veneration.

SCENE II.

Cato and *Domitius.*

Cato reproaches *Domitius* for having ſided
with *Cæſar.* *Domitius* defends himſelf by
plauſible

plausible Reasons, and runs out in *Cæsar's*
Praise. At last he desires an Interview between *Cæsar* and him, to deliberate upon the
Interests of *Rome*. *Cato* consents to it, and
asks him what Surety *Cæsar* demanded.
Domitius answered him, that *Cæsar* insisted
on no other Surety than the Virtue of *Cato*,
but told him that he ought not to trust *Pharnaces* in *Utica*. *Cato* informs him, that
Pharnaces depended on him: He describes
the Situation of the Castle, into which *Cæsar*
might come and talk with him without
being seen by any Body: He says *Pharnaces*
is on the Sea-Shore viewing his Fleet; that
his Soldiers durst not come near him; that
every thing was carefully looked after, and
especially the Motions of *Pharnaces:* That
Cæsar might therefore have an Interview
with him in the Castle; and that the Affair
might be transacted with the greater Secrecy,
he proposes to remove the Guards from its
Entrance. He adds, Tell *Cæsar*, nevertheless,
that *Cato* sees very far into the Heart of
Man, and that Artifice and Disguise cannot
blind him.

S C E N E III.

Arsene, Phenice, and *Domitius.*

Arsene at her Entrance orders *Domitius*,
since he had heard of *Cæsar's* Love to her,
to

to inform him that she should always look upon him with Contempt and Disdain, &c. She takes her Leave of *Domitius*, and seeing *Pharnaces* approach, endeavours to avoid him.

S C E N E IV.

Pharnaces, Arsene, and *Phenice.*

Pharnaces begs her to stay. *Arsene* loads him with Reproaches, putting him in Mind of her Brother's Death. *Pharnaces* inflamed with Wrath and Rage, tells her, that every Body condemned her Conduct; that *Cato* and the *Romans* complained of her, and were even ready to deprive her of her Hereditary Throne and Kingdom. He then proposes that she should go on board his Fleet, and go off with him. She answers, that if *Cato* should condemn her, she would submit; and upbraids her Lover of Cowardice, protesting that she never will marry him; but that she will think herself happy, could she be revenged on him with her own Hand. Upon this *Pharnaces*, in a Passion, reproaches her in very harsh Terms

S C E N E

S C E N E V.

To Them, *Porcius.*

Arſene informs *Porcius* of *Pharnaces*'s Pre-
tenſions, and begs his Support. *Porcius* enraged at the Calumnies with which *Pharnaces* loaded his Father, makes great Proteſta-
tions to *Arſene*, and propoſes to marry her.
Arſene quits the Stage.

S C E N E VI.

Pharnaces and *Porcius.*

Pharnaces with a haughty Air aſks *Porcius* if he thought to gain a Kingdom by
loving *Arſene*, and treats him with Contempt.
Porcius ſpeaking with Diſdain of Royalty,
adds, That without any Views to that, he
ſhould have thought of marrrying *Arſene*,
and that he wiſhed ſhe had been by Birth a
Roman. Pharnaces tells him, that ſhe is ſo
in reality, and that *Cato* declared ſhe was no
Queen, and inſinuates that *Cato* muſt want
Candour, or ſhe can be no Queen. *Porcius*
anſwers, *It muſt be ſo,* ſince his Father had
ſaid it, and departs in Haſte to ſatisfy himſelf. *Pharnaces* remains alone, and ſays he
is confirmed in his Thoughts of *Porcius*'s
loving

loving *Arsene*, and that all his Hopes were destroyed if she should find that she was not a *Parthian*. He threatens to kill *Porcius*, &c.

S C E N E   VII.

Felix and *Pharnaces.*

Pharnaces tells *Felix* that the Face of Affairs would soon be altered, and that the Troubles of *Africa* would soon cease; that the *Romans* having laid down their Arms, deplored the Death of their Friends; and that at last the Sweets of universal Peace were relished. He asks him if *Cæsar* approved of his Design, and the Proposal he had made him by *Timon* and *Arbates*, of securing to himself the Sovereign Power at the Price of *Cato*'s Head, and if *Timon* and *Arbates* are returned? *Felix* replied, They were not. *Pharnaces* is willing to execute his Design with all possible Dispatch, and discovers the Stratagem which he intended to use for causing his Troops to enter *Utica* to kill *Cato*, and carry off *Arsene*. *Felix* tells him that the Guard was removed from the Gate of the Castle, and that this Circumstance would render his Enterprize so much the more easy. *Pharnaces* enjoins him Secresy, and departs to execute his Design; and thus the Act ends.

R   A C T

ACT III.   SCENE I.

Cæsar and *Domitius.*

Cæsar fays, it is for *Cato*'s Intereſt that he demands this Interview; but that he would wiſh, if poſſible, to fee *Arfene* before-hand. *Domitius* informs him that he ſhould fee her, but that it would be to no Purpofe, fince ſhe defpifed him. After fome Reafoning upon his own Love, and upon the War, he fees the Queen approaching, and takes his Leave of *Domitius.*

SCENE II.

Cæsar and *Arfene.*

Arfene, upon feeing *Cæfar*, knows him to be the *Roman* with whom ſhe was in Love. She aſks him if it was he who came to her Father's Court with the Complaints of *Cæ-far.* He anfwers, It was; and that he him-felf was *Cæfar. Arfene* is troubled. *Cæfar* begins to explain himfelf more freely, and complains that his Paſſion was repaid with Difdain and Hatred, *Arfene* briefly informs him

him that fhe did not hate him: By this Confeffion, *Cæfar* is tranfported with Joy. *Arfene*
blufhes at the Declaration fhe has made, but
at laft confirms it, and fays, that without her
own Knowledge, fhe had hated what fhe
moft loved. At laft fhe intercedes with him
for the Deliverance of *Utica*, and for the Life
of *Cato*, telling him, that nothing in the
World was fo dear to her as the Glory of
Cæfar and the Life of *Cato*, &c. Then fhe
goes off the Stage.

S C E N E   III.

Cæfar and *Cato*.

Cæfar advifes *Cato* to banifh all Sentiments
of Hatred, and promifes to make him Part-
ner in the Government with himfelf. With
Horror *Cato* hears the Propofal. *Cæfar* on
the one hand attempts to juftify himfelf, and
demands that *Cato* and his Friends fhould
allow him to reign. *Cato* on the other hand
accufes him of Tyranny, and rejects all Offers of Peace upon any other Terms than
the *Liberty of Rome*. *Cæfar* reprefents to
him the Danger to which they were reduced,
and that they could hope for no Affiftance
from *Pharnaces*, who fought nothing fo
much as his Deftruction. That he had fent
two Traitors to make an Offer of his Head

to

to him, and that he had caufed them to be detained. *Cato* commends him for his Magnanimity; but obftinately perfifting in his ardent Wifhes for the Liberty of *Rome*, he tells them that he would acquaint the *Romans* with his Offer, and that if they accepted of it, and affented to their own Ruin, for his Share he would chufe to die, and fo he makes his Exit. *Cæfar* in a fhort Soliloquy breaks out into an Admiration of his Virtue, and fays, That if he were not *Cæfar*, he would wifh to be *Cato*, and to have fuch Sentiments of Liberty. *Pharnaces* comes up.

S C E N E IV.

To Him, *Pharnaces.*

Pharnaces is furprized to fee *Cæfar* in *Utica*, and tells him that he impatiently expeds the Return of *Timon* and *Arbates*, whom he had fent to acquaint him that he would prefent him with the Head of *Cato:* That this was a Propofal which he ought not to treat with Indifference, as he could thereby finifh a War which might be fatal to him if *Cato* lived. *Cæfar* rejeds this Propofal with a becoming Horror, calls him Traitor, and hints to him, that the fame may one Day be his Fate. On this he leaves him. *Pharnaces*

com-

complains that *Cæsar* had not so much as thanked him for his Offer; but, says he, His Haughtiness may chance to cost him dear. He then flatters himself with the Hopes of carrying off *Arsene*, which finishes the third Act.

A C T VI. S C E N E I.

Cato and *Porcius.*

Porcius requests of his Father to know the Answer which the Senate had made to *Cæsar*'s Offers. *Cato* tells him, That he saw with great Pleasure an Unanimity among them in rejecting a Peace that was inconsistent with the Liberty of *Rome*, and that the *Romans* were determined to revenge the Injuries of their Country: He then requires him to swear an invincible Hatred against *Cæsar*. *Porcius* complying, asks of his Father whether or not the Queen of the *Parthians* was a *Roman. Cato* asks him how such a Thought came into his Head. *Porcius* answers, That *Pharnaces* had acquainted him that *Cato* himself was the Author of the Report. *Cato* asks if he loved him, advises him to have no Thought but of War; and tells him,

him, that tho' she was a *Roman*, his Views on her would be to no Purpose, as he should very soon know.

S C E N E II.

To Them, Arsene *and* Phenice.

Arsene tells *Cato* that she was come with a Proposal to spare the Effusion of *Roman* Blood: She tells him that she must be unhappy while the Divisions of *Rome* continue: That she loved the *Romans* better than even the *Parthians*; and that tho' she was a Queen, she could not help wishing well to the Enemies of Kings. *Cato* declares, that if all the *Romans* had the same Regard for him, their Misery would soon end. At last *Arsene* tells him that the Suspension of Arms was almost expired, and begs him to prolong it, because she flattered herself with obtaining every thing of *Cæsar*. *Cato* seems to be amazed at this, and asks how that could be. *Arsene* says, that she will touch the Heart of *Cæsar*; that Heaven had bestowed upon her a Kingdom that could satisfy the whole Extent of his Ambition; that *Cæsar* might with her enjoy the Kingdom of *Parthia*. She vows that *Rome* never shall be disturbed; and that all the Fruits of her Love should be Peace. *Cato*, astonished

to

to hear that she loved *Cæsar*, complains that his Virtue was exposed to the Indignity not only of seeing her attired as a Queen, but of her bearing a Heart susceptible of a Passion for a Tyrant. *Arsene* asks the Reason of this Astonishment; and *Cato*, without any other Answer, gives her *Arsaces*'s Letter to read. After she has read it, she is transported with an Extasy of Joy to find herself the Daughter of *Cato*, as is *Porcius*, to find her his Sister. At last *Cato* tells her in a resolute Manner, that Royalty ought to be no Happiness to her, and that her Love for *Cæsar* was a Disgrace to her Birth and Character. He then exhorts her to act as a *Roman*, and at once to put an End both to her Ambition and Love. *Porcia*, after many Reflections, at length determines to prove her Birth by her Actions, however dear it may cost her Passion. *Cato* upon this embraces her. He then sees *Cæsar* approach them, that they may be Witnesses of the Interview.

SCENE III.

To Them, *Cæsar*.

Cæsar desires *Cato* to let him know what were the Senate's Demands. *Cato* answers, That they demanded the very thing with which *Cæsar* threatned him, his Death, and

R 4   that

that in fhort they wifhed that the War would determine their Fate. *Cæfar* afks what he had done, and enumerates his Actions and good Offices. But *Cato* ftill treats him as a Tyrant. *Cæfar* puts him in Mind of the Difproportion of their Strength; and turning to the Princefs, complains of the Harfhnefs of *Cato*, which he faid was no longer tolerable. *Porcia* reproaches *Cæfar* with infulting an Enemy whom he ought to honour, and at laft tells him that there was one prefent who claimed his Refpect. Whom have I to dread? fays *Cæfar*. Know, replies the other, that *Cato* is my Father. This Point being cleared up, *Cæfar* makes Ufe of that as a Handle to propofe a Match with *Arfene*, which might give Peace to the World. But this *Cato* rejects with great Firmnefs, telling him that he always had before his Eyes the Death of *Pompey*, who was Son-in-Law to *Cæfar*, a miftaken Happinefs which haftened his Ruin; and that in fhort, he looked upon the Propofal as ignominious for him.

SCENE IV.

To Them, *Domitius.*

Domitius acquaints them with the Treachery of *Pharnaces*, who with an armed
Body

Body had made his Way as far as the Caſtle: That three or four *Romans*, together with the Confident of *Arſene*, had bravely reſiſted him; and that *Cato's* Son *Marcus*, having darted himſelf with great Courage into the Middle, attacked *Pharnaces*, whom he had killed; but that the latter had Strength enough, while *Marcus* was turning towards the other Enemies, to run him thro' the Back, ſo that the one died as a Hero, the other as a Villain; but that the reſt of the Enemies were diſperſed. *Cæſar* mentions the Treachery of *Pharnaces* with Horror; he takes leave of *Cato* by telling him, that ſince he has rejected Peace, he muſt prepare for War; and ſays to *Porcia*, To-morrow, if the Gods ſhall give me the Victory, I will lay my Sword at your Feet; and then goes off.

SCENE V.

Marcus carried by the Soldiers.

Cato, Phocas, Artaban, and Attendants.

Cato looks upon the Body with great Reſolution; pronounces an Encomium upon his Son; gives *Porcius* his beſt Advice, and exhorts his Friends to ſet ſail and flee from the Vengeance of *Cæſar*; he gives them his laſt Adieu, and the Act ends.

A C T

A C T V.   S C E N E I.

Cato, *alone fiting by a Table with a Book before him, a naked Sword lying on the Table, and a Couch on the other Hand.*

Cato pronounces the Difcourfe upon *the Immorality of the Soul,* as it is to be found in Mr. *Addifon's Cato.*

S C E N E II.

To him, *Porcius.*

Porcius, alarmed at the Sight of the naked Sword, wants to carry it off; but *Cato* prevents him, and then orders him to leave the Room. *Porcius* renews his affectionate Expreffions; upon which *Cato* embraces him, and defires that he would go and fee if his Friends were embarked, telling him that he himfelf in the mean while would endeavour to take fome Repofe. This comforts *Porcius,* and he leaves his Father in Bed with the Curtains drawn.

S C E N E III.

Porcius and *Porcia.*

Porcius acquaints his Sifter with the pleafing Hopes he entertained, that all would be
well,

well, and that there was a Probability of the Public Tranquillity being reftored: He informs her of the Orders he had received from his Father, and of his repofing himfelf, and leaves the Stage.

S C E N E IV.

Porcia and *Phenice.*

They talk of their own Situation, and that of *Cato*'s, for whom they tremble.

S C E N E V.

To Them, *Phocas.*

Phocas enters with an Encomium upon the refrefhing quiet Slumbers that arife from Innocence, and tells them that he had feen *Cato* afleep.

S C E N E VI.

To Them, *Artaban.*

Artaban informs them that the Troops of *Cæfar* were making no Difpofitions for an Attack ; perhaps waiting the Anfwer of *Cato.*

S C E N E VII.

To Them, Porcius, *in a great Emotion.*

He informs them that he has been at the Harbour, where his Father's Friends were
obliged

obliged to wait for want of a favourable Wind to carry them away. He tells them likewife that a Veffel was arrived from *Pompey*'s Son, to acquaint his Father that he was doing his utmoft to fend him Reinforcements from *Spain*, to affift him to act againft the common Enemy. — A Noife is heard — *Porcius* goes out, and immediately returns in a great Agony, telling them that *Cato* was killed. *Porcia* fwoons.

S C E N E VIII.

To Them, Cato, *carried in wounded.*

Cato, as he is dying, enquires at *Porcius* about his Friends; and if they are gone: He orders him to apply neither for Pardon nor Favour to the Enemy, but to do his beft to reftore the Liberties of his Country. He embraces *Porcia*; gives her his beft Advice; efpecially that fhe would efpoufe the Man who fhould revenge the Wrongs of *Rome*. He comforts his weeping Friends, and dies.

The Play ends.

A small Treatife *of* M. DE FENE-
LON, *Archbishop of* Cambray,
and Author of The Adventures of
TELEMACHUS.

IMmediately after the Tragedy follows a
fmall Treatife of Mr. *de Fenelon,* inferted
in his Reflections upon Grammar, Rhetoric,
Poetry, and Hiftory. The Author tranflates
it, and he quotes it in his Anfwer to the Criticifm that has been paft upon him. This
Tract gave me great Pleafure; I had never
read it before, nor did I know that Mr. *de
Fenelon* had wrote upon that Subject. As
the Sentiments of that great Man can't be
too public, I thought it not enough to quote
them, without tranflating them as the *German* Author has done, that the Public may
be entirely acquainted with his indifpenfible
Precepts.

The Sentiments of Monfieur FENE-
LON *upon a Plan of* TRAGEDY.

TRAGEDY ought to be characteri-
ftically different from Comedy. The
firft reprefenting great Events to excite violent

lent Paffions; the other is confined to the Reprefentation of Manners in private Life.

As to Tragedy, I am far from thinking that any Rules are to be given for bringing thofe Entertainments to Perfection, wherein corrupted Paffions are reprefented only to excite them. We know that *Plato*, and the Sage Legiflators in the *Pagan* World, prohibited all Inftruments of Mufic which might melt a Nation into Effeminacy, from a well-ordered State. What a Severity then ought to be obferved by Chriftians with regard to loofe Entertainments! Far from endeavouring to bring them to Perfection, I am pleafed that all of that kind which we have is but lame and imperfect; our Poets having rendered them as languifhing, trifling, and ftale as Romances. All is filled up with Fires, Chains, and Tortures, and a Man there dies in good Health of Body and Mind. The Beauty of the Sun, or the Charms of *Aurora* are afcribed to very indifferent, very infipid Perfonages; their Eyes are two Stars; every Term is a Hyperbole, and not a Spark of true Paffion enters into the whole. So much the better; for by this Means the Weaknefs ef the Poifon prevents the Decreafe. But I think that Tragedy may receive a wonderful Force, fhould its Authors, without minding that giddy Romantic Love which makes fuch Havock in
their

their Plays, follow only the true Philofophic Ideas of Antiquity.

Among the *Greeks,* Tragedy was entirely independent of unfanctified Love. For inftance the *OEdipus* of *Sophocles* admits of no Paffion foreign to the Subject. That great Man obferves the fame Conduct in his other Tragedies. Mr. *Corneille* in his *OEdipus* has weakened the Action, rendered it double, and diftracted the Spectator by the Epifode of a cold Amour betwixt *Thefeus* and *Dirce.* Mr. *Racine* falls into the fame Abfurdity in his *Phedra:* He has made a double Plot, by joyning with the furious *Phedra* the whineing miftaken Character of *Hippolitus.* Had *Phedra* been abandoned to all the furious Tranfports of her Paffion, the Action had then been fimple and fhort, affecting and rapid. But our two Tragic Poets, with all the real Merit they poffeffed, were carried away by the Torrent of Cuftom, and yielded to the prevailing Tafte for Romances. Wit had become the Fafhion, and Love reigned thro' all. They imagined that it was impoffible for an Audience to have fat two Hours without yawning, if fome amorous Intrigue was not brought on to relieve them : They thought themfelves obliged to hurry over the greateft and moft affecting Subject, to make way for a languifhing Hero who interrupts it. Farther, his Sighs muft be ornamented with

Quibbles,

Quibbles, and his Defpair tagg'd with Epigramatic Points. This made the greateft Authors deviate into the groffeft Abfurdities, that they might pleafe the Public. I fhall give an Inftance in the following Lines;

Unrelenting Thirft of Glory,
  Whofe tranfporting Joys I breathe,
That my Name may live in Story,
  Bids me give myfelf to Death;
Yet thy commanding Rage controul,
  Before Eternal Life I prove.
To Death e'er I bequeath my Soul,
  Let me bequeath a Sigh to Love.

Here was a Man who durft not die without Points and Witticifms.

I fhall give another Inftance of a Bombaft Flowry Defpair.

———————— *Pierc'd to the Heart*
With an unlook'd-for, yet a fatal Dart,
The accurs'd Avenger of a righteous *Wrong;*
The unhappy *Victim of a Hate too* ftrong.

What a bombaft affected Language is this for ferious Grief! In my Opinion a certain empty Swelling, which is in the higheft Degree improbable, ought to be cut off from Tragedy; as for Example, the following
                                          Verfes

Verſes have ſomethng in them very forced
and unnatural.

O eager Paſſion for a great Revenge,
To which my Father's Death hath given
    Birth;
Impetuous Progeny of my Reſentment,
How my great Sorrows claſp you to my Boſom!
You fill my Soul with your unbounded Sway:
O give, O give me a ſhort Time for Reſpite,
That I may think on this my preſent State,
On what I wiſh to win, *and what I'd* bett,
        Corneille's Cinna, Act I. Scene I.

Mr. *Boileau* found a kind of Genealogy
in the foregoing Verſes; firſt, *Eager Paſſions,*
which produced an *impetuous Progeny,* and
theſe again were claſped to the Boſom by
Sorrows. The Speeches of great Characters
in Tragedy ought to be all noble and lively,
if they are in the paſſionate Strain ; but then
the Language of Paſſion is always natural,
and without any ſtudied or affected Turns,
for no Man would bewail his Misfortunes
in that Manner.

Mr. *Racine* was not exempted from this
Fault, which Cuſtom had rendered as it were
neceſſary. Nothing is more unnatural than
the Narration of the Death of *Hippolitus*
at the End of the Tragedy of *Phedra,* which
in other Reſpects is very beautiful.   *Thera-*

S   *menes*

menes, who comes to acquaint *Theseus* with
the Death of his Son, ought to have pronounced the Fact only in two Words, and
even these he ought to have wanted Strength
to pronounce distinctly. " *Hippolitus* is dead.
" He died by a Monster sent from the Bot-
" tom of the Deep by the Wrath of Heaven.
" I saw it." A Person thus affected, in such
an Agony, and out of Breath, can he ever be
supposed to amuse himself with the florid
pompous Description of the Dragon?

Her Eye and drooping Head appear'd
To speak her mournful Purpose, &c. ———
The Earth was mov'd, the Air diffus'd Infec-
　　tion,
The Billow, on whose Backs he rode, recoil'd.
　　　　Racine's Phedra. Act V. Scene I.

Sophocles is far from this unseasonable improbable Elegance. On a like Occasion he
puts in the Mouth of *OEdipus* the following broken agonizing Sentiments:

All, all is now disclos'd. I see thee now,
O Light! But soon must never see thee more.
Unhappy Man! To what a Pitch I'm wretched!
Whence, whence this sudden Falt'ring of my
　　Tongue ———
My Fortune, whether art thou fled! Wretch!
　　Wretch!

　　　　　　　　　　　　　　　Madness,

Madnefs, Defpair, are link'd with the Remem-
    brance
Of what I was, and am. Is there, my Friends,
An Object now that I can fee or love;
That I can talk to, or can hear with Comfort?
All, all is now Defpair. Hence with a Tyrant,
An execrable Villain, doom'd to be
Abhor'd by Gods and Men.
———————— Perifh the Wretch,
That in the frightful Defart, where expos'd
And bound I lay, preferv'd this hateful Life.
O barbarous Pity, what a Cup of Sorrow
Had I and mine ne'er tafted, but for thee!
A Father's Murder ne'er had ftain'd my
    Hands,
Nor had my Love defil'd a Mother's Bed ———
I'm giddy when I view my Depth of Guilt.
Both, both my Parents ruin'd! — and by me!
Who have a Brood by her who gave me Life.

This is the Language of Nature when fhe
finks under Calamity. Nothing can be more
diftant from *quaint Phrafe* and *Witticifm.*
We have five other Inftances of the lively
and fimple Expreffion of Grief in the Characters of *Hercules* and *Philocletes.*

If Mr. *Racine*, who had ftudied the great
Models of Antiquity, had formed a Plan of
a *French* Tragedy upon the Subject of *OEdipus*, in the Manner of *Sophocles*, without any
fubornate Intrigue of Love, and in the *Greek*
Sim-

Simplicity, fuch an Entertainment muft have been curious, affecting, rapid, and interesting. It might not indeed have been applauded, but it muft have commanded the Affections, and poured forth the Tears. No breathing Time muft have been left. A Love for Virtue, and a Horror for Crimes, muft have rufhed upon the Soul. In fhort, it muft have had all the Effects defigned by the moft wholefome Laws. It could have given no Alarms even to the Purity of Religion itfelf. All that was neceffary, was to cut off the falfe and the improper Ornaments.

The Narrownefs of our Verfification, and the frequent Returns of Rhime oftentimes oblige our beft Poets, for the fake of a Jingle, to load their Lines with Epithets. In order to make one good Verfe, they tag it to another poor one. For Inftance, I am charmed when I read thefe Words:

——————————— *Let him die.*

But it puts me out of all Patience, when that Line introduces another to this Purpofe,

Or with a brave Defpair gain Victory.

This unnatural Bombaft is really difgufting; it can convey to us no Idea of Men who

who are engaged in ferious, noble, and paf-
fionate Converfation. When Probability is
taken away, the Spectator lofes all the Pleafure of the Entertainment. I own that the
Ancients a little exalted the Strain of the
Bufkin:

An Tragica diffævit & ampullatur in Arte.
Horat. Epift. I. Ep. iii. v. 14.

But he never could mean that the Bufkin
fhould deviate from the Imitation of true
Nature. It is her's to give us a beautiful and
a great Reprefentation of her: But ftill a
Man ought to fpeak as a Man. Nothing is
more ridiculous than for a Hero, in the greateft
Actions of his Life, not to join an unaffected
Simplicity to the Grandeur and Strength of
Expreffion,

Projicit ampullas, & Sefquipedalia Verba.
Horat. Art. Poet. v. 97.

It is fufficient to make *Agamemnon* haughty, *Achilles* fierce, *Ulyffes* wife, and *Medæa*
furious; but a pompous and bombaft fpoils
the whole; and the greater the Characters, or
the ftronger the Paffions one would reprefent
are, the more he ought to ftudy a noble irre-
fiftible Simplicity.

I can't help thinking that too bombaft
Speeches are often put in the Mouths of
Romans: It is indeed true that their Thoughts
had fomewhat of a noble Elevation, but they
always chofe to exprefs them in a natural

S 3 and

and eafy Manner. Tho they were, in *Virgil*'s Phrafe, * *Populum late Regem*, a People whofe Power and Conquefts were very extenfive, yet they were as calm and moderate in expreffing themfelves in Converfation, as they were induftrious in fubduing thofe Nations who were jealous of their Power.

> *Parcere Subjectis, & debellare Superbos.*
> *Virg.* Æneid VI. v. 853.

Horace has in other Words drawn the fame Picture of them.

> *Imperet Bellonte prior, jacentem lenis in hoftem.*
> Carm. Sæcul. v. 51, 52.

There feems not to be a fufficient Agreement betwixt the Language of *Auguftus* in the Tragedy of *Cinna*, and that modeft Simplicity with which *Sueton* adorns all his Actions and Behaviour; for he left in *Rome* fo great an Appearance of the ancient Liberty of the Common-Wealth, that he would not be called *Lord*. *Sueton*'s Account of him runs thus: " Not only by his Autho-
" rity, but even by his Countenance, he
" checked this infolent Flattery, and next
" Day

Virg. Æneid 1. v. 25.

" Day made a very severe Edict against it;
" nor after this would he suffer himself to
" be stiled MY LORD, no not by his Chil-
" dren and Grand-children, either in Jest or
" in Earnest. ———— During his Consul-
" ship he walked generally on Foot; and
" when not Consul, he often appeared
" in an open Chair, and received even the
" Compliments of the most promiscuous
" Mob. ———— In every Election of
" Magistrates he went about with his three
" Candidates, and sollicited in the accu-
" stomed Manner. He likewise gave his
" Vote in the Tribe, like one of the People.
" ——— He trained up his Daughter and
" Grand-daughter in Spinning and House-
" wifry. ———— He lodged in an ordinary
" House belonging to *Hortensius*, remarkable
" neither for its Largeness nor its Ornaments,
" the Galleries of it being very short: ———
" Famed neither for Statues nor fine Walks;
" and for forty Years he lay in the same
" Chamber both Summer and Winter. ———
" His Frugality, with regard to Furniture,
" appears from the Beds and Tables he left
" behind him, most of which scarce came
" up to the Elegance of a private Gentle-
" man. ———— His Supper consisted only
" of three, or at most, six Dishes, not of
" the most sumptuous kind, but given with
" the most social Benevolence. ——— His

Dress

" Dreſs was generally home-ſpun, and made
" by his Wife, his Siſter, his Daughter, and
" Grand-daughters. —— He eat very little,
" and what he did eat, was for the moſt
" Part ordinary Food."

Pomp and Shew did not ſo well agree
with what they called *Roman Politeneſs,* as
with the Luxury of a *Perſian* Monarch.
Notwithſtanding the Severity of *Tiberius,* and
the ſervile Turn for Flattery the *Romans* had
in his Time and under his Succeſſors, yet
Pliny informs us that *Trajan* even then behaved like a good Fellow Citizen, and lived
in an amiable Familiarity with thoſe about
him. The Anſwers of this Emperor are
ſhort, ſimple, void of Ambiguity, and free
from the ſmalleſt Tincture of the Bombaſt †.
All we read of the *Romans* in *Titus Livius,*
Plutarch, and in *Cicero,* repreſents them as
Men of an elevated Turn of Thought, but
ſimple, natural, and modeſt in their Expreſſions. They bear no Reſemblance to the
ſtiff and over-grown Heroes of our Romances. A great Man ſhould not declaim
like a Player; but ſhould neverthleſs uſe
ſtrong and plain Words in his Converſation:
He ſhould ſay nothing low; but at the ſame
time he ſhould ſay nothing *affected* or *bombaſt.*   *Ne*

---

† The Bas-reliefs on his Pillar repreſented him in the
moſt modeſt Poſture, even when at the Head of his Army.

Ne Quicumq; Deus, Quicumq; adhibebitur
    Heros,
Regali Conspectus in Auro nuper & ostro,
Migret in obscuras humili Sermone Tabernas,
Aut dum vitat humum, Nubes & Inania captet,
Ut festis, &c.
      Horat. Art. Poet. v. 227 & Sequ.

The Sublime of Tragedy ought not to
hinder Heroes themselves from speaking with
a Simplicity adapted to the Nature of the
Subjects on which they talk to one another.

Et Tragicus plerumq; dolet Sermone pedestri.

CRITICISMS *upou* CATO, *by an* Anonymous Friend.

NOT only I myself, but all my Countrymen who have reaped any Advantage from the Progress of our Poetry, ought
to acknowledge the Obligations we lie under
to Mr. *Gottsched,* who has chalked out to us
the Road (if I may so speak) of *Tragedy.*
Should I attempt to give him all the Praises
his Merit deserves, my Abilities would be
unequal to the Task. However, tho' I am
surprized at his Perfections, (which I am
                    forced

forced to pafs over in Silence) yet I can't help owning that I have found fome Things in his *Cato* which I look upon as fmall Blemifhes.

This Author, who fo much blames the empty Scenes in the *Englifh Cato*, has done his beft to avoid the fame Fault. The Expedient he ufes for this Purpofe is, *Naming the Perfon who next appears*, as *Cato comes, He appears*. In the four firft Acts, confifting fome of two, and fome of three Scenes, he endeavours to extricate himfelf from *that Difficulty*, by this Stratagem, which I don't like, becaufe, in my Opinion, it does not repair the Lofs arifing from the Scenes being empty.

As the Rules of the Drama make it neceffary to let the Spectators into the Character of the chief Heroes of the Tragedy, our Poet makes *Arfene* defcribe to *Phenice* the true Character of *Cato* very fully. But becaufe this happens juft as *Cato* enters, and their Difcourfe lafts a confiderable Time after he makes his Appearance, it is not probable but *Cato* muft have heard fome Part, which might have been avoided by his not entering fo foon.

Two of my Friends are of my Opinion that *Cæfar*, as characterized in this Tragedy, is more reafonable than *Cato*. *Cato* is blameable for rejecting every Propofal with fo much

much Obftinacy, and prefenting himfelf to the polite *Cæfar* in a harfh, furly, nay, next to clownifh Manner: For Example, in the third Scene of the fourth Act, Cæfar *afks* Cato *what the* Roman *Senate in* Utica *wifhed for?* Cato anfwers, *That that fhould befall thee with which thou threatneft her*; that is to fay, Thy *Ruin*, thy *Overthrow*, and in fine, thy *Death*. Some Foreigners have faid, *It was not to be wondered at if* Cæfar *loft all Patience*.

As to *Cæfar* and *Cato*'s being reprefented equally great, what follows in the fame Scene is a Proof of it, and in my Opinion, from the Sentiments of both, one may fay of *Cæfar* and of *Cato*, what was faid in *France* of the *Alexander* and *Porus* of *Racine*, *Either* Cæfar *is too great for* Cato, *or* Cato *too diminutive for* Cæfar; both the one and the other is a Stranger to true Grandeur; for *Cæfar* is too thirfty of Power, and *Cato* too ftiff in Principle.

Pharnaces and *Porcius* fometimes ufe very trifling Expreffions; I have likewife obferved that *Porcius*, whofe Character is elfewhere well enough fuftained, fays fomething out of Character in the laft Scene. He propofes that the Corps of his Father fhould be prefented to *Cæfar* with a View to move his Pity. He muft have by this time forgot the Advice of his Father, when dying; *But thou fhalt ſhalt never aſk a Favour at the Hands of thy Enemy, and ſhalt never neglect any thing for the Liberty of* Rome. I think he would have, with more Propriety, made *Cato*'s Son ſay every thing that could encourage the reſt of his Friends to take Advantage of the News they heard of *Pompey*, and promiſe, if the Exigency required, to imitate his Father by dying, rather than abandon them.

The Author of the *German Cato* finds Fault with the *Engliſh* Performance, becauſe in it the Actors make their Entrances and Exits without the Spectators knowing why; but in my Opinion he himſelf has fallen into the ſame Fault, at leaſt in one Place: For in the fifth Scene of the Second Act *Porcius* appears upon the Stage with *Arſene*, to whom he thus eagerly ſpeaks, *Princeſs, be not uneaſy about your Safety; ſhould all periſh,* Porcius *ſhall be thy Friend. Tread in your Father's Footſteps, by protecting Innocence. Give but the Word, and my Sword ſhall be unſheath'd in your Defence.* At theſe Words *Arſene* turns her Back upon the Defender of her Liberty, and goes off without ſpeaking one Syllable; I could never be reconciled to this dumb Departure.

In ſhort I think *Cato* in one Place ſpeaks a little out of Character. In the third Scene of the Firſt Act, when he receives the News of his Daughter's being alive, he burſts out into

into thefe Expreffions ; *How? What? My Child alive? What do you fay?* This fure is not the fame *Cato,* who when he faw the Corps of his Son, appeared fo calm, that one would have rather thought him tranfported with Joy, than depreft with Sorrow.

As for the Verfification I fhall only obferve that *you* is often ufed inftead of the *thou*; but I remember to have read in a Performance of the fame Mr. *Gottfched,* that even in Profe Dialogues we ought rather to ufe the *Tu* of the *Latins,* than fpeak in the Plural Number like the *French* and *Germans,* who, one would think, were addreffing themfelves to a Dozen of People. Thus I believe he might lawfully (according to his own Obfervation) make Ufe of the *Tu,* fince the Characters are *Roman.* Thefe few Remarks I have made in running over *Cato,* (which in other Refpects is an excellent Performance) without any Intention to detract from the real Merit of its Author.

The Author's Anfwer *to the above* CRITICISM.

THIS Tragedy has had the good Fortune to fall into the Hands of able Critics, nay, in fome meafure, to meet with Applaufe.

Applaufe. I therefore don't at all repent the Pains it has coft me, and I am infinitely obliged to any Gentleman who fhall communicate to me his own, or his Friend's Sentiments.

I never imagined that either an *Epic* or *Dramatic* Poem can be quite faultlefs. Human Imperfection will not admit of Perfection in the fmalleft Pieces of Poetry; therefore we can't flatter ourfelves to think it can enter into Works of greater Importance and Extent. *Homer*, who, by the Confeffion of all the World, has produced two Mafterpieces in his *Iliad* and *Odiffey*, and who was fo much admired by *Horace*, is by the fame *Horace* owned fometimes to have flept, tho' in the following Verfe he defends him.

" *Verum Opere in Longo Fas eft obrepere*
  " *Somnum.*"

" But in a Work of confiderable Length it
" is pardonable fometimes to fleep."

He has even before obferved, that there are Faults which may be overlooked by a Poet, even when he has fucceeded in the greateft Part of his Work.

Sunt delicta tamen, quibus ignoviffe velimus.

Yet

Yet there are some Faults of such a Nature, that they may be pardoned by us.

This my learned Critic has undoubtedly had in his View, when he deigned to honour my *Cato* with his Remarks; for I am persuaded that the great Gentleness with which he has treated this Attempt in Tragedy, has prevailed with him to overlook more considerable Faults than these he has marked. Therefore, if I shall answer his learned Criticisms, it can never be thought to be with a View of vindicating myself entirely, nor to make the World believe that what he has criticized ought to pass for Beauties. No, I am not so much bewitched by Self-love; I own, and am sincerely conscious, that I am liable to Faults. Let me be allowed however to advance somewhat in my own Defence, and to intermix it with some Reflections which may revive a Taste for Dramatic Poetry.

The first Fault I am charged with, is not without Foundation; for one may easily perceive a Fault in another, yet be guilty of the same himself. *Horace* says,

In vitium ducit culpæ fuga, si caret arte.

I own that I have too often repeated this Connection of the Scene, *I see him coming, He appears*, &c. and it is only the Repetition
that

that makes the Fault, for the Thing itself is none. When two Actors are upon the Stage, and one of them sees another coming up, for him to say *I see him, or there is the Man I expected, or I hope he has not over-heard us,* is no Fault. This I can prove by the Example of our best Dramatic Poets. *Peter Corneille* in his *Cid,* Act III, Scene I, makes *Elvira,* who sees *Chimene* coming, say, *She returns. She comes. I see her* ‡ .

I believe the Reader will dispense with more Examples either from *Corneille* or other Poets, for they are easily to be met with every where: I have brought the Examples from the best Piece of *Corneille* on Purpose; for it is certain when he wrote that, he was unacquainted with the only true Connection of the Scenes in which he has been so often defective

---

‡ Our Author here brings five Examples from the *Cid;* but we are to remark that the Poet has distinguished this Connection of Scenes into two Kinds. The first of the Actor who enters, which connects the Conversation with those on the Stage: The second of the Actor who comes in unexpectedly, and makes the other retire. But the Examples which the Poet has cited in his Answer, and which I did not think proper to be inserted here, because all the World knew them, are all Examples of the first kind ; and it is very easy to prove in such a Case that there is no Fault in naming the Actors who enter. As to the second Case, which is that of the Actor who comes on the Stage, and who occasions those who are already on it to make their Exit, which is the principal Point, we shall see how he proves that this Connection of the Scenes does not leave the Stage empty.

defective in many Respects. How often does it happen, that two Actors don't see one another, and other two appear without knowing why? But *Corneille*, without knowing the Rule for the Connection of Scenes, or without chusing to follow it, has put into the Mouths of his Characters the Connections we have seen, and in the natural Method we have quoted; and pray why may not I do the same in *Cato?* *

As to the second Remark of my Article, he seems to think, that the Recital made by

T *Arsene*,

---

* In my Opinion, the Author defends himself very weakly upon this Point. All the World knows, he speaks true; but it was of this second Kind of Connection of Scenes, rather than that of the first, that he ought to have given us Examples. After all, tho' he really gave us these Examples, he was not authorized to follow them at the Expence of good Sense. It is very probable, that two Actors, in seeing a third come up, by whom they would be neither seen nor heard, should leave the Stage in naming him aloud; but he is not named only, that the Scenes do not remain empty: and it is not ordered by *Aristotle*, that this Connection should be accounted a just one. Let us examine the *OEdipus* of *Sophocles*, which the same *Aristotle* gives us as a Model, thro' the whole of his Art of Poetry, and we shall find none of those Connections of Scenes. From the Beginning to the End, all the Actors who appear have a Reason for their doing so, and the Scene never remains empty. This is the Rule for the Connection of Scenes, and these, who for their own Ease have found out another, are much to be blamed. Our Poet has for his Vindication produced Examples of this new Rule, which will never gain Credit with Posterity, unless an universal Corruption should prevail; for, as I said before, it is repugnant to good Sense, and our Masters in this way will not admit of it.

Arſene, to deſcribe the Character of *Cato*, is defective, becauſe that Actreſs, after declaring the Arrival of *Cato*, goes on in her Recital in ſuch a Manner, as that *Cato* muſt have heard her. Theſe are her Words: Phenice, *don't you ſee how the Splendor of his Wiſdom ſhines, even amidſt his Grief! Admire then that Hero to whom no Mortal is comparable. The Gods have in vain ſtruck him with reiterated Blows of adverſe Fortune. He yet remains firm and unſhaken, and boldly encounters their Wrath by his Conſtancy.*

I agree that on a ſhort and narrow Theatre, ſuch as that of *Leipſic*, *Cato* coming ſlowly up, might have heard ſome of theſe Words: But upon a larger Theatre, ſuch as that of the Elector of *Dreſden*, this could not be the Caſe, and the Actreſs might have ended her Speech before he was within hearing. If we ſuppoſe that a Man, ſo ſage and venerable as *Cato*, ought not to enter the Stage running, in the time that eight Verſes were repeating, he may reaſonably be ſuppoſed to make twelve or fifteen Steps before he came ſo near as to hear her.

But tho' one ſhould ſuppoſe that *Cato* hears a Part of *Arſene*'s Diſcourſe, what Harm can ariſe from that? Perhaps ſhe does it on Purpoſe to let him know the high Notion ſhe had of his Virtue; and one can't reaſonably conclude that it is from a Principle

ple of Flattery she commends *Cato* when he appears, or from her thinking that he hears her, becaufe she begins his Encomium with the Scene, and before he appears. Therefore neither the Rules of the Stage, nor of Probability, can be violated.

As to the third Remark of my Critic, it indeed affects the very Effentials of Dramatic Poetry. It is certain that the principal Character in the Play ought to be moft ftrongly marked; and the Poet ought likewife to endeavour all he can to intereft the Audience in its Favour, that it may be the Object of all their Cares and Compaffion. This is the Rule in which I am faid to fail, and if the Charge is true, it is no doubt a monftrous Blunder.

To vindicate myfelf in this Particular, I might inftance Mr. *Defchamp*, who has done the fame thing in his *Cato*. But that can't avail me; and it may be told me that I ought not blindly to follow the Miftakes of my Original; I muft therefore vindicate myfelf by Arguments *à priori*, and prove that in my Tragedy *Cato* is much greater than *Cæfar*; and if this laft appears as at firft great as *Cato*, his Greatnefs ferves only to add to that of the principal Hero.

For this Purpofe we are previoufly to remark that the Character of a Hero confifts in Patriotifm, in a virtuous Magnanimity;

nor can a Love of Power, nor Tyranny difguifed in the Shape of Virtue, pafs for *true
Greatnefs*. For inftance, *Marcus Aurelius* is
forced to make War for the Happinefs and
Safety of his Country. He is deftitute of
Money, and rather than opprefs the *Romans*
with a Tax, he puts up to Sale his moft precious and richeft Moveables: The Senators
and Citizens flaunting and fhowing away in
his Royal Spoils and Imperial Equipage,
give him no Concern, provided he can beat
the Enemy without impoverifhing his Subjects: He pardons the Life of *Caffius*, who
had rebelled againft him, and intercedes
with the Senate for his Wife and Children.
Nero, on the contrary, affects a boundlefs
Magnificence; he diverts the City with pompous Entertainments, but it is with the
Money of the Citizens and People, and the
Plunder of the Exiled and Profcribed. He
refufes, it is true, to fign one Dead Warrant,
but he wifhes the *Roman* People had but one
Neck, that he might cut it off at a Stroke.
There is not a Man who will not prefer the
Poverty of *Marcus Aurelius* to the Magnificence of *Nero*; and the Interceffion of the
one for the Offender, to the Pity of the
other for the Criminal.

Thefe very characteriftical Differences are
found betwixt *Cæfar* and *Cato*. *Cato* is
greater thro' Misfortunes. *Cæfar* dazzles by

a

a political Clemency; but this Virtue is coun-
terfeit, and at the bottom a Paſſion for Revenge and Power. The Pardon he offers is
but a Snare to entangle the Oppoſition to his
Views. *Cato*, on the other hand, will have
nothing for himſelf, but all for *Rome*; and
if he can't obtain her Freedom, he chuſes to
die. *Cæſar* offers him Favours, but he rejects
them all without the Liberty of his Country.
This *Cæſar* refuſes to comply with ; and
Cato deſparing to force him into a Compli-
ance, reſolves to kill himſelf.

Is not unfortunate Virtue infinitely greater
than the Happineſs ariſing from the Tinſel
Virtue of *Cæſar ?* *Cato*, it is true, is obſti-
nate ; but ought not the Hero of a Tragedy
to have ſome Faults to excite our Compaſſion ? This is taught us by *Ariſtotle.* Was
not *OEdipus* in ſome manner the Cauſe of
his own Misfortune, when by his unaccoun-
table Raſhneſs he killed his Father, tho'
without knowing him? Did not the Rage
and Fury of *Oreſtes* occaſion the Murder of
his own Mother, a Thing which to him
proved the fruitful Source of Woe? Is not
Phedra to be blamed for her own Death,
ſince ſhe declares her Love for *Hippolitus*
to her Confident, and even before the Chorus? It is then neceſſary that ſome Part of
Cato's Misfortunes ſhould be owing to his
own Faults, which in his Circumſtances can

only

only happen from an Obſtinacy, either the Effect of Stoical Philoſophy, or his own Conſtitution. But ſtill Compaſſion prevails; he is ſo virtuous, ſo diſintereſted, ſo zealous for the Good of his Country, ſo unſhaken under his Misfortunes, ſo magnanimous, ſo upright, that one muſt admire, love, and pity him in Death. If *Cato* had been perfect and faultleſs, the Spectators muſt have been unaffected with his Fate. It is objected to me, that my way of ſpeaking and thinking is low, and ill adapted to the Characters. This Obſervation is really of the higheſt Importance; and I don't know if I ſhall be able to clear myſelf of the Charge. The common Opinion is, that the Stile of Tragedy ought to be very lofty and ſublime; but I don't know if they who think ſo have not adopted this Maxim by reading *Seneca*'s Tragedies, who is always ſo lofty, even upon the moſt common Subjects, that he loſes Sight of Nature and Probability, and has already been ſo much blamed by the moſt learned Poets, that we ought to take for our Models the Tragic Authors of *Greece*, who make Uſe of noble and unaffected Expreſſions, but never of Thoughts that are forced or bombaſt.

The modern *French* Poets have been found fault with upon this Account in a very lively Manner by *Riccoboni*, in his *Diſſertation*

upon

upon Modern Tragedy, and by an anonymous *Italian* Writer, in a Piece intitled, *Paragone Della Poesia Tragica* ; as also by Mr. *Bocelli*, in the Preface of *Merope de Maffei*. That these three Foreigners should condemn the *French* Tragedians for this Fault, does not seem strange to me ; for Mr. *Fenelon* in his Thoughts upon Dramatic Poetry, which I have subjoined to my Tragedy, has blamed them for the same Fault. *Father Brumoy*, in his *Theatre of the Greeks*, does the same in many Passages ; and *Horace* had done it long before him in these Words:

Et Tragicus plerumq; dolet, &c.

Thus the Tragic Poet ought to make *Telephus* speak in a simple Stile. When he represents him as an exiled and misfortunate Prince, he ought to banish from him the Sublimity of Language, and every thing swelling either in the Thoughts or in the Expressions, if he would move the Spectator to Compassion. This *Seneca* did not believe. And this *Lohenstein* did not advert to † .

Probability is the true Rule for the Tragic

T 4   Stile,

---

† An excellent *German* Poet, who lived at the Time of the first Reformation of that Stage.

Stile, and the Poet is indispensably obliged to stick close to Nature, according to *Horace*,

Respicere Exemplar vitæ Morumq; jubebo Doctum Imitatorem, & veras hinc ducere Voces.

How should I have observed this Rule, if I had made young *Porcius* speak like *Cato*, or like the low-spirited head-strong and malicious *Pharnaces*, or like *Cæsar?* Must not the Difference of their Characters appear in their Conversation? The Personages in Tragedy are not all Poets, nor can they talk and think in the artificial Manner of *Seneca* and *Lohenstein*, who are condemned by all the World. No! they are Men who talk a Language agreeable to their State, their Age, their Sex, their Fortune, and their Character, left, as *Horace* has beautifully observed,

——————————— Forte Seniles Mandentur Juveni Partes, Pueroq; Viriles; Semper in Adjunctis Ævoq; morabitur aptis.

This I believe may be a sufficient Answer to the first Exception of my Critic upon this Head. As to the Expressions of *Porcius* and *Pharnaces*, which are thought too low, I answer, That in the last Scene *Porcius* resembles himself no more, since he has forgot his

his former Courage, and propofes that his
Father's Body fhould be carried to *Cæfar* in
thefe Words: " Come, carry the dead Body
" into *Cæfar*'s Prefence, we don't know but
" his unrelenting Heart may be moved,
" when he fees that *Hero bathed in his own*
" *Blood.*" In effect, *Porcius* is no more like
himfelf. Neither can we fuppofe him to be
fo, confidering his Youth and Circumftances;
for if I had made him like his Father, how
would he have refembled a young Man? Or
how fhould I have obferved *Horace*'s Rule
with regard to the Character of Youth, the
Fiercenefs, the tumultuous Paffions, and the
Inconftancy of which he has beautifully defcribed in one Line,

Sublimis, Cupidufq; & amata relinquere Pernix.

Thefe three Qualities are very plainly difcovered in *Porcius.* He is fierce and head-
ftrong, while his Father was alive, to fupport
him, and it is for this Reafon that he oppofes
Pharnaces with fo much Warmth and Keen-
nefs: His Paffion for *Arfene* is impetuous,
and in the end he proves inconftant: For
after having anfwered, with a noble Refolution, that he would never difregard the In-
ftructions his Father gave him, nor fail to
follow the Courfe of Life he had prefcribed
him, he quits this laudable Defign, and ftruck
with

with the Death of his Father, endeavours to gain *Cæfar* by the mildeft Meafures. This is the true Character of fuch a young Man as Nature and Experience prefent.

I am likewife blamed with committing the fame Fault with which I have charged Mr. *Addifon*, by making *Arfene* in the third Scene of the fecond Act leave *Porcius*, who promifes to defend her againft *Pharnaces*, without anfwering one fingle Word. But is there any thing furprizing in this, efpecially when fhe fees *Pharnaces* coming up, her Brother's Murderer, and her own hated Lover; in fine, a Man whom fhe induftri-oufly fhuns?

My Critic farther objects to me, that I have altered the Character of *Cato*, efpecially in the Paffage where he rejoices at finding his Daughter alive, after he had believed her dead. He fays that *Cato* ought not to be fo tranfported as to enquire about her Life four times, as he does. But I afk, whether *Cato*, in fpight of all his Philofophy, is not ftill a Man? The Stoics never maintained that the Affection of a Father ought to be quite ftifled. The Emperor *Marcus Aurelius* fhed Tears for the Death of his Mafters; and when fome of his Courtiers afked him if fuch a Conduct became an Emperor as well as a Philofopher, he anfwered them, *Allow me for once, I befeech you, to be a Man as well*

as

as an Emperor. Why might not *Cato* have the same Privilege granted him? The Stoics prepared themselves to encounter the most terrible Calamities of human Life; and it is partly for this Reason, and partly because his Son *Marcus* has fallen so gloriously, that *Cato* hears the News of it with so little Emotion, and even with an Air of Pleasure; but all the Philosophy in the World can't have such an Effect upon a Father, as to make him quite unconcerned when he hears that his Daughter, whom he believed dead, is still alive. In this Case *Cato* ought to be allowed to give way to the Sentiments of Humanity.

Besides, if I had made any of the Personages in my Tragedy address one another in a clownish rustic Manner, I believe our *Germans* would have been highly shocked at it. In fine, if we heard an Inferior say, *As for thee, my Prince,* &c. or a Son to his Father, *I will tell thee, my Father,* we could not have bore it, and this has made me endeavour to light upon an agreeable Medium, by serving myself alternately, and as the Case required, of the *you* and the *thou.* I must nevertheless confess, that it had been better, had I always used the latter; if I was after this to write a Tragedy, I should lay it down as a Rule to myself, *always to make Use of it, and likewise to imitate the noble Simplicity of the ancient Manners* to recommend them to the Stage; but others will perfect what I have so weakly laid the Foundation of.

——————— *Fungar Vice cotis, acutum Reddere quæ ferrum valet, exors ipsa secandi.*

There are also added the Author's Answers *to some* Criticisms *that were made upon him after his Letter was printed; wherein he very handsomly defends himself for not making* C A T O *die altogether, according to Historical Truth. The* Critic *would have wished that he had tore out his very Intrails; and our Poet, upon just Grounds, shews the Impossibility of doing so, even in Ricital.*

I FLATTER myself I have not judged amiss, when at the Beginning I said People might reap some Advantage from the Reflections of Mr. *Gottsched*, which to me appear very solid. And as for the Public, tho' it should only learn, that in *Germany* Authors think as justly as in any other Nation, and that the Theatre, and the Laws of it are as well known there as elsewhere, yet I hope it will think this an useful Piece of Knowledge.

I

I thought it would be agreeable to the Public to give fome Account of the Number and Nature of the Pieces wrote by *Hannf-fach*, the firft Dramatic Poet who appeared in *Germany*, as alfo of the Works of *Opitz*, *Gryphius*, and *Lohenftein*, whom I have already mentioned, and a Catalogue of whofe Works I fhall hereafter add for the Reader's Satisfaction.

The

The Design proposed by the first Writers of Greek TRAGEDY. *The Rise, Progress, and Ruin of* Italian TRAGEDY. *Of the* New Italian TRAGEDY.

WITHOUT repeating what has been often said of the Original of Tragedy, it is sufficient for my present Purpose that I explain the Purposes for which the ancient *Greeks*, its Inventors, designed it.

One thing is plain, that every *Greek* Tragedy had two Purposes; one of the Fable, the other of the Poet. The first had stated Rules, as it served to mend the Heart, and regulate the Passions; the other to correct the State, and improve political Virtues. For Instance, in the *Palamedes* of *Euripides*, the End which the Poet proposed was to put the Injustice of the Sentence of the *Athenians* against *Socrates*, upon the Accusations of *Annitus* and *Aristophanes*, into a strong Light, by representing the Persecutions of *Palamedes* by *Ulysses*: Hence it happened that *Aristophanes*, to be revenged upon *Euripides*,

Euripides, who had expofed him in his Tragedy, wrote his Comedy of the *Frogs*, which
is a Satyr on the *Tragic Poet*.

We have no reafon to doubt that the *Greek*
Poets, in their Tragedies, had it in View to
excite and keep alive the public Deteftation
of Tyranical Government, then fo abhorred
by the *Athenians*; and on that Account they
have reprefented the Vices of Princes as the
fruitful Sources of all the Calamities attending their Royal Families. It is true that
Ariftotle, who lived fo near the Times of
thefe *Dramatic* Poets, would have over-
looked, or been ignorant of the Purpofes I
have mentioned, if they really had any fuch
Meaning.

But this Objection may be anfwered, by
obferving that the Defign of the Poet, to
correct or counfel the Government, was kept
as fecret and dark as poffible, left he might
have irritated the Adminiftration by his
Liberties in Writing. Befides we may eafily
conceive that *Ariftotle*, who was the Tutor
of *Alexander*, the Mafter and Enflaver of
Greece, had the Glory and Intereft of his
Mafter too much at Heart, or perhaps was
too dextrous a Courtier, to tell the World
that the End of all Tragic Poets was to create an Abhorrence of Kings; and that they
never met with fo univerfal Applaufe, as
when

when they reprefented Princes in the moft odious Colours.

After the *Greeks*, the *Romans* compofed Tragedies, but without any other Aim than to tranfport to *Rome* all the *Greek* Arts and Sciences; the *Italians* and *French* likewife have wrote Tragedies, but without having any political Ends in View; they having wrote them purely as public Entertainments, proper to make their Countrymen Sharers of the Diverfions common in other Countries.

Before Tragedy appeared in *Italy*, which was about the Year 1520, the *Italians*, for the fifteenth Century, had been ufed to fee frequent Reprefentations of the Paffions of *Chrift*, the Lives of Martyrs, and of Virgins; but thefe Shews were commonly played only during Lent, and in Churches. And as the Spectators repaired to them from a Principle of Devotion, when the Reprefentation was over they were charmed to feel the Emotions of Grief and Tendernefs in their Hearts; which they looked upon as a Proof of their Senfibility for the Truths of their Religion.

But, excepting thefe Times of Lamentation and Mourning, the *Italians* had no other View in feeing a Play, but to laugh and amufe themfelves. The firft Poets who exhibited Tragedies to the People, having fent the Spectators home melancholy and
grieved,

grieved, the Public was foon weary of this new kind of Diverfion: The Authors of thofe Pieces upon cruel Subjects, not reflecting that the political Views of the *Greek* Poets in the Cataftrophes which they wrought up before the Eyes of a Republic, the jealous Enemy of Tyrants, could have no Place among the *Italians*, a People, whofe Government was more regular, and their Manners more gentle. However, Tragedy kept its Footing for fome Time in *Italy*, by the Pleafure which that Lettered Age took in feeing the ancient Reprefentations revived. Men of Learning had before their Eyes only the wonderful Productions of the *Greek* and *Latin* Poets: But the Heavy and the Dull, on whom, in *Italy*, the Succefs of a Play depends, being infenfible of this Pleafure, Tragedy was foon loft, and exhibited only at Feafts, on Occafion of the Births and Marriages of their great Men. But now the World is quite weary of them, they being thought very improper for public Rejoycings, and Comedies are fubftituted in their Place, as I have faid elfewhere.

Treffino, whofe Ideas were commonly very juft, was the firft who prefented a Tragedy in the *Italian* Language: He chofe a well-known Subject, becaufe he wanted that the Spectators fhould be well acquainted with it. I believe the Reafon of his taking a Fable

U   from

from Hiftory, rather than one of his own Invention, in which he was very fruitful, was to prevent Criticifms upon his Undertaking.

I fhall not here enter into the common Queftion, whether a Poet, in writing a Tragedy, ought to adopt a hiftorical or a fabulous Plot. *Caftell-vetro* has treated that Subject fo copioufly, that I fhall prefume to fay nothing after fo great a Man. *Treffino* exhibited the firft Tragedy, and chofe *Sophonifba*. The Action and Cataftrophe are entirely hiftorical: For that Princefs dies by the Poifon fent her by *Mafiniffa*. The Action is interefting, and very proper to move; but not of fo horrible a Nature as to oblige the Spectators to leave the Play-houfe with melancholy Looks and diftorted Features. If the Dramatic Authors, who followed him, had imitated him in this Tragedy, they might have not only got Footing, but might have flourifhed to a great Degree in *Italy*. But Men of Learning, at that Time, probably judged that this Tragedy was no Pattern to copy after; and in comparing it with *Greek* Originals, they perhaps did not find enough of Blood and Murder in it. They were fond of copying exactly after the *Greek* Poets, and even wanted to improve upon them: And fince the Time of *Treffino* we have feen *Lorbeche del Giraldi*, *La Semiramide del Manfredi*

Manfredi, la Canace di Speron Speroni, and a great many others which have frightned the *Italian* Spectators out of their Wits.

If one were at Pains to compare the Tragedies I have named, together with fome others, with the *Greek* Tragedies, one might there fee an exact Imitation of the *Greek* Originals, and confequently they muft be owned to be complete Tragedies. It is true that at prefent, becaufe the Stile has nothing of the Bombaft, and becaufe their Maxims and Sentiments are quite fimple and natural, the *French,* and even fome *Italians,* refufed to look upon them as Tragedies.

The Tragedies which continued in *Italy* for the following Age, remained buried in the general Corruption of Learning. Since that Time it has never recovered; and if very rarely fome *Italians* write a Tragedy, it is quite neglected. Among all the Tragedies wrote fince the Year 1620, I believe we cannot find a complete Model, for if any of them have Beauties, thefe Beauties are mingled with very great Imperfections. For Inftance, the *Ariftodemo of Dollori* is an excellent Tragedy, and upon the Stage has a wonderful Effect; but it is wrote in fo Lyric a Stile, that the Language is quite unfupportable: On the other hand, thofe who fucceed him to the Year 1700, and which are but few, are acknowledged by the learned

Men

Men of *Italy* themselves to have succeeded no better.

Since that Period, the *Italian* Theatre has taken a new Form. Mr. *Martelli* has wrote a good many Tragedies in Alexandrine Verses that rhime. These kind of Verses were at once both admired and censured, and are not unknown in *Italy*, because they are two Verses of seven Syllables joined together; and because we have some ancient Stanzas of a *Sicilian* Poet's Verses of the same Measure, which perhaps may give the Hint to the *French* Alexandrine; for this *Sicilian* is one of the most ancient Rhimers. Some time after, Mr. *Gravina* wrote five Tragedies; and the Marquis *de Maffer* brought his *Merope* upon the Stage: But hitherto the *Italians*, so far as appears, have never established any Standard with regard to Tragedy, that may be accommodated to our Age and Manners; the Form of the *French* Tragedy not being at all agreeable to their Taste, as I shall shew by and by.

Gravina has been perhaps too zealous an Imitator of the *Greeks:* But the Marquis *de Maffer* has not been so scrupulous upon this Head; tho' his *Merope*, as to its Fable, is *Greek*, yet it is accommodated to our Manners, so as not to offend the Spectators; and tho' in the *Action, Cresfonte* is bound, a Javelin brought to dispatch him, and *Merope*
introduced

introduced upon the Stage with a Hatchet in her Hand, all which have been blamed, yet thefe two Incidents have been applauded by every Audience in *Italy*, who have a Tafte for, and admire thefe ancient Manners. It is faid that the fame Author has wrote another Tragedy, which is now locked up in his Clofet. I don't doubt of its Excellence; and if it has not yet been brought on the Stage, it muft be owing to the *Italian* Players. For thefe ten Years they have played only wretched Tragi-Comedies; and having thrown up Tragedy, that Author is perhaps unwilling to truft his Piece with Actors who have fallen into a Defuetude of acting true Tragedy.

Of the Rife *and* Reformation *of* FRENCH TRAGEDY.

ITALIAN Tragedy began with the fixteenth Century, long before Tragedy appeared in *France*. If they who talk of *Italian* Tragedies, would be at Pains to compare them with the *French* of the fame Age, they will find the former grave, majeftic, wrote with Dignity, conceived with Good-fenfe, and exactly according to the fevereft

Rules

Rules of the Drama. On the other hand, we ſhall find the *French* confuſed and artleſs, languid in its Sentiments, improbable in the Fable, and irregular in its Conduct. In ſhort, if we compare the *French* with the *Italian* Tragedies, with regard to Stile, the *Italians* have this Advantage, that the Stile of their firſt Tragedies has never grown antiquated, while that of the *French* is become quite ſhocking, and entirely baniſhed the Stage. It is far otherwiſe in the Caſe of *Italian* Tragedy which began in the Age of *Petrarch*, who embelliſhed that Tongue with all its finiſhed Graces and Perfections: And I my-ſelf have, with Applauſe, played in 1712, in the *Sophoniſba* of *Treſſino*, and the *Oreſtes* of *Ruccelai*, who were their two moſt ancient Tragic Poets.

Peter Corneille reformed and brought the *French* Tragedy to its utmoſt Perfection. *Rotron* himſelf, who had trod the compleat Round of Theatrical Extravagance, when he ſaw the firſt Tragedy of *Corneille*, cor-rected his Faults, and compoſed his *Vin-ceſlaus*, which may be looked upon as a good Play. We may therefore call Monſieur *Cor-neille* the Father of the *French* Stage, nay, the very Inventor of *French* Tragedy; be-cauſe his Tragedies, thoſe of his Brother, thoſe of *Racine*, and of all ſucceeding Poets, reſemble neither the *Greek*, the *Latin*, the

Italian,

Italian, nor the ancient *French* Tragedy. But thefe great Men lived at a Time when the *French* Court was the Model of Gallantry, and the Pattern of Tafte.

They thought proper to foften the Severity of Tragedy, in order to recommend it to the Liking of their young King and Court ; and for this Purpofe they made Love the Mafter and Controuler of their Stage. I don't know if I fhould be much in the wrong, if I declare that *French* Tragedy is the elder Daughter of Romance, fince a romantic Strain is fo predominant thro' it all. This Tafte was then fo prevailing, that *Thomas Corneille,* in his *Timocrates,* has done nothing but copied *Calander.* In a fhort time Love became the Tyrant of their Stage, and their Dramatic Authors have forced it into Subjects not only where it was improper, but where I thought it impoffible it fhould have Place.

Mr. *Corneille,* by adapting the *OEdipus* of *Sophocles* to the *French* Stage, has altered the Originals, and in Place of *Creon* has introduced *Thefeus,* and given him a Miftrefs, that he may the more eafily work up fome whining Scenes. But before *Corneille,* I believe it never entered into any Man's Head, that it was proper to introduce Love into the *OEdipus* of *Sophocles.* Monfieur *de Voltaire,* in the fame Tragedy of *Sophocles,* has not

U 4   imitated

imitated *Corneille:* He has not introduced any ſtrange Characters into the Action, that they may talk of Love: However, not willing to be entirely defective in that Point, without which it is thought a Tragedy would be very unſucceſsful, Mr. *Voltaire* has not indeed added a Woman more than is in the Original *Greek*, but he introduces *Philocetes,* who he ſuppoſes was in Love with *Jocaſta,* before ſhe was married to *Laius.* And theſe two old Men, for ſurely they muſt have been old, are repreſented, as calling to Mind their paſt Amours.

Can we imagine that, in a Sacred Tragedy, the profane Love of *Polenetes* ſhould affect the Action of the Piece! In the Tragedy of the *Maccabees,* the young *Maccabee* loves a *Pagan* Woman, whom he wants to convert. That I may not run thro' all the Tragedies, I will cloſe, by inſtancing in that of *Sertorius,* in the firſt Recounter of that old General with young *Pompey,* after the moſt ſerious and political Reflections upon the State of the Public. Theſe two great Men finiſh this ſolemn Dialogue with a Diſſertation on their Love-Intrigues. I believe in the firſt Place it will not be unneceſſary to examine the Effects which this kind of Love produces in Tragedy; and this will deſerve an entire Chapter.

Of

Of the Effects which Love *produces in* FRENCH TRAGEDY. *The Cutting of the* Choruses, *and the Introduction of* Confidents.

ROMANTIC Love generally takes up three Fourths of the Action in *French* Tragedies. If we take away the tender Scenes, and reduce the principal Action to its true Object, the Tragedy would be ended in an Act and a Half, or two Acts at most. For Example, let us take out of *Nicomedes* the ten Scenes of *Laodice*; out of the *OEdipus*, the six Scenes of *Dirce*; out of *Poleuetes*, the Love-Scenes of *Severus*; from the *Phedra* of *Racine*, the six Scenes of *Aricia*; and we shall see that the Action will not only be uninterrupted, but that it will be more lively and brisk; and thus it plainly appears that these tender Scenes serve only to damp the Actions of the Piece, and to render the Heroes insipid and little. If, after these two best Writers of *French* Tragedy, we examine others, this Truth will be more plain: But when Love is the Subject of the Tragedy, that Passion, which in itself is so interesting, enters into the Action with
Propriety

Propriety enough. It is generally thought in *France*, that a Tragedy without Love could never pleafe the *French* Ladies who compofe the Bulk of the Audience in *Paris*. However, about the Beginning of the Year 1716, when the Players firft acted *Athalia*, it had a great Succefs; and in the *OEdipus* of Mr. *Voltaire*, which had univerfal Applaufe, the only thing which was difliked was the Recital of the Loves of *OEdipus* and *Jocafta*. Notwithftanding thefe Examples, they never have recovered themfelves from this Practice. They are willing to preferve Love in Tragedy; and I believe I can guefs the Reafon. The Difpofition of a Fable is not eafy; there muft concur in it all the Steps of an Action in Life, the Beginning, the Progrefs, the Plot, the Unravelling, and the End. Half a Dozen Love Scenes help thefe infenfibly forward; thro' thefe we muft march for the right Conduct of an Action; and by making up thefe Blanks, you are made to jump infenfibly from the Beginning to the Middle, and from the Middle to the End. By lopping off what I have mentioned, by taking the Love Scenes out of many Tragedies, which may be done without interrupting the Action, we can eafily point out this Truth, and then will fee the dangerous Jumps that Authors muft otherwife be obliged to make in the Conduct of their Plays: I had a great Pleafure

fure in making this Experiment. I propofed
to my Companions the Plan of a Comedy
which might comprehend all the Dramatic
Entertainments in *Paris :* The Propofal was
relifhed, and in a little time three of them
undertook to execute it : After the Prologue,
we had an Act of Comedy in the *Italian*
Manner; the fecond Act was a Tragedy,
and the third a comical Opera. The Sketch
of the Tragedy was given by me, and the
three Authors executed in fuch a manner, as
to do them Honour, I fpeak of the *Arcagambis,* which was acted with Applaufe,
and of which it is needlefs for me to give any
Account as it is in Print. In one Act we fee
a complete Action; the Princefs *Thamira*
takes up but one Scene; and if any Scholar
will weave into that Action ten Love Scenes
betwixt *Thamira,* the King, the Prince, and
the Nurfe; I fay, if this fhall be done hand-
fomely, with fome diftant Relation to the
Subject, one fhall be furprized to fee a complete Tragedy of five Acts grow up without
any other Difficulty.

I own that when the *Arcagambis* was
played, I had a complete Pleafure: I was
complemented by every Body upon that
Comic-Tragedy; and what was moft furprizing, was to fee all the Parts and Degrees
of a complete Tragedy in five Acts. To
tell the Truth, Sir, I was not a little proud
of

of the Merit of having reduced into one Act the entire Notion of a Tragedy, and can perform the fame Operation upon other Originals which I could mention, purely by cutting off the Love Scenes.

When Tragedy was reformed in *France*, the Chorus and the *Choriphee* was cut off. The *Choriphee* is the Chorus that enters into the Action, and fpeaks along with the Actors. They have thought that this Part was ufelefs to Tragedy, and void of Probability: And indeed upon the Plan of *French* Tragedy they may be in the right; for moft Part of their Tragedies are upon private Subjects tranfacted in the Palaces of Princes, where Chorufes are certainly introduced abfurdly, and againft Probability. But they found themfelves at a Lofs by thus cutting off the *Chorus* and the *Choriphee:* Therefore, to fupply the Abfence of the latter, their Authors have had Recourfe to Romance; they have taken from the Character of the 'Squire the Idea of a Confident, either Male or Female, who are linked to, and attending their principal Perfonages.

It is true that in the *Alexander* and the *Athalia* of *Racine* there are none of thefe Confidents. But I don't think that this was the Effect of any Scruples that arofe in the Mind of that excellent Poet on this Point; but owing to both the prophane and facred Hiftory

History furnishing a Sufficiency of principal Characters, without the Authors being obliged to have Recourse to Fiction to help him out with Conduct. His *Andromache* convinces one of this Truth : For if he had entertained the least Scruples on this Head, he never would have given a Confident to *Andromache* and *Hermione*, nor a Tutor to *Pyrrhus*, three Characters quite useless in the Play : As for *Orestes*, the Author was so happy, that he found a *Pylades*, furnished by History, to his Hand.

By taking away the *Chorus* and the *Choriphee* from Tragedy, and introducing Confidents, I am mistaken if the Authors, by endeavouring to avoid a small Inconveniency, have not fallen into a considerable one. For their Heroes, in Imitation of *Cyrus* and *Orondates*, and other romantic Captains, make Confidents not of Noviciates in the Art of Knighthood, as 'Squires were, but often of a Slave to whom they entrust not only their Loves, but even the most delicate Plots. Often this Confident is brought upon the Stage with no other end but to hear and explain that Subject, and is quite useless thro all the rest of the Play.

Of

Of the Unity *of* Place *in* FRENCH TRAGEDY.

THE chief Point that is mentioned, with regard to Dramatic Performances, is the Observation of the three Unities in Tragedy and Comedy, I mean those of *Action, Time,* and *Place:* These direct us to judge of the true Merit of Tragedy and Comedy. *Aristotle,* in his Poetry, has not mentioned the Unity of Place; but the Nature of the thing alone has suggested the Reasonableness of it to Dramatic Poets: When *Aristotle* confined the Action of a Tragedy to twelve or twenty four Hours, the Unity of Place was absolutely necessary for so short a time, for it can't be supposed that the Action in that time can measure a great deal of Ground.

Besides, in the Infancy of Tragedy, the Representation was very simple: It had no Machines, no shifting of Decorations, yet these Shiftings are necessary for aiding the Imagination of the Spectator when the Place is changed. The first Actors therefore were obliged to make Choice of Subjects that were transacted upon one Spot of Ground.

These

Thefe Entertainments having pleafed the People, and the principal Citizens of every Republic being fond of encreafing their Magnificence, Machines, and Decorations, were introduced; but thefe Decorations ferved only to adorn the Scene, and not to fhift it: As to the Machines, they were ufeful for the Gods who were introduced into the Place of the Action which never was changed: Thus we find there are no Shiftings of the Stage in *Sophocles* or *Euripides*.

It will be doubtlefs objected to me, that the Learned in Antiquity affure us there were Shiftings of the Stage. To prove this, *Bulanger* and *Lelius Geraldus* quote this Verfe from the third Book of *Virgil*'s *Georgics*,

Vel Scena ut Verfis difcedat frontibus.

I agree with them, that in the Entertainments of the Ancients there were Changes of Decoration; and I know that *Servius*, in his Note upon this Paffage of *Virgil*, fays, *But the Conftruction of the Scene was fuch, that it could be either quite changed, or drawn afide. It was faid to be changed, when by the Help of Machines a quite different Face of the Picture was prefented. It was on the other hand only faid to be drawn afide, when by opening the Curtains, a concealed Picture was here and there expofed to them.*

It

It is neverthelefs certain that we have no ancient Tragedy, the Subject of which requires a Shifting of the Scene. Thefe Changes of Decoration were therefore only made at the End of the Reprefentation of a Piece, when they wanted to reprefent another : For it was cuftomary to make a Piece of a comic or a mimic Nature fucceed a Tragedy; and often in one Day three or four different Shews fucceeded one another on the fame Theatre.

Some may perhaps take the Opening of a Door, by which a Meffenger enters, or that Part of the *Afinaria* of *Plautus,* where the Father, the Son, and the Miftrefs, are feen at Table together, as a Change of the Theatre. But upon an accurate Examination of the Matter, one will eafily perceive, that thefe different Changes of the Theatre, fpoke of by *Servius,* do not take Place in thefe two Inftances.

In my Catalogue, when fpeaking of the Olympic Theatre of *Palladio,* in the City of *Vicenza,* I have given *Vitruvius's* Account of the Conftruction of Theatres. The Theatres had three principal Doors, and two on that Side where the Actors entered. Every one of thefe Doors fronted different Streets, and different Buildings; and when in the Action a Stranger or a Meffenger was to enter the City, they opened one of the two laft mentioned

mentioned Doors, fo that without any Change
of the Theatre, the Spectators, through that
Door, faw the City itfelf. In the fame
manner in the *Afinaria* they opened one of
thefe two Side-Doors which prefented to the
View of the Spectators the Gallery of the
Houfe, where the Actors fat eating at a Table.
But to return ; by long Cuftom the Unity
of the Place had become fo common among
the *Greeks*, that there was no Occafion for
prefcribing it formally, fince it was authorized by Practice, and always prefumed to
be underftood. The Moderns have not followed this Probability ; but not to name
them all, I fhall only inftance in *Calvaret*,
who, probably being no Stranger to the Objec-
tions made to his Predeceffor, upon this Account, has endeavoured to avoid this Fault,
by putting thefe Words under the Lift of his
Dramatis Perfonæ, in the Tragedy called the
Rape of Proferpine. *The Scene is in Heaven,
in* Sicily, *and in Hell, where the Imagination
of the Reader may reprefent to itfelf a kind of
Unity of Place, by conceiving this Scene to be a
perpendicular Line drawn from Heaven to Hell.*
To remedy fo monftrous an Abfurdity, the
Critics, who have wrote fince that Time, have
laid down a pofitive Rule for this Unity of
Place, which was only formerly confequen-
tially deduced from the Rules fo judicioufly
eftablifhed by *Ariftotle*. They have, as for-

X   mally,

mally, required the Unity of Place as *Ari-stotle* did that of Action and Time, that by this Means the Sallies of the Poets Imagination might have some Check. But the late Tragic Poets following this Rule of the Unity of Place more servily than their Predecessors, have perhaps paid too religious a Regard to it. Is it not strange that the Place where a Tragedy is acted should be the Closet of an Emperor or a King; and that the Action of this Tragedy should be the Intrigues and Secrets of a Conspiracy wrought up and concerted under the Eyes of the very Prince intended to be murdered? Would not one be rather tempted to admit of a Change of Place, as the *Italians* have done since the Year 1600, in their Imitations of, and Translations from the *Spanish* Theatre.

The late Commentators on *Aristotle* are seriously employed in discovering whether this Unity of Place is to be understood of the *Extent of Ground taken up by the Actors at the Beginning of the Tragedy*, or of *the Town or City where the Action is laid*. But without stopping to discuss their several Reasonings in this Place, we shall in few Words lay before the Reader our own Sentiments of the Matter.

The first of all the Rules, and that which *Aristotle* lays down as the Basis and Foundation of all the rest, is to *observe Probability.*
Thus

Thus neither the Unity of Place, nor any of the reſt of *Ariſtotle's* Maxims ought to be followed at the Expence of Probability, which is the Source of all the Rules obſerved in Poetry; and I don't think that this Probability is ſufficiently obſerved in the Unity of Place ſo ſcrupulouſly adhered to by the *French* Poets.

The Spectators, in my Opinion, would be leſs ſhocked by ſeeing the Actors paſs from one Apartment to another in the ſame Palace, (as in *Italy* and *Spain* was the Cuſtom in the laſt Age,) than by ſeeing a Conſpiracy concerted and carried on in the Cloſet, and under the Eye of the Tyrant who was to fall the Victim.

Let us, for inſtance, take one of the beſt Tragedies of the excellent Mr. *Corneille*, and examine the Effects of that great Man's ſcrupulous Attachment to the Rule preſcribing the Unity of Place. Let no one charge me with an Intention to criticiſe upon him; I only intend to ſhew, that by ſtraining Things leſs, he ſhould have preſerved Probability more, and that if he has given Occaſion for Criticiſm, it is owing to his being over-cautious in this reſpect.

In his Tragedy of *Cinna*, the Place of Action is the Emperor's Cloſet; and it is in the ſame Cloſet that *Æmilia* bawls out that ſhe will kill the Emperor. In the ſame Clo-

ſet

let *Cinna* concerts the Confpiracy with *Æmilia* and *Maximus*. After the Converfation betwixt *Auguftus*, *Cinna*, and *Maximus*, the Emperor has fcarce left the Clofet, till *Cinna* tells *Maximus*, That if he had advifed *Auguftus* not to throw up the Empire, it is with a View that his Victim may be the more illuftrious, and that he may kill *Auguftus* on the Throne. If the Confpirators, during all the Action, run a rifque of being heard, they run ftill a greater upon this than upon any other Occafion; for the Emperor having juft left them, could not be far gone, and might liften to know if they fpoke the fame in his Abfence, they had done in his Prefence. It appears then contrary to all Probability to make them fpeak fo loud immediately when the Emperor leaves the Room. The Poet himfelf has been fenfible of this, and for that reafon, he makes *Cinna* fay, *Friend, we may be over-heard in this Palace.* But this Reflection comes too late: I don't know but the Spectators might have been better pleafed with a Change of Place, than with fo imprudent Conduct in fuch Perfons as *Cinna* and *Maximus*. Mr. *Corneille*, in the Examination of this Tragedy, endeavours to defend himfelf againft this Objection, which had probably been made againft his Tragedy in his own Life-time: His Words run thus: *It is true, it has two Places of Action; the*

one

one Half is acted with Æmilia, *and the other
in the Closet of* Auguſtus. *I ſhould have juſtly
deſerved to be ridiculed, had I made this Emperor deliberate with* Maximus *and* Cinna
*whether he ſhould abdicate the Empire, pre-
ciſely in the Place where* Cinna *informs* Æmilia *of the Conſpiracy which he has formed
againſt him.*

According to Mr. *Corneille's* Confeſſion,
the famous Deliberation betwixt *Auguſtus,
Cinna,* and *Maximus,* happens in the Cloſet
of the Emperor; and the Emperor leaves
them there, when he ſays, *Adieu, I will
carry the News to* Livia.

And it is in the ſame Cloſet that *Maximus*
and *Cinna* held the imprudent Conference
we have juſt now mentioned. *Corneille* does
not allow us to imagine that they had gone
out of it into the Apartment of *Æmilia,* or
anywhere elſe, ſince he makes *Cinna* ſay, at
the End of the Scene, *My Friend, we may
poſſibly be over-heard in this Palace; and we
ſpeak perhaps with too much Imprudence in a
Place ſo improper for communicating our
Secrets. Let us remove.* They remained
then in the ſame Cloſet; and all we have
ſaid of the Want of Probability in their
Conference, continues in its full Force; and
Mr. *Corneille* could not remedy this without
ſhifting the Scene of Action.

But let us return to what Mr. *Corneille* ſays

X 3   upon

upon the Place of Action, agreeable to the Principles which he lays down in the Examination we have juſt now mentioned. All the firſt Act ought to paſs in the Apartment of *Æmilia*; all the ſecond, in the Cloſet of *Auguſtus*; and as for the third, it ſeems to ſtand in need of a third Place. Is it proper that *Maximus* and *Euphorbus* ſhould talk to one another in the Cloſet of *Auguſtus* concerning the Conſpiracy againſt the Emperor? Or that in the Apartment of *Æmilia*, *Maximus* ſhould talk to *Euphorbus* of his Love to her; and that *Euphorbus* ſhould adviſe him to abandon the Conſpiracy, and betray *Cinna*? Mr. *Corneille* muſt then have another Apartment to preſerve Probability. The three firſt Scenes of the fourth Act, betwixt *Auguſtus*, *Euphorbus*, and *Livia*, neceſſarily paſs in the Cloſet of the Emperor: At the End of the third Scene the Stage is empty; and the fourth Scene paſſes betwixt *Æmilia and her Confident*, without any thing bringing them on the Stage. For this Reaſon Mr. *Corneille*, in his Examination, ſays that this Scene, and all the reſt of the Act, paſſes in *Æmilia*'s Apartment. But how is the Spectator acquainted with this Change of Place? Does he not always ſee the ſame Decoration? He is then unavoidably ſhocked with two Blunders, *viz.* The Emptineſs of the Scene, and the hearing *Æmilia*, *Fulvia*, and *Maximus*

mus talk to one another of the Confpiracy in
the very Place from which *Auguſtus* and
Euphorbus had but juſt come. The Change
of Decoration would have remedy'd the former of thefe Faults; but the latter is irreparable. What ought we to conclude from
all this? Why, that there are fome Actions
which, on account of their continual Change
of Place, are not proper for the Theatre;
and that if one might, without offending
Probability, admit this particular Change of
Place, it is ſtill neceſſary to acquaint the Spectators of it by a Change of Decoration; for
perhaps it is not fufficient to make the Actors
tell that they have changed the Place, as
when *Chiméne*, in the *Cid*, teſtifies to *Roderick* her Surprize at feeing him in her Houfe.
This Difcourfe is contradicted before the
Spectators, by the Decoration which reprefents to them all along the fame Royal Palace. *Racine* has made an admirable Ufe of
the Change of Decoration in his *Athaliah*,
which I look upon as the Mafter-piece of
Dramatic Poetry. The Place of Action for
this Tragedy is the Porch of the Temple;
and when the Poet wants to fhew the King
on his Throne, furrounded with his armed
Levites, he has no more to do but to open
the Doors of the Temple: This deferves
the Name of an ingenious Obfervation of the
Rules, and a faithful Adherence to Proba-
X 4   bility.

bility. In this refpect he has imitated the *Greeks,* who difpofed their Theatre in the Manner which beft fuited the Natures of their Pieces. Thus *Sophocles,* in his *OEdipus, the Tyrant,* ftanding in need of the King of *Thebes* Palace, and an Altar, choofe for the Scene of Action the public Place in which the Altar and the Palace of the King were built. *Guarini,* in his *Paſtor Fido,* has like-wife ordered his Theatre in fuch a Manner, that without any Change of Decoration, the Spectators fee the Temple on the Top of the Mountain, the Grotto at the Foot of it, and the Valley where all the Scenes pafs.

Of the Unity *of* TIME, *and the* Unity *of* ACTION *in* FRENCH TRAGEDIES.

THE *French* are not always exact Ob-fervers of the Unity of Time, or in other Words, of the Rule enjoining twenty four Hours for the time of the Action: To prove this, I might produce many Examples; but for Brevity-fake, fhall only take notice of the *Horatii.* This Tragedy begins the very Moment in which one would think the *Roman* and *Alban* Armies were juft about to

engage

engage one another; and the firſt Scene repreſents to us the Anxiety of the *Sabines*,
about the Event of the Battle. At the End
of the firſt Act, *Curiatius* comes to inform
Camilla that there was to be no Engagement,
ſince the contending Parties had agreed to
ſingle out, from their reſpective Nations,
three Combatants, who were to fight for the
common Cauſe. The Difficulty that now
remained, was to know who were the moſt
proper Perſons to be made Choice of. The
Romans chooſe the *Horatii :* The *Albans* the
Curiatii. Preparations are made for the
Combat; the People flock to the Camp ; a
Suſpenſion of Arms is agreed to ; the Oracle
is conſulted ; and by it the Choice of the
Romans is applauded : The People return to
the Camp; the Battle is fought ; *Horatius*
comes off victorious ; he makes his Entrance
into *Rome* ; the People receive him with
Acclamations, and welcome him with Shouts
of Joy. He goes into his own Houſe ; he
kills his Siſter. The King pays a Viſit to
Old Horatius, whoſe Son *Valerius* accuſes of
having murdered his Siſter. *Horatius* pleads
the Cauſe of his Son; and the King acquits
him. Thus the Tragedy ends. Without
conſulting *Titus Livius*, I believe we need
only reflect on the Extent of Time which
theſe Events may reaſonably be ſuppoſed to take up, in order to be convinced
that

that they could not happen in leſs than two or three Days.

With regard to the Unity of Action, I find a great Difference between the *Greek* and the *French* Tragedies; I always perceive with Eaſe the Action of the *Greek* Trage-dies, and never ſo much as loſe View of it; but in the *French*, I own I am often at a Loſs to diſtinguiſh between the Action itſelf, and the Epiſodes with which it is intermixt. What, for inſtance, is the Action of the *Cid* of *Mithridates*, and of ſome others? In the *Cid*, *Roderick* kills the Father of his Miſtreſs, puts the Enemies to Flight, has a Beating-bout with his Rival, obtains the King's Par-don, and the Hand of *Chiméne*. Theſe are all the Events in the Piece; but which of them ought to be regarded as the principal one, or the main Action of the Tragedy? Is it the Pardon which *Roderick* obtains of the King? That Pardon is granted in the Mid-dle of the Piece. Is it the Defeat of the *Moors*? That happens in the Interval betwixt the third and fourth Act. Is it, in fine, the Marriage of *Chiméne*? Not one of the Events of the Piece leads to that End.

Mithridates returns to rally his Forces, and march forth againſt *Rome*: He finds his Son in Love with *Monimia*, whom he him-ſelf was to marry. The *Romans* advance; *Mithridates* goes out to engage them: He

returns

returns wounded; and dying, orders the Marriage of *Monimia* and his Son.

Will any one fay that the Death of *Mithridates* is the Action of this Tragedy! But the Death of a Hero can never be the Subject of a Tragedy, unlefs the Poet direct every Part of his Piece to that particular End. The Death of *Britannicus*, for inftance, is juftly looked upon as the Action of that Tragedy, becaufe the Author's Intention is by different Events to lead us on to this Cataftrophe, upon which he all along fixes our Views; but in *Mithridates*, what Circumftance, what Confpiracy makes us dread, or even expect the Death of that Prince? There is nothing in *Mithridates* which fixes the Death of that Prince as the Subject of the Tragedy.

The Death of a Hero, or a Tyrant, may fometimes be the Hinge on which the Action turns; or it may be the Effect and Refult of it.

For inftance, in the Tragedy of *Heraclius*, *Phocas* is killed, and the Action of the Piece is *the owning the rightful Succeffor to the Empire, and his Re-eftablifhment upon the Throne*: To bring this about, *Phocas* is flain; and in this Cafe the Death of the Tyrant is not *the Action itfelf*, but the *Effect* and *Refult* of it.

In the *Death of Pompey*, *Pompey himfelf* is dead before the Tragedy begins; and his
Death

Death is, as it were, the Spring from which the whole of the Action flows. In this Case the Hero's Death is the Cause of the Action: The Death of the Count *de Gormas* produces several Actions in the *Cid*; but in *Mithridates*, the Death of the King is by no means either the Cause, or the Effect of the *Action*. As there would be no end of examining them all, I shall only say, that in the far greater Part of the *French* Tragedies, the Action is very often a Mystery, into which the Authors themselves cannot let the Spectators. This is far from being the Case with the *Greek* Tragedies; in them you discover the *Action* at first View.

In *OEdipus*, for instance, a Pestilence lays waste the City *Thebes*. On that Account the Oracle is consulted, who declares that the unavenged Murder of *Laius* is the Cause of all their Woes. Upon this *OEdipus* binds himself by an Oath to avenge it; a Scrutiny is made, and *OEdipus* is found at once to be the Son of *Laius*, and Murderer of his Father. This is the Subject of the *OEdipus*, and one will at first perceive the Action of this Tragedy, for every Part of the Actor's Conduct tends to discover the Murderer of *Laius*, and prepare the Woes of *OEdipus*.

After having spoke of these *French* Tragedies, in which it is not easy to perceive the true Action, let us now speak of those wherein

wherein the Unity of Action is not sufficiently obferved, and where Matters are fo ordered, as to force one to acknowledge two Actions.

I fhall begin with *Andromache*, which is inconteftably one of the fineft of Mr. *Racine*'s Pieces. The true Subject of this Tragedy is the Marriage of *Pyrrhus*: The *Greeks* charge *Oreftes* to oppofe it; but upon his Arrival at the Court of *Pyrrhus*, he finds himfelf fway'd by a more prevalent Intereft than that of *Greece*, which was entrufted to him: His Love for *Hermione* makes him wifh that *Pyrrhus* might marry *Andromache*: The Command of *Hermione* obliges him to kill *Pyrrhus*: The Paffion which rages in the Breaft of that Hero, his Fury, his Jealoufy of *Hermione*, and in fine, his Death, are all Circumftances which intereft the Spectators more than thofe relating to *Pyrrhus* and *Andromache*, and might of themfelves make the Subject of a Tragedy. On the other hand, the Fate of *Andromache*, and the Love of *Pyrrhus* for her, are Subjects fufficiently interefting to fupply a Poet with the Matter of a good Tragedy; and, upon Reflection, any one will eafily fee, that a Poet of Mr. *Racine*'s Abilities, could have eafily worked out his Tragedy without *Hermione*'s being at the Court of *Pyrrhus*, and without affigning any other Intereft to hinder
the

the Marriage of *Orestes* with *Andromache*, than the Instructions given him by the *Greeks:* *Pyrrhus* would have had the same Struggle betwixt his Passion for *Andromache* and his Dread of drawing out against himself the united Forces of all *Greece*. *Andromache* in like manner would have appeared to us racked on Account of the Love she bore her Son, and by her Horror at a Marriage with the Murderer of *Priam*'s Family, even the Son of that hated Man who murdered her Dear *Hector*.

If Mr. *Racine* had stuck by the Simplicity of this Subject, his Piece had been more regular and more moving; for it is not the Multiplicity of Interests that renders a Piece interesting; on the contrary, it interests more when one single Event, without any thing foreign or adventitious, attracts the whole of the Attention : Mr. *Racine* undoubtedly knew this well enough; but he has been forced to accommodate himself to the Genius of the Nation, which is chiefly touched with the Fate of Lovers in Dramatic Performances; and as it is absolutely necessary that Love should have a Part in all Subjects that are truly tragical, the Poets, who have brought these Subjects upon the *French* Theatre, have not only been obliged to make Use of Episodes for that Purpose, but often to work up these Episodes with

more

more Care and Accuracy than the principal
Subject of the Piece. Hence it is that there
are so many Episodes in the *French* Tragedies.
To this it is owing that the Personages in
their Episodes interest the Spectator as much
as the principal Hero of the Piece.

We may form a Judgment of this Affair
from the *Severus* of *Poleucles*, the *Eriphile* of
Iphigenia, the *Aricia* of *Phedrus*, and from
the Amours of *Theseus* and *Dircé* in the
OEdipus.

If the Necessity of always introducing
Lovers upon the *French* Theatre, has produced Faults in the Works of the greatest
Masters, we may easily guess at the Fate of
the inferior Class of Authors who have gone
into this Practice; but to speak the Truth,
this Usage has perhaps been of singular Service to help them to maintain and keep up
their Dialogue, since there is no Passion that
furnishes out a greater Number of *common-
place Topics*, than that of Love.

Of Character *in the* FRENCH TRAGEDY.

THE *French* Writers of Tragedy seem
not to have been careful enough in
marking the Differences as to the particular
Species

Species of Heroifm, peculiar to different Nations. The *Greek* Poets and Hiftorians paint their Heroes grand, but for the moft Part fierce and cruel. The *Roman* Heroes retain the fame Grandeur, but it is heightened and fet off by Humanity and Generofity.

In the *French* Tragedies, *Cæſar*, *Alexander*, *Pompey*, *Mithridates*, *Auguſtus*, and *Achilles*, feem all born under the fame Climate, and trained up in the fame Maxims.

Every Hero, befides the predominating Character of his Nation, ought to have one peculiar to himfelf: We know that *Pyrrhus*, the Son of *Achilles*, was impetuous and cruel; and that *Hippolitus*, the Son of *Thefeus*, was favage, auftere, and fteel'd againft the Impreffions of Love; neverthelefs, in *Racine's* *Phedra*, this *Hippolitus* is finical in his Sentiments, and blubbers for his dear *Aricia*; *Pyrrhus* is humbled, tender, and trembling at the Feet of *Andromache*; it may be anfwered, that if *Pyrrhus* is fufceptible of Love, and fubmiffive to his Miftrefs, there are certain Starts in which he difcovers his true Character, and fpeaks with Haughtinefs to *Andromache* herfelf. By attentively examining thefe Paffages, we find that it is lefs the Fiercenefs of his Character which makes him talk in this harfh Manner to *Andromache*, than the Impatience which muft be natural to every Lover in his Situation.
While

While his Miſtreſs was continually bewailing the Loſs of her Huſband, and touched with the afflicting Remembrance of her Son's Situation, the moſt tender Lover would have ſaid as much as *Pyrrhus* on a like Occaſion; and it is not ſo much the Character as the Situation, that Mr. *Racine* has here followed. If this great Poet has ſo much altered two ſo remarkable Characters, what muſt we imagine others to have done?

That we may be able to view this Fault in a true Light, it will not be amiſs to make ſome Obſervations upon Characters in general.

Every Man, and eſpecially every Hero, has ſome predominant Branch of his Character, which gives a particular Stamp, if I may ſo ſay, to his Thoughts, and allows him to reliſh nothing but what is accommodated to it: If at any time he feels the Workings of theſe Paſſions which are common to Humanity, there is no Occaſion for thinking that they are different in him, from what they are in other Men: The ſame Paſſions do not render different Men alike. On the contrary, the different Characters of Men give a different Turn to the ſame Paſſion in every individual Man. All Men may poſſibly be in Love, but every one is ſo in his own Way, and this Way depends upon the prevailing Part of his Character, which is more

Y or

or lefs influenced by thefe accidental Paffions, as he is more or lefs able to refift their Impreffions.

We find Examples of the juft Combination of thefe Paffions in fome of the Tragedies of *Racine* and *Corneille*.

In the *Iphigenia* in *Aulis*, when *Achilles* is afraid of lofing his Miftrefs, he does not abandon himfelf to vain Regrets: But that impetuous Hero, impatiently bearing the Superiority of *Agamemnon*, flies into a Paffion, and threatens him even in the Prefence of *Iphigenia*. *Prufias* exceffively fond of his Wife, and giving himfelf up to be entirely managed by her, is deaf to the Calls of Nature in favour of his Son *Nicomedes*. Thus Love, which in *Achilles* meets with a fierce and haughty Character, allows him ftill to act agreeably to it: But finding in *Prufias* a Character where Sweetnefs and Condefcenfion reign, it quite fubdues him, and imparts all its Weakneffes to him. The two Poets have been equally happy in working up thefe two different Characters, and have obferved all the Rules of Probability, which are but indifferently obferved by the other Writers of *French* Tragedy, who beftow upon their Heroes that Gallantry and thofe Sentiments they have borrowed from Romances, without caring whether thefe Heroes would have loved in fuch a Manner,

or

or whether their Method of loving be agreeable to the Characters which History and Fable give them.

I shall not spend time in running over all the Pieces of the modern Poets, to point out their Faults of this kind; we may easily apply to every one of these Pieces, what I have said concerning the prevailing Character of every Hero, and the proportionable Alterations which the Passions make in it.

I shall close this Chapter by observing that the Word *Character* is often improperly used. Most People find *Characters* where there are really none: Is there, for instance, a single Character in the *Cid*, except that of the Count *de Gormas?* In *Roderick* is there any other than that of *Cleopatra?* Is there *any at all* to be found in *Titus* and *Berenice?* In fine, in the *Horatii* I can only find two Characters marked, that of *Horatius*, and that of *Curiatius*; and in *Cinna*, those of *Augustus* and *Æmilia*.

I don't pretend to give what I have said of the Character of these different *Pieces* as a formal Decision: I only let the Reader know what Impression they made upon myself; and perhaps what I have advanced may lay a Foundation for their being examined with greater Accuracy for the future. I have not taken upon me to criticise these Tragedies in which I find so small a Number of

Cha-

Characters, a great Number of which are by no means neceſſary to denominate a Tragedy good. When the Action is ſimple, and turns upon one or two Perſonages, it is ſufficient that their Characters be maintained and marked: Thus in *Roderick*, the Character of *Cleopatra* is ſufficient for the Piece.

Of the Sentiments *of the* FRENCH TRAGEDIES.

ONE of the ſix conſtituent Parts of Tragedy, according to *Ariſtotle*, is what the *Italians* call *Sentenza*: As I don't find a *French* Word which correſponds exactly to it, I ſhall in its ſtead ſometimes uſe the Word *Sentiment*, and ſometimes the Word *Maxim*.

The *French* Tragedies chiefly excel in this Point, which is the Rock on which thoſe Authors ſplit, who, by indulging the Fire of their Imagination too much, ſwerve from that *Probability*, which is the moſt ſolid Foundation of true and genuine *Beauty*.

Is it, for inſtance, probable that a Hero, amidſt the Tranſports of the moſt violent Paſſion, ſhould enter upon the moſt refined and abſtract Speculations in *Metaphyſics?*
This

This pretended Beauty produces an Effect quite contrary to the Intention of Tragic Poetry.

At the very Moment the Heart is touched with the deplorable Situation of a Hero, boiling with Fury and madden'd with Defpair, there flows from his Mouth a Thought fo delicate and refined, a Sentiment fo little expected, and fo much above the common Pitch, that it in fome meafure deftroys the Sentiments of the Heart, by attracting the Attention of the Mind.

Read, for inftance, in *Corneille*, the Difcourfe of *OEdipus* to *Dircé*, when he is found to be the Son of that fame *Jocaſta* whom he had married; and you will obferve, that in order to exprefs the Situation in which he is, he ufes Thoughts fo grand and noble, that they force our Applaufe, but at the fame time weaken our Compaffion. In the Tragedy entitled *The Death of Pompey*, *Cornelia* alone is capable of moving the Paffions, and touching the Heart. Yet the noble Sentiments with which fhe fo much abounds, both with regard to *Cæfar* and the Afhes of *Pompey*, are only capable of dazling the Mind, but not of moving the Heart; the Spectators, inftead of being touched with Pity, are ftruck with Admiration, which is far from being the End of Tragedy, in which the Skill of the Poet confifts in hiding Art,

Y 3

and

and fhewing only Nature. The Sentiment
of the Soul, expreffed in a manner agreeable
to one's Situation, is of itfelf fufficiently able
to move the Spectators, which a ftudied
Thought will never do.

If we obferve in what manner *Sophocles*
makes *OEdipus* fpeak, when he brings him
upon the Stage, together with his two young
Daughters, we will perceive that the real
Situation of that misfortunate Hero, who
was at once their Father and their Brother,
is not in the leaft altered, or weakened by the
Wit of the Poet. If Poets tranfgrefs the
Rules of Probability, by putting into the
Mouths of their Heroes, whofe Circumftances demand the moft natural Sentiments,
too far-fetched Expreffions, they are equally
culpable if the Language they put into their
Mouths is not fuited to their Rank, Age, and
Sex.

We muft agree however, that Elevation of
Sentiments admits of many Degrees, but the
manner of Expreffion is different, according
to the Difference of Age and Education.
Many of the *Greek* and *Latin* Poets have
been juftly blamed for not having obferved
the Rules of Probability in the Language
they put into the Mouths of their Characters; and the fame Cenfure may be paft,
with Juftice, upon *French* Writers of Tragedy; among them we often find Heroes,
and

and their Confidents, Women and Children, talk in the fame Strain, and equally fhow away with Maxims and Sentences. The *French*, who are naturally full of Wit, with Pleafure purfue that Part of Tragedy which we call *Sentiments*, and frequently facrifife to it all other Confiderations: In this they are encouraged by the Applaufe which a fine Maxim always gains from the Audience; and it has been known that a Tragedy has fucceeded purely upon the Merit of the pretty Maxims that were fcattered thro' it. But this Succefs has impofed upon Authors, who have not perceived that a Piece, which has no other Merit, has never a durable Reputation: If they want that their Pieces fhould be longlif'd, let them apply themfelves to the Conduct of the Fable; let them take care that that in itfelf, when ftript of the Ornaments of Speech, fhall be affecting and interefting for the Spectators; let them employ their Wit in the Obfervation of the Character and other Circumftances, and they fhall then be fure to pleafe for ever.

Thus it is that *Racine* has acquired immortal Fame. Some have imagined that he has not excelled in Sentiments, or pretty Sayings; but they make this Reflection becaufe they don't obferve that elevated Thoughts, which ftrike in other Writers, are formed in *Racine* in as great a Number as in other

Poets;

Poets; but in thefe they ftrike more, becaufe
the Inequality of their Stile fhews them in it
a Contraft which is more dazzling. They
are not fo eafily difcerned in *Racine*, whofe
Stile is always equally noble, and his Expreffions always juft and natural, but never confounded with founding Bombaft; and this is
the true Pattern of Stile. Let the *French*,
who reproach the *Italians* with their *Con-
cetti*, or Conceits, do Juftice to themfelves
and the *Italians* both: To the *Italians*, by
owning that thefe Conceits are not agreeable
to their Men of Learning, and difapproved
by them; and to themfelves, in guarding
againft a Fault for which they blame the *Italians*, and which is become but too common
among modern Writers: It is true, it is lefs
frequent among good Authors, and I will
inftance two in *Racine* himfelf, which are as
abfurd as any among the *Italians*.

    Pyrrhus, in the *Andromache*, Act **I.** Scene
IV. fays,

I feel thofe Ills that I have dealt to **Troy**
Vanquifh'd and bound, confumed with fruitlefs
    Plaints,
Burnt with more Fires than thofe I kindled
    there.

                              I

---

    † See likewife an Inftance of this kind from the fame
Author in Page 258.

I have quoted thefe Paffages of *Racine*, not fo much with any Defign to reflect on that great Man who has fo rarely been faulty in this refpect, as to fhew how much we ought to guard againft thefe bombaft Sentiments, fince they fo eafily infinuate themfelves into the Writings of the greateft Mafters.

I believe I have faid enough on this Subject, becaufe it will be eafy for the Reader to apply thefe Obfervations to the feveral Dramatic Performances he fhall have Occafion to examine.

Of the Intention *of the* French *Tragic* POETS, *and fome* REMARKS *upon* FRENCH TRAGEDY.

THE End of Dramatic Poetry is to pleafe, and for this the Poets ought to conform themfelves to the Tafte of the Nation. Among the *Greeks*, the People having a great Share in the Government, nothing interefted them fo much as the Revolutions of Kingdoms: They were pleafed to fee the Paffions drawn in fuch a manner as to occafion them, and to hear the Theatre adopt political Maxims. In the firſt Chapter we have ſeen that their Poets brought upon the Stage Subjeƈts and Cha-raƈters agreeable to their Genius. The *French*, contented with their happy Government, through a long Succeſſion of Years under the wiſe Direƈtion of their Princes, are leſs touched with Piƈtures reſembling the Intrigues of Ambition: They with Joy behold Love and Jealouſy keep Poſſeſſion of their Stage ; and Romances, which have had ſuch a Run among them, have naturally led their Poets to repreſent that which they took a Pleaſure in reading : This has given Riſe to *French* Tragedy as we have it at preſent, where Love, in the Taſte of Romance, poſ-ſeſſes always the firſt Part; and this predo-minant Paſſion may be looked upon as the Charaƈteriſtic of their Tragedy, which di-ſtinguiſhes it from that of *Greece* and *Italy*.

Perhaps it were to be wiſhed that they could put into the Mouths of ſome other Heroes, beſides thoſe of *Greece* and *Rome*, who were of ſo oppoſite a Charaƈter, Senti-ments of Tenderneſs and Love : Why may they not make their Princes repreſent Dra-matic Heroes, as the *Engliſh* have done ? But don't let us inſiſt too much on this Point, for it would carry us too much out of our Way; only we may obſerve that their Poets having given them *French* Sentiments, have thought fit to give them even *French Civility*.

Thus

Thus on the Head of *Achilles*, or *Cæsar*, we see a Hat and a large *Nodding Plumage*, like thofe over a Canopy, and Strangers who are not ufed to fee thefe Heroes fo burlefqued, can't help calling them Monfieur *Cæsar*, and Monfieur *Achilles*.

Don't let us blame the *French* Poets, but rather the Tafte of the Spectators, who could be pleafed with nothing but thefe Pictures of Jealoufy and Love: To this alone are owing the Faults which we have taken Notice of in the Works of their great Mafters; fuch as their failing, in the Unity of Place, as in *Cinna*; of Action, as in the *Andromache*; of having fo ftrongly altered Characters, as in the *Cid*; in fhort, of introducing upon the Stage, Confidents, thofe eternally cold and infipid Characters.

‖ If I ever fhall have the Happinefs of knowing the *Englifh* Stage, I fhall inform you of my Sentiments of it; at prefent I fhall fpeak of their Tragedy of *Cato*, which has been tranflated into our Language, and acted upon our Stage with Applaufe. For my own Part I am of Opinion, that in this Play may be found the true Plan of a well conducted Confpiracy, and the Language of a Hero who ftill thinks nobly, but within the Compafs of Nature. *Cato* is greater than
all

‖ This was wrote before the Author had been in *England.*

all Heroes either ancient or modern, yet I ftill know him to be a Man. It may be objected that it is unnatural to reprefent *Cato* as denying to fhed a Tear for the Death of his Son; but I affirm that there is no Point in which the Character of *Cato* is better fuftained, without his deviating from Nature. *Cato* furrounded with the thin Remains of the Senate, muft have difcouraged them had he given any Proof of Weaknefs. But even tho' he had been by himfelf, perhaps he might not have fhed Tears, for thefe don't always accompany Grief, and agree ill with the Character of *Cato*; but if we examine the Sentiments of the *Englifh Cato* upon this Occafion, we fhall find them both great and tender in the higheft Degree at the fame time.

I don't fpeak here of the Underplot containing the Loves of *Cato's* Son and *Lucia*, and *Juba* with *Marcia*; thefe I difapprove of, as not immediately affecting the Subject of the Play; but probably the Neceffity of introducing Women put him under another, that of making them *young*, and therefore he could find no other Bufinefs for them upon the Stage but Love. It is to be hoped that if the *Englifh* and *Italians* follow the fine Models that are before them, they will give the World good Plays. I likewife flatter myfelf that the *French* Audiences will lofe the Tafte

for

for thefe fwelling Thoughts which ftun the Mind, and fhock the Underftanding. They begin already to fet up againft the Impieties and the infernal Politics, and licentious Maxims, which fome Moderns have derived from polluted Sources, which have only a falfe Appearance of Greatnefs. Then fhall we have lefs Love upon the Stage, the Manners and Characters better preferved, the Unities obferved, and the Sentiments and fine Thoughts ufed on proper Occafions.

But I do not expect to fee Rhime banifhed from the Theatre; a Man muft be a *Frenchman*, and from his Infancy have his Ears accuftomed to the Return of Rhime, otherwife they muft be grated by its continual Monotony, not only of Rhime, but of the Period, which always takes up the Space of two. This Form, which never alters, produces on your Mind the fame Effect that the Billows of the Sea do upon your Eye: Thefe at firft pleafe the View, but afterwards fatigue it, and the Spectator turns his weary Eye to the Shore for Relief.

F I N I S.

[N.B. *The following Catalogue should have been plac'd immediately after the Account of the* German *Theatre.*]

Tragedies and *Comedies* of § HANS-SACH from 1516, till 1558.

Adam and *Eve.*
Virginia.
Guesmund.
Absalom.
Lucians Charon.
The Six Champions.
Jocasta.
The Two Gentlemen of Burgundy.
The False Empress.
The Innocent Empress.
The Elizabeth.
The Unequal Children of Eve.
Jacob and Esau.
Esther.
Tobias.
The Messias.
Griselda.
The Miser and the Gentleman.

Palidis.
The Prodigal Child.
Juno and Jupiter.
Job.
Judith.
The Judgment of Solomon.
The Rich Man dying.
The Folly of Erasmus.
The Judgment of Paris.
Plautus's Menechmes.
Henno.
The Half Friends.
The Queen of France.
The Banish'd Empress.
Mucius Scevola.
Oliver and Artus
The Chevalier Galmi.
The Bianceffora.
The Violanta.

---

§ This Poet died in 1567, in the 81st Year of his Age; his Works have been printed at *Nuremberg* in 1570.

Dramatical

Dramatical Pieces of MARTIN OPITZ.

Daphne.

The Antigona of Sophocles.

The Trojans of Seneca.

Judith.

Dramatical Pieces of ANDREW GRYPHIUS.

Tragedies.	Comedies.
Leo of Armenia.	The Nurse.
Katharine of Georgia.	The Wandering Shepherd.
Cardenio and Celinda.	
Charles Stewart.	Piasta.
The Death of Papinian.	
	Farces.
The Constant Mother.	Petez Squens.
The Gibeonites.	Horribilicribrifax.

Dramatical Pieces of LOHENSTEIN.

Cleopatra.

Sophonisba.

Ibraim Bassa.

Agrippina.

Epiccharis.

A

A

TABLE

OF THE

MATTERS *contained in* RIC-
COBONI's Reflections *upon*
DECLAMATION.

Z

Heathen

Action

The T A B L E.

There

Italian.

                     What

  Their

Had

The T A B L E.

The T A B L E.

The T A B L E.

The T A B L E.

Extract of the Tragedy called dying CATO.
Dramatis Personæ.

Table of Matters contained in FENELON'S
  Thoughts *on Tragedy.*

                                       Mr.

Answer

The T A B L E.

F I N I S.